FAIRWING – BRAZIL

TALES OF THE SOUTH ATLANTIC

U.S. and Brazilian Allies Battle Axis Forces for Control of Vital Sealanes

Stories of Allied Service Personnel 1941-1945 On-Duty and Off-Duty

Photos and Commentary on Brazilian Bases, People, Cities, and History, 1941-1945 and Contemporary

By John R. Harrison
PhoM2/c-USNR

Schiffer Military History
Atglen, PA

FAIRWING BRAZIL - WORLD WAR II

Tales of the South Atlantic

John R. Harrison - PhoM 2/C

From early December, 1941 through much of 1945, many U.S. Navy and U.S. Army Air Force and Army personnel served at joint Brazilian – U.S. bases in the coastal cities of Brazil and on two islands in the Atlantic Narrows between that country and Africa. The U.S. Fourth Fleet, based in Recife, Brazil and its Fleet Air Wing 16, based at several coastal cities, were there to wage war on Axis Power submarines, surface raiders, and blockade runners. The U-Boats and armed raiders were sinking Allied ships at an alarming rate. The blockade runners were carrying vital war materials to the Axis Powers.

The U.S. Army Air Force established a major air base at Natal, Brazil for use as the southernmost point of its Ferry Command (later the Air Transport Command, or ATC), which shuttled many thousands of airplanes and troops, as well as war material to all the theatres of war during World War II. As a result, Natal's Parnamirim air base became known as the "Crossroads of the World".

This compilation of anecdotes, photographs, and maps, with the accompanying captions and text, is presented to provide the reader with a perspective on the experiences of U.S. service personnel who were lucky enough to serve in Brazil, a beautiful country populated by friendly people. This story also illustrates that in addition to providing vital military bases, the Brazilians were staunch allies who sent an infantry division and a squadron of fighter planes to fight in the liberation of Italy. It is hoped that the commentary on the history of Brazil and its people will inspire greater interest in that country and the realization of its importance in the future of South America and the entire western hemisphere.

Review of Book

John (Jack) Harrison has presented us a book that unveils the complex role Brazil played in World War II. Besides providing new material regarding the Atlantic Ocean-wide strategy of the United States (U.S.) Navy in weakening the ability of Germany's U-Boat and surface raider fleets to harass Allied shipping, Harrison's book provides new data concerning U-Boat operations in the Pacific Ocean and the U.S.' ability to rapid ferry aircraft from the Americas to fighting in north Africa and southern Europe from bases in eastern Brazil. The book has terrific anecdotal stories of servicemen stationed there during the war, as well as follow-up information on their lives. Harrison's photography and that of his compatriots of wartime activity and life then in Brazil's cities, also with updates, is outstanding. This is truly a remarkable story told from first-hand experience.

Joseph Lake
Delaware Historian

The Cover Photographs

The photo on the front cover shows a PBM (Martin Mariner) of Fairwing 16 flying over Guanabara Bay, near the Santos Dumont Airport section of Rio de Janeiro. Fairwing 16 had seaplane and landplane bases all along the Atlantic coastline from Amapa (Belem) in the north to Florianapolis in southernmost Brazil.

The photo on the back cover shows the German anti-aircraft crew of U-848, an IXD2 type U-Boat commanded by Wilhelm Rollmann attempting to avoid gunfire and depth charges from a VB-107 Liberator (PB4Y) of Fairwing 16 during a battle which took place between Brazil and Africa on November 5, 1943. This particular battle lasted about six hours and primarily featured attacks by PB4Y's from Ascension Island piloted by Lieutenants C.A. Baldwin, W.R. Ford, W.E. Hill, and Samuel K. Taylor. After hours of battle, a final attack by VB-107-B-4 piloted by Lieutenant Taylor finally blew up U-848. Twenty survivors were spotted, life rafts were dropped, and a nearby British freighter was notified of the location, but only one German crewman was eventually rescued 30 days later. While this photo was taken during a battle in which planes of Fairwing 16 were the victors, in other engagements, the anti-aircraft gunners on the U-Boats shot down the attacking planes and the entire air crews were killed.

In the introduction, a notation refers to Clay Blair's books entitled *Hitler's U-Boat Wars*.[1] In a photograph four pages beyond page 288 (in Volume II, *The Hunted*), Mr. Blair captioned a photo of the attack on U-848 with the sentence, "note the unmanned anti-aircraft array on the U-Boat's bridge". This was incorrect, as the cover photo clearly shows there were at least four German sailors crouching down behind the two dual sets of anti-aircraft cannon on the bridge of the U-Boat.

In general, Mr. Blair's book has excellent detail, but he also tended to downplay the serious nature of the U-Boat war. Winston Churchill is quoted as saying that the U-Boat menace was the only thing that really frightened him during World War II.

After the war, the British people and government diverted much of the Marshall Plan aid to purchase much needed foodstuffs to feed a malnourished populace. As a British colleague told me many years later, "we should have used the aid to rejuvenate industry but we were so hungry, we ate most of it." They were hungry because of the U-Boat activities. Their military forces also suffered serious shortages of supplies during the 1940-43 period due to the successes of the German submariners.

The capability of Admiral Doenitz's small U-Boat fleet was severely restrained by diversion of U-Boats to the Mediterranean because of land battles, otherwise the total number of Allied ships sunk in the 1939 through 1945 period would have been much greater and the final outcome more problematic.

Fortunately for the Allied powers, Hitler was land minded and had inadequate knowledge of the importance of sea power and essentially little comprehension of Naval strategy. Morison (Ref. 5) has a particularly relevant section on this subject:

"Military men are often accused of planning every new war in terms of the last one. Now the pattern of World War II in the Atlantic turned out to be very similar to that of World War I; yet nobody planned it that way. Hitler had endeavored to build up a high-seas (surface) fleet and neglected U-Boats, while Britain, France, and the United States were far better prepared to deal with a surface than an underwater Navy. Until the German Admiralty records were examined, almost everyone in the United States and Great Britain thought that the U-Boat campaign had been prepared long in advance. Nothing could be further from the truth.

"Submarine warfare was unwanted and unexpected by Hitler, unprepared for by the German Navy; when adopted perforce it was improvised until well on into 1943 when all German Naval effort and large share of production was concentrated on making it a success"

When the war started Admiral Doenitz had only 43 U-Boats. After the war a justifiably bitter Doenitz said, "Germany was never prepared for a Naval war against England, a realistic policy would have given Germany a thousand U-Boats at the beginning." One can only say, "God looks after fools and the United States of America."

DEDICATION

This book is dedicated to my wife, Doris Bennett Harrison, and to my mother, M. Ella Parke Harrison. To Dorie, my partner in life for 67 years, and to Mom, who inspired my interest in photography by her skilled use of her Kodak box camera. I am deeply indebted to them.

IN MEMORIAM

Frank Burgess
Billie Goodell
Sam Taylor
Ed Krug
Marshall Jamison

Book Design by John Harrison.

Library of Congress Control Number: 2013954823

Printed in China.
ISBN: 978-0-7643-4665-1

We are interested in hearing from authors with book ideas on related topics.

Published by Schiffer Publishing, Ltd.
4880 Lower Valley Road
Atglen, PA 19310
Phone: (610) 593-1777
FAX: (610) 593-2002
E-mail: Info@schifferbooks.com.
Visit our web site at: www.schifferbooks.com
Please write for a free catalog.
This book may be purchased from the publisher.
Try your bookstore first.

The Basis of an Alliance

Personal Diplomacy

Success in the South Atlantic depended on cooperation with the Brazilians. This photo (I-1) is emblematic of the excellent relationship between FDR, Getulio Vargas, and Admiral Ingram, which provided the foundation for the eventual victory of combined US-Brazilian forces in their battles with Axis power submarines, surface raiders, and blockade runners. Getulio Vargas called Jonas Ingram - "My Admiral". By 1943, FDR had a six-year friendship with Vargas and his foreign minister (O. Aranha) - Photo from FDR Library.

ACKNOWLEDGEMENTS

Several of my World War II friends contributed photographs, stories, and anecdotes, which appear in this book. In compiling this work, I have also had the good fortune of being helped by a number of new friends who have supplied photos and materials.

Notable among those who served in the war and also helped me are the following: Billie Goodell, a bona fide American hero of VP-83/VB-107; Arthur and Bernice Sykes, both who served as photographers in the US Navy; Moo Thick Soo Hoo, who has a life story and a parental family story which constitute an example of the courage of immigrants who overcame great challenges, with Moo becoming a navy photographer of note and a Lieutenant Commander who served 30 years in the US Navy; Lieutenant Commander Ed Krug of VP-83/VB-107, who had served his country in the army horse calvary starting in 1937, before his distinguished career as a US Navy aviator; Lieutenant Commander Paul Richter of VP-83/VB-107, a 30 year navy veteran who served with distinction and whose parent's and grandparent's immigration life story is an example of the fortitude of the type of people who made this country great and is illustrative of how the "Greatest Generation" was nurtured; Lieutenant Carrell I. (Zoom) Pinnell of VP-83/VB-107 who worked his way up from apprentice seaman in 1936, served as one of the original Naval Aviation Pilots, later was commissioned and spent 20 years in the navy; Lieutenant Frank Burgess of VP-83/VB-107, an orphan from the Dust Bowl of Oklahoma who after enlisting in 1938 was promoted from Yeoman 2/c to Naval Aviation Pilot and then commissioned officer during his 20 years of naval service; Commander Samuel K. Taylor, Jr.. of VP-83/VB-107, the Tennessee Ridge-Runner who came from a rural farm background and enlisted in early 1941 for pilot training and after a very effective career in naval aviation stayed in the organized reserves for 20 more years; Richard Wilson, an aviation radioman who saw combat while serving in VP-83/VB-107 and became the squadron historian and a leader in the many annual reunions held by VP-83/VB-107 personnel after World War II. Richard's two editions of squadron history and his help were invaluable contributions to this book.

Among the latter day friends who helped is Dr. Clyde Smith, Jr., an American expatriate who has just retired from his professorship at the University of Rio Grande do Norte at Natal where he and his Brazilian wife have lived for many decades. Clyde had written two editions of "Trampoline to Victory: The Story of the Americans in Natal, Brazil During World War II" which had much detail on the role of the US Army Air Force at that location.

Lieutenant Colonel Marshall Jamison of the US Army Air Force who was the first American officer into Natal on December 17, 1941 and who performed valiant improvisational leadership for the air force personnel during the first six months after Pearl Harbor has reprised to me the details of his experiences in those early days.

Regina Fontes Foster, a Brazilian expatriate born in 1950 in Recife, Brazil but who from ages 6 to 14 lived in the USA where her Brazilian air force colonel father was going to college. Regina is the niece of Guinora Pinheiro Machado who was a beautiful 17-year-old living in Natal during the war years and who I photographed for one of my navy buddies. Guinora, who now lives in Rio de Janeiro, put me in touch with Regina and her husband (Leroy) and they have provided much assistance to me.

Sheila Carper Adkins, daughter of Wallace Richard Carper, aviation chief radioman in VP-83/VB-107, kindly loaned me her father's photo album which she found in a cedar chest where it had been for many decades. Her father, Dick Carper, had a distinguished navy career. His son, Thomas Carper, now a US Senator from the state of Delaware had previously been a US Congressman and Governor of Delaware. The Senator was helpful.

A most helpful friend who made many contributions to this book is Fred Nicolau, a Brazilian engineer who is an avid student of history and all things American. Fred's help has been invaluable.

Manuel Gentil Marinho Pessoa Neto, Eduardo Maia and Augusto Maranhao, current residents of Natal also supplied information and photos. Christian Fehr and Roberto Costa Pinto of Salvador da Bahia, Hans Von Manteuffel of Recife, Margi Moss of Brasilia, and Marie Christine Pinheira also very kindly provided photos of modern Brazilian cities.

My wife of 66 years, Doris Bennett Harrison, has well tolerated all the long hours, days, months, and years I have spent on this work and our daughter, Nancy H. Geoghegan, has worked in producing all this verbiage, hopefully in readable and interesting form.

CONTENTS

PREFACE

> This generation of young Americans has a rendezvous with destiny.
>
> Franklin Delano Roosevelt – 1941

December 7, 1941 was a relatively warm and pleasant day for winter time in Northern Delaware. I had been bouncing and shooting a basketball in our backyard when my mother came to the back shed door and called me to come in, that there was an important announcement coming in on the radio about the Japs and an attack on Pearl Harbor. This was about three weeks after my seventeenth birthday and I expected to graduate from high school the following June. Our immediate thoughts were about my brother, Bill, who we had learned was due to leave from San Diego Naval Base to go to Hawaii in December. Fortunately, he was not due to leave until December 10, 1941, so he was safe for the moment.

Even though many events tended to indicate that our country would sooner or later be involved in the conflict raging around the world, we did not expect that we would be catapulted into the conflict by the Japanese at that particular time. Our country had just been starting to emerge from the depths of the Great Depression in the 1939-1941 period and it was not an era of "Great Expectations." High school graduates from our small rural village where economic life depended on four local industrial mills, or on farm labor on the many surrounding family farms, could largely expect to become either mill workers or farm laborers. While my two older brothers and I, as well as our boyhood friends, had the benefit of stable and loving family life in a fine rural village and had obtained a good education through the 12th grade level, there were very limited affordable opportunities for college education. I had always wanted to go to the US Naval Academy at Annapolis but lack of 20-20 vision made that impossible.

So, on that fateful Sunday, it can be stated accurately that my future course in life was largely unplotted and unknown. It was also primarily subject to external world affairs, which were certainly outside my control. Very soon I would fully comprehend the meaning of President Roosevelt's words when he said, "This generation of young Americans has a rendezvous with destiny."

Many stories have been told, books have been published, and motion pictures made about World War II and the experiences of the people who were participants in that momentous conflict. Amazingly, there is still more to be revealed and reflected upon, particularly about the Battle of the South Atlantic and the valiant efforts of the Brazilians. There were several "theatres of war," and most of the activities of the armed forces of the combatants and the local civilian populations in the other sectors of conflict have been well described in the many publications which are available. However, not much has been written, published, or distributed about the conflict in the South Atlantic Ocean between the Axis Power submarine and surface vessel forces and the combined forces of Brazil, the United States, and Great Britain. Nor does the American public realize the scope and depth of the efforts made by the Brazilians as our allies.

Since I had the good fortune to serve in Fleet Air Wing 16 in Brazil during 1943-1944, and preserved many photographs which depict wartime activities in that area, I have been able to assemble this collection of photographs and accompanying commentary by my shipmates and myself to help delineate some of the historical record. I have also supplemented this material with maps, photos, and commentary from references to put things into context and complete the picture. It was a privilege and an honor to serve our country and the cause of freedom during World War II. One month after graduating from high school in June, 1942, (at the age of 17) I enlisted in the U.S.. Navy for a "minority cruise." It was clear that service in the military was certain and I had always wanted to go to sea in the Navy. In addition to fulfilling my obligation as a citizen, my intent was to pursue interests in photography and aviation which had started with building detailed models of military aircraft and subsequently photographing the models.

From an initial assignment (after boot camp at Newport, Rhode Island) I was sent to Patrol Wing 9, headquarters squadron at Quonset Point, Rhode Island Naval Air Station to serve as a "striker" (apprentice) in the Photo Laboratory. Initially I was to go to Pensacola to attend the Navy's school for aerial photographers but the class had already started so I was sent to Quonset Point instead.

During the fall of 1942, I began flying as a lookout in PBY patrol planes escorting convoys in the North Atlantic on their way to Britain or Murmansk, Russia. The evening before I was to go on a convoy coverage flight, I would try to be asleep by 2000 because a very early wakeup call was impending. Normal reveille was at 0600 at which time the Master-at Arms (MAA) (a salty and assertive Boatswains Mate first class) would walk down the line of metal bunks clanging his night stick on the feet of the bunks and saying "all right, hit the deck". However, when we were due to go out on a patrol flight, the MAA would tap one on the shoulder and whisper "get up and dressed, you have 45 minutes to get down to Seaplane Hangar no.2 for your flight." That wake-up call would be at about 0400 and we would have to hustle because putting on long john underwear, 2 pairs of woolen socks, two sweaters, dungaree pants, heavy fur lined arm pit length leather flying pants and flight jacket, along with mukluk type lined flight boots, gloves, and helmet took a fair amount of time.

The jump seat in the "blister"* on the side of a PBY gets a bit chilly and uncomfortable during a 10 to 12 hour flight over the North Atlantic in the winter time in an unheated airplane. Electrically heated clothing was not available in the early months of the war. We usually ate most of the flight rations early in the flight because after a few hours the bread froze hard as a rock. Despite the heavy fur lined leather flying gear it was not possible to keep ones feet warm.

Our discomfort paled into insignificance contrasted to the potential perils faced by the merchant marine seamen who would be sailing into the "Black Hole," that area in mid-ocean where no air cover could be provided to the convoys at that time. They, for a long time, were the unsung heroes of World War II.

Most of us were too young to realize the full extent of the peril we would encounter if the plane crashed or was shot down. Periodically during our slow circling around the convoy, the pilot would make a run down through the center of the ships, about 15 feet over the water, apparently to break the monotony. When he did that I could look out at the seamen on the rail of the ships at eye-level. We would continue covering the convoy until about 1630 before heading home. That evening, after having left Quonset at about 0500, we would be pleased to see landfall, either off Long Island or Block Island, depending on the convoys' route. During that early phase of the war we did have some form of radar but it very seldom functioned as designed.

*See Photo I-91, P. 129

Photo I-2: The author in winter flying gear - 1942

The PBY (or Catalina, as our British allies dubbed it) was a fine long-range patrol plane which fulfilled several functions well. It did not have as much speed, or bomb and armament capacities as the PB4Y 's Liberator (the Navy's version of the B-24), some of which were just beginning to pass through Quonset Point from the aircraft factories in late 42, early '43, but the PBY was a very important airplane.

In June, 1943, five of us from the Photo Lab were informed we were being transferred to Fleet Air Wing 16 in Brazil. Our contingent included a man named Robinson who clearly was well over 50 years of age when he enlisted in 1942. He had recently been promoted from his entry rank of Photographers Mate First Class to Chief Photographers Mate.

Also included were Jim Tracy, Bill McKeehen, Bill Rodman, and myself. Robbie Robinson (I can't recall his first name) had been in charge of the Photo Lab when I arrived at Quonset. Robbie had a portrait photo studio in New Rochelle, New York. I remember how he taught us to smear Vaseline on the camera lens before taking a portrait. What possessed him to enlist in the Navy, I did not know.

The Photo Lab at Quonset Point had later become managed by a regular Navy Chief Petty Officer, with three gold hash marks on his sleeve denoting 12 years with a good record, one Emmett O'Neill Sanders.A group photo of Quonset Point photographers appears at the end of the Preface. He was a good manager and good disciplinarian and was also well connected in the hierarchy of the peace time photographic section of the Air Force, Atlantic Fleet. Regular Navy men sometimes had a natural tendency to stick together in important matters.

Orders for transfers of Navy photographers originated through VD-2 (Photographic Squadron 2) located at Norfolk Naval Air Station. VD-2 functioned as the photographic personnel pool for the Atlantic Fleet. I suspect Robbie's hurried promotion to Chief had its origin in the orders for the transfer of a Chief to Brazil. While I, in my teenage state of bliss and naiveté, did not have any apprehension about being sent to Brazil, even when Chief Sanders said we were going to a very hot place, Robbie was clearly upset.

We first went to Norfolk, Virginia and joined about 115 other sailors being sent to Brazil. We took a very hot and dirty two day trip by railroad (the rail cars were of the 1880 or so vintage) to Gulfport, Mississippi to a large (and 99% empty) Port of Embarkation (P.O.E.) base where we spent about seven days learning to shoot rifles and drilling.

We left Gulfport in trucks and went to New Orleans where we boarded a Liberty Ship that had been converted into an Army transport; the U.S.S.. William Evarts. The next day we were joined aboard ship by a battalion of colored Seabees (Naval Construction Battalion) who were on their way to Trinidad to construct a Naval Air Station with Blimp hangars. The rows and rows of bunks in the ships hold contained metal piping bunks, about four or five high in each stack, with canvas sacking to serve as beds. When we looked down into the hold we saw all the colored Seabees and the scene looked eerily like one would envision occurring in a slave ship, except of course, there were no manacles or chains. Fortunately, the convoy, which formed outside New Orleans, only lingered overnight before heading out into the Gulf of Mexico toward Guantanamo Bay, Cuba. It took several days to get to Gitmo because, like many convoys of that time, the speed was restricted to that within the three to six knot pace of a Greek freighter or two.

The water turned a beautiful blue and the breezes were fine on-deck when we got into the Caribbean. Sailfish and dolphins and small bobbing escort vessels were included in the panorama of the sea. The food; we were fed two meals per day, was horrible. None of us gained any weight. Several of the tiny escorting vessels were Canadian or British. Apparently the Pacific war and other convoys were commanding most of our surface vessels and trained sailors; an early indication of how unprepared for war our country had been in 1941.

After stopping for a day in Gitmo (we did not disembark) the convoy headed toward Trinidad. We had been told at Gitmo that several ships in the convoy just preceding us toward Trinidad had been sunk by U-Boats. At that period Trinidad was also known as Torpedo Junction. We passed by Aruba and Curacao and arrived at Trinidad after what seemed like a week or so at sea. The Seabees departed to their work and we were billeted at the Naval Air Station for a week waiting for a new convoy to be formed going toward Brazil. During our stay at Trinidad Robbie "jumped ship" in a desperate effort to avoid being sent to Brazil. He clearly felt that Chief Sanders comment about Brazil being a "very hot place" was accurate. The Shore Patrol caught up with Robbie and the last time I saw him they were leading him to the brig in handcuffs. I never found out what happened to him after that. Perhaps some reader of this book will know?

The great tragedy of the whole episode with Robbie was that all of the air bases of Fleet Air Wing Sixteen were in comfortable coastal areas of Brazil which had excellent year round climates due to sea breezes (except Belem where no photographers were based). Had he not been misled by others he would have enjoyed his service at Recife or Natal, just like the rest of us did. Some of the sailors who were rotated back to the states in '43 or '44 requested a return to Brazil when the opportunity arose. Those who had earlier gone to Brazil in December 1941 or 1942 were faced with living in tents or in some cases sleeping in planes. However, by mid 1943, when we got there, the U.S. Engineering Department and the Army Corps of Engineers had, with Brazilian cooperation, constructed good barracks, mess halls, and other air base facilities that were very adequate.

Those who were fortunate enough to serve significant portions of their naval service in Brazil also had two other benefits. They served under an Admiral (Ingram) and an Air Wing commander (Rossmore Denham Lyon) who were officers who fostered good morale by treating all the men serving under them in a fine manner. Of equal importance, we were serving in a friendly allied country with the Brazilian populace, who despite their own widely varying economic conditions, were almost uniformly convivial. Many of them had a standard of living much lower than the average American but that did not seem to negatively affect their friendly demeanor. It is now very clear to me that Chief Sanders decision to include me in the transfer orders to Brazil was a very fortuitous defining moment in my life. Unfortunately I never had or took the opportunity to thank him.

During my service primarily at Recife and Natal (I spent one month on Fernando de Noronha, an island off Natal), I was able to photograph some of the people, places, and facilities of those Northeastern cities. I also had the good fortune to travel on leave to Bahia (now called Salvador, capital of the state of Bahia) and to that jewel of a city, Rio de Janeiro.

When, in the year 2000, I installed darkroom equipment in my basement and began making enlargements of my photos from Brazil my purpose was to send copies to my old squadron mates and possibly prepare a photo exhibit. Then, in 2001 I happened to read an article in the New York Times about Natal, Brazil written by one Larry Rohter which described wartime occurrences there as well as current efforts to memorialize the cities' role in the war. Several names were mentioned in that article which prompted me to contact the persons named therein to share knowledge on the role of Natal in the 1941 – 45 period.

The gentlemen contacted, Dr. Clyde Smith, Jr., an American expatriate and professor of history at the Federal University at Natal, and Captain Marshall Jamison of the U.S. Army Air Force who had been the first U.S.. Air Force officer to arrive in Natal in December 1941, both expressed an interest in my photographs.

Intrigued by those contacts and by memories prompted by viewing my enlarged photos, further contacts were made with a number of men who also had served in Fleet Air Wing 16 in Brazil. One of them (Billie Goodell) put me in touch with a Brazilian (Fred Nicolau of Natal - blackrivercousins@yahoo.com). Fred proved to be an Americanophile with a strong interest in World War II events, particularly regarding the joint efforts of the Brazilians and the Americans. Since 2001, I have had a running dialogue with all four of these estimable friends.

To supplement knowledge about Brazil as I had known it in the 1940's, a review of books about that fascinating and important country accompanied my work in reproducing both my photographs and photographs from my Navy friends. As I learned more about Brazilian history and Brazil's current role in the world it became clear that additional contemporary photos of the four cities in which I had served would be interesting to demonstrate how much that dynamic country had changed in the past 60+ years. My Brazilian friends have kindly supplied these contemporary photos.

The attempts to memorialize the Brazilian-American joint actions in World War II continue currently at Natal. Several of my Brazilian friends are playing a key role in this effort. Since the Allied actions in the Battle of the South Atlantic were a very important part of the tremendous logistics struggle to win a world-wide war it is important that additional information on that subject be disseminated. Those war years were also a high point in U.S.-Brazilian relations so recounting those activities and memorializing them could have a positive effect on the current relationship between Brazil and the United States.

Photo Lab Personnel Quonset Point

Photo I-3; Photographers at Quonset Point Naval Air Station

This group is made up of 27 men of Headquarters Squadron Fleet Air Wing Nine plus two photographers of Airasdevlant seconded to FAW 9. (1943).

First Row - Left to right = Bill Rodman, J.M. Shafer, CPO E.F. Dolezal, Lt. Monosson, CPO E.O. Sanders, Jim Tracy, E.L. Kraft

Second Row - Thibodeaux, K.G. Watland, M.H. Benham, J.J. Breen, P.G. Braudis, J.R. Harrison, Bruce Rose, J.E. Hartmann, C.N. Wofford, Maro Nelson Bartlett, R. L. Hatch

Third Row - A. R. Hallgren, F.J. Moore, T.C. Schoettner, Carl M. Rowe, P.E. Miller, Theron Donald Goble, Gene Wolf, ___?___, C.K. Ainsworth

Chiefs Dolezal and Sanders are leaning on a Fairchild F-56 aerial camera used for aerial mapping photography.

List of Acronyms

1. Fairwing – Fleet Air Wing
2. ATC – Air Transport Command
3. MAA – Master at Arms
4. VD-2 – Photographic Squadron Two
5. Gitmo – Guantanamo Bay, Cuba
6. PBY – Patrol Bomber – Consolidated
7. PBM – Patrol Bomber – Martin
8. FDR – Franklin Delano Roosevelt
9. Pan Am – Pan American Airline
10. OS2U – Observation Scout Two – Sikorsky
11. USO – United Service Organization
12. Hedron – Headquarters Squadron
13. CPO – Chief Petty Officer
14. USAAF – United States Army Air Force
15. PT – Patrol Torpedo Boat
16. PhoM2/c – Photographers Mate Second Class
17. PV-1 Patrol Ventura (Lockheed)
18. U-Boat – Untersee Boat
19. PB4Y – Patrol Bomber Four – Consolidated
20. ACFC – Air Corps Ferry Command
21. C-47 – Cargo Plane 47 (Douglas DC-3)
22. C-87 – Cargo Plane Version of B-24
23. ADP – Airport Development Program
24. "ASIMOW" – Name of UCLA Professor and of a Joint Ford Foundation sponsored industrialization project for north east Brazil – 1960's
25. "RITA" – A joint US Agency for International Development and Brazilian Government Agency Industrialization project of north east Brazil – 1960's
26. PX – Post Exchange
27. USED – United States Engineering Department
28. TVA – Tennessee Valley Authority
29. USACE – United States Army Corps of Engineers
30. NASA – National Aeronautics and Space Agency
31. K-20 – Fairchild Aerial Camera
32. F-56 - Large Fairchild Aerial Camera
33. 2000 is 8:00 PM; MilitaryTime Used Throughout The Book
34. NAS - Naval Air Station
35. A.C.I. - Air Combat Intelligence

INTRODUCTION

You were in Brazil during World War II, what were you doing there?

A question frequently asked of the author

FAIRWING – BRAZIL contains a collection of photographs, most of which I, as an 18 year old enlisted photographer, or my colleagues, took during our service in Brazil with Fleet Air Wing 16, the aviation component of the U.S. Fourth Fleet which was headquartered in Recife, Brazil under the command of Admiral Jonas H. Ingram. The commentary in this book focuses primarily on events during World War II in and off the coast of the northeastern Brazilian cities of Natal, Fortaleza, Recife, Salvador/Bahia, and the southeastern city of Rio de Janeiro. The Map No.1 shows the location of these coastal cities of Brazil within the entire large country (the Estados Unidos do Brasil). This is a modern map which shows the modern highway system and Brasilia, neither of which existed in the 1940's. This map is from the 5th edition of the Rough Guide to Brazil,[(2)] published by Rough Guides Ltd, in 2003, reproduced with the permission of the publisher. Map No. 2 (from Reference_3_) shows that the northeastern coast of Brazil is the western hemisphere's closest point to Africa.

The objective of the Fourth Fleet was to dominate the strategically important Atlantic Narrows between Natal, Brazil and the Freetown – Accra portion of Africa by finding and destroying Axis Power submarines and blockade runners who were funneling essential war materials from the far-eastern Japanese empire through the South Atlantic Narrows between Brazil and Africa into Europe. An additional purpose was to halt the sinking of Brazilian and other Allied merchant ships by the Axis Power's naval units. Because the Mediterranean Sea was hazardous for Allied shipping, control of the South Atlantic Narrows was strategically critical.

Though Recife, population about 250,000 in 1943, was where both the Fourth Fleet and Fleet Air Wing 16 were eventually headquartered; Natal, then with a population of about 50,000, which is about 200 miles north of Recife, was the earliest, largest, and most important joint U.S.-Brazilian airbase facility in Brazil. Within a few days after Pearl Harbor, both a few Army Air Force personnel and a 6 plane detachment from a U.S. Navy squadron of PBY amphibious patrol planes arrived at Natal which already had limited air base facilities previously developed by Panair do Brasil, a subsidiary of Pan American Airways. These facilities were for the Pan Am Clipper, a large seaplane. Since Natal was the closest point to Africa it was the obvious place to base patrol planes (which at that time had somewhat limited range) to counteract the Axis Powers naval units.

Natal also subsequently became the southernmost point for the transit of airplanes, personnel, and war material to U.S. Allies in Europe, the Mediterranean, the China-Burma-India, and Pacific theatres of war. Accordingly the U.S. Army Air Force Ferry Command, later the Air Transport Command (ATC), made Natal the "Crossroads of the World", starting in 1942. Many thousands of Allied armed forces personnel (as well as USO celebrity entertainers and political personages) passed through Natal and the Parnamirim Air Base after it was greatly expanded in 1942-43.

Recife, which had the requisite harbor facilities, was the main base for the surface ships of the Fourth Fleet which consisted of destroyers, cruisers, service vessels and eventually (1944-45) Jeep aircraft carriers. Ibura field at Recife also became the second largest Brazilian-US air base and was used by squadrons from both countries. Ultimately, Fairwing 16 had joint air bases all the way from Belem in the north down to Florianopolis in southernmost Brazil, with some of the bases being strictly for seaplanes.

The Brazilian Air Force and Navy and the other U.S. forces worked together in the battles with the Axis Powers naval forces. Many Brazilian personnel were also involved in the construction of the jointly controlled air bases and seaport facilities and also were employed in base operations. Fairwing 16 and its Brazilian allies, in their battles with the U-Boats, lost a lot of fine men in the South Atlantic Ocean from accurate anti-aircraft fire from surfaced submarines.

I-4 Map No. 1: Brazil and neighbors, from 5th Edition of the Rough Guide to Brazil published by Rough Guides Ltd. in 2003. Reproduced with the permission of the publisher.

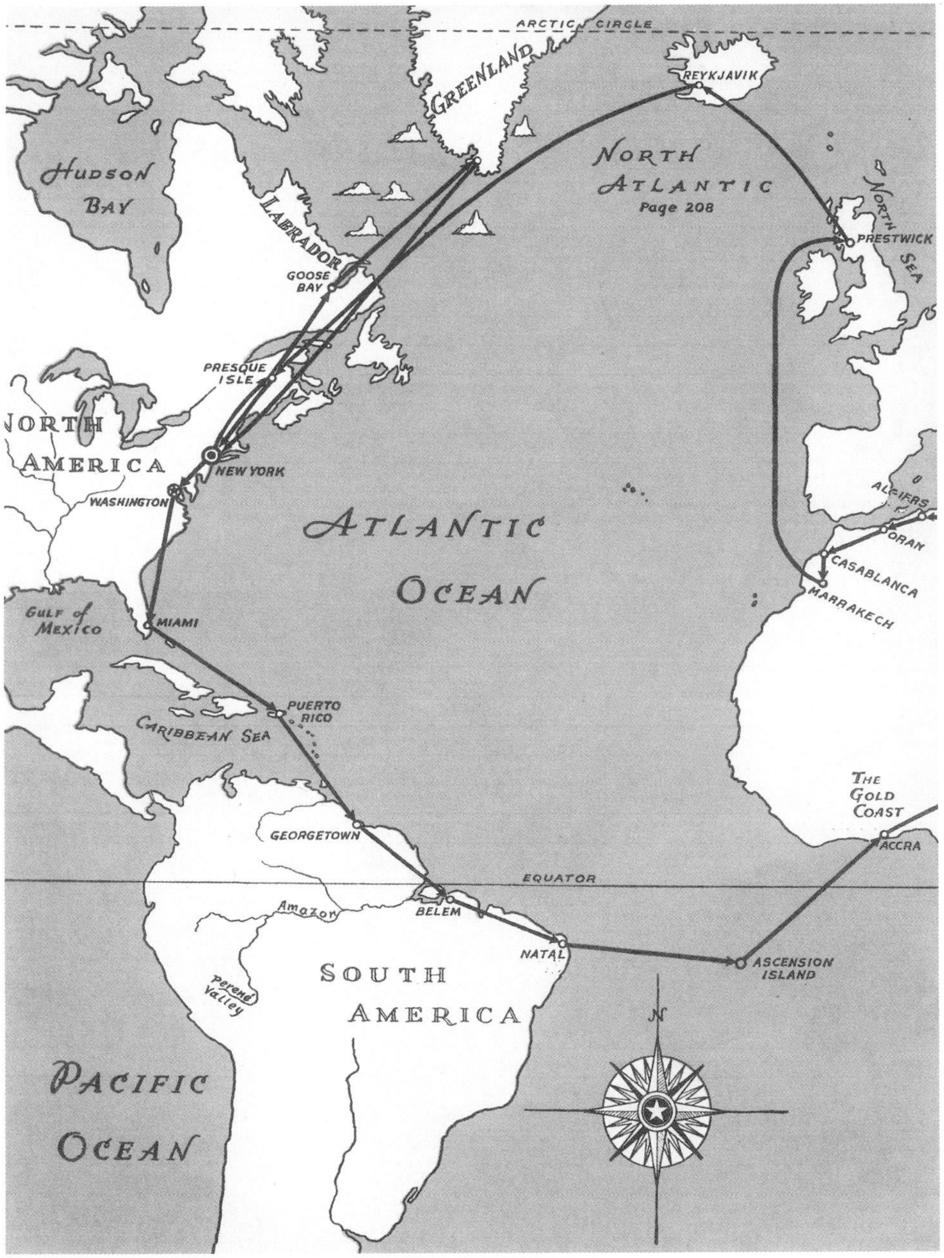

I-5 Map No. 2: Atlantic Ocean air routes, credit Whittlesey House-McGraw Hill Book Co. "Flight to Everywhere" by Ivan Dmitri

ATLANTIC OCEAN AIR ROUTES

During World War II the useful range of heavily loaded transportation planes was a limiting factor in the selection of acceptable air routes from the USA where the planes were produced to the various theaters of war. Smaller bombers and particularly fighter planes were even more limited in ranges. In addition to the distance factor the weather conditions and the potential interdiction of supply and plane delivery flights by enemy planes were also factors in selection of the best route.

While Map No. 2 shows that Natal to Freetown in Africa is only 1,600 miles and New York to London is over 3,100 miles, Natal is still in the southern hemisphere and about 3000 miles from Miami, USA.

When all the factors: weather; length of over water flight segments'; possibility of enemy interdiction, and; base availability in friendly or allied countries were considered, the Southern Route was logically chosen as the primary air transport command route. Once the Ascension Island base was available even short range fighter planes like the P-38 could be flown across the South Atlantic.

The PBY's, PB4Y's, PBM's, and PV-1's of that time had to dive close to the U-Boats to accurately bomb or depth charge the enemy. These planes were slow and relatively easy targets and some of the air crews paid the ultimate price whenever the U-Boat crews were sufficiently alert.

For those who seek further detailed knowledge of the role and performance of Fairwing 16 and the Fourth Fleet and their Brazilian counterparts we suggest a review of a book entitled "Galloping Ghosts of the Brazilian Coast" by Alan C. Carey[4] and its list of other works on this subject. Also of particular note are two volumes from Samuel Eliot Morison's "History of Naval Operations in World War II, the Battle of the Atlantic Volume I and II".[5] An additional two book set of interest is entitled "Hitler's U-Boat War, Volume I – The Hunters, 1939-1942, and Volume II, The Hunted 1942 – 1945" by one Clay Blair. Mr. Blair's work (1998 vintage) is a very scholarly and detailed review of epic proportions and well worth extended study. The three referenced works give a broad and detailed account of the activities of Allied and Axis Power forces in the naval battles of the Atlantic.

To learn more about the activities of the USAAF Air Transport Command at Natal and elsewhere, the reader is referred to the excellent pictorial history by Ivan Dimitri of the Saturday Evening Post entitled "Flight to Everywhere" (Reference 3). Dr. Clyde Smith, Jr., of Natal has also published two editions of his "Trampoline to Victory" about Natal's role in World War II (References 6, 7)

For those who served in Brazil and wonder what has happened there over the past 60 plus years we recommend the following 3 publications:

- "Brazil – the Rough Guide", by Cleary, Jenkins and Marshall, ISBN 1-84353-077-5, www.roughguides.com. As implied in the title this work is an excellent guide for tourists.

- "Brazil" – (Travel Survival Kit 3 @ 1996 Lonely Planet Publications)[8]; Draffen, McAsey, Pinheiro, and Jones. ISBN-0-86442-3179. This book has an excellent review of the history of Brazil among other things. It is very informative.

- "Brazil, Past and Present" – by Beppe Ceccato, Edizioni White Star, Italy ISBN: 88-8095-395-5. Outstanding history and photographs

Brazil has long been, in the author's opinion, the best friend the USA has in South America. It is a large, important, complex, diverse country which has been able to develop into a democracy that holds much as yet unfulfilled promise for a better life for all of its people in the future. It is important to realize that the population of Brazil has grown from 46 million in 1940 to 164 million in 2000 (a 256% increase) while the population of the United States has grown from 131 million to 280 million (only a 113% increase). Further, Brazil has a land area which is 8% larger than the mainland USA, with vast natural resources. Brazil has become the world's largest exporter of soy, beef, tobacco, chicken, sugar, coffee, orange juice, and alcohol fuel in the world. It has also developed large automobile and aircraft manufacturing industries. Recently large undersea deposits of petroleum have been discovered off the coast of Brazil.

Like many countries around the world Brazil classified groups of its states by sections. Map No.3 shows the way Brazilians' denote geographic areas or sections of their country and also delineates the names and capitals of the states. This Map No.3 is reproduced with permission from Brazil Travel Survival Kit 3 ©1996 Lonely Planet publications. [8]

There are striking differences in; climate, degree of industrialization, population density and distribution, economic status, and racial mixtures in the different sections of Brazil, a Land of Great Contrast. The Southeast and South are more industrialized, generally have more dominantly European ancestry, and can be classified as modern, developed areas. The Central West and North are less populated and relatively less developed.

The Northeast population is largely concentrated along the coast because of the more favorable climate conditions by the sea. After World War II there was a significant migration of people from the Northeast to the Southern sections in order to seek economic improvement. In the past few decades the beauty and favorable climate of the coastal areas of the northeast have been rediscovered and tourism has greatly increased.

The Northeastern cities of Fortaleza, Natal, Recife and Salvador have also experienced significant growth in population and diversity in industry and economic activity. This has tended to materially decrease migration to the more southern areas.

European migration into the Northeastern cities has also increased.

I-6 Map No. 3: Regions and states of Brazil, reproduced with permission from Brazil Travel Survival Kit 3© 1996 Lonely Planet Publications

1

Brazil, Strategic Ally in World War II

Brazil and World War II: The Forgotten Ally; What did you do in the war, Zé Carioca?*

Frank D. McCann, University of New Hampshire

PREWAR MILITARY PLANNING

The general public and the ruling political classes of the USA were ambivalent on the question of if, when, and how we should begin to oppose and confront aggressive policies of the Axis Powers as the year of 1939 progressed. We were still in the throes of the Great Depression. The unemployment rate was still near 20% in early 1940. We were more anxious about improving economic conditions at home rather than being concerned about geopolitics and Karl Haushofers' theories about world domination via control of the Heartland of Europe; a perspective which had dominated the thinking of Hitler. Accordingly, we did not, in general, well prepare our meager armed forces for the challenges they were to face after December 7, 1941. On Pearl Harbor Day there were fifteen other countries which had armed forces larger than those of the USA. Portugal, Sweden, Switzerland, and Romania had larger military forces than the USA. Many good men and women died unnecessarily due to this failure of the body politic, which occurred both in the U.S.A. and Great Britain.

However, fortunately we had a Joint Planning Committee of the U.S. Army-Navy Board which realized in the 1938-39 period that Nazi Germany and Italy might start a more general and successful aggressive war aimed at first establishing their hegemony over Europe and the Mediterranean areas to be followed by eventual incursions into South America. The Planning Committee further deduced that any invasion of the Western Hemisphere would be aimed at crossing the Atlantic Narrows between West Africa and Brazil and landing on the sea coast of Brazil in the area from Belem on the Amazon south to Bahia, Brazil. Our strategic military planners needed to forestall either an outright invasion from Africa (after a looming defeat of the British forces there) or the conversion of the Brazilian and Argentinian governments into regimes more friendly to the Axis Powers. Skeptics sometime maintain that Germany never really threatened Brazil. However, Adolf Hitler made the following statement about Brazil; "We shall create a new Germany there. We shall find everything we need there."

Our efforts in this area became more active shortly after the fall of France in May, 1940 since this event increased the possibility of Axis Power incursion into Brazil from French Colonies in Africa. We began to ship military equipment and armaments to Brazil under Lend-Lease arrangements. As a result of this effort Brazil did agree to first: allow U.S. Navy surface forces to begin operations off the coast of Brazil, and second; to allow Pan American Airways and the U.S. Army Corps of Engineers to start construction of airfields in Brazil starting in November, 1940. This was part of a secret agreement between the USA and Brazil. This agreement was facilitated by concurrent U.S. economic aid to Brazil. Despite these secret arrangements, not all elements of the Brazilian authorities were pro-American and Brazil did not declare war on the Axis Powers until August, 1942. Given the course of events up until the battle of Stalingrad this is easy to understand.

The aforementioned concern in the American Military establishment about the potential for Axis Power invasion of Brazil also led to construction of a large port of embarkation (P.O.E.) Army base at Gulfport, Mississippi during that period. When I was on my way from Quonset Point, Rhode Island, Naval Air Station (Fleet Air Wing Nine) to Fleet Air Wing Sixteen at Recife, Brazil in mid-1943, I spent several days at the large P.O.E. base at Gulfport prior to shipping out on a convoy from New Orleans. I noted that row after row of barracks at Gulfport had never been used.

* Ze Carioca refers to Jose Carioca, a Disney character emblematic of Brazilians in a movie. See photo I-73 for a drawing of Ze Carioca on a PB4Y airplane.

This, of course, was a good thing because it meant that by mid 1943 the Axis Powers had been stopped well before they could contemplate an invasion of the western hemisphere via Brazil. America and its people would be well advised to learn more about Brazil and cultivate an even stronger relationship with its government and people. This writer does not fault the U.S. military planners in building the Gulfport P.O.E. since prior to the events of December 1941 through November, 1942, the general perspective was that the USSR would soon be totally defeated and the Axis Powers free to complete the conquest of the Mediterranean, the African coasts, and the Middle East.

A NARROWLY AVOIDED CATASTROPHE

It should be noted that the offensive capability of the German Wehrmacht in the Soviet Union was not fully compromised until its defeat in the titanic battle of Kursk in July, 1943. Kursk was the largest tank battle ever and the field of battle was larger than the country of Wales.[15]

A fortuitous outcome of the early work on cooperative efforts by Brazil and the United States armed forces was that we could jointly develop an effort in late 1942 to combat the depredations of the U-Boats and disguised German surface raiders in the South Atlantic and also begin to intercept the Axis blockade running surface ships as they sailed through the Atlantic Narrows toward Europe or toward the Pacific.

The current general public is not fully aware as to how close the Axis Powers came to winning their war for world domination. From June, 1940 until June 22, 1941, when Hitler turned east against the Soviet Union, only the valiant British people and their Commonwealth partners stood between the Axis Powers and complete victory. Only the arrogance, cruelty, racism, and overconfidence of Hitler and Mussolini and the lack of coordination with the Japanese allowed the gallant soldiers (men and women) of the Red Army to stop the conquest of the Soviet Union at Moscow, Stalingrad, and Kursk.

Our supply of military equipment to the Red Army also had a pivotal effect. Over 50% of the Red Army's gun powder was made in American ordnance plants.

In the early fall of 1941, the Germans, and their Italian, Romanian, Hungarian, and Slovakian divisions were so confident that the Red Army was defeated that they did not supply all the troops with winter clothing, indeed the German soldiers later stripped winter clothing from captured Soviet soldiers. The Germans had previously considered a small demobilization.

Fortunately for the cause of freedom, the Japanese (who had signed a non-aggression pact with the Soviet Union in April 1941) did not dramatically threaten Siberia so Stalin was able to bring the Siberian divisions to the Moscow front in November, 1941. This and the Germans' awful treatment of captive areas sparked the realization within the Soviet Republics (particularly the Ukraine) that the German occupation would be even worse than the occupation and policies of the Russians who had subjugated and murdered many of them after 1919.

It is also fortunate that negotiations between Molotov (Foreign Minister of USSR) and Ribbentrop of Germany at Kirovograd in June of 1943 did not result in a separate peace agreement between the USSR and Germany.

Apparently Hitler and Stalin could not reach an agreement on how they would divide up Central and Eastern Europe between Germany and the USSR.

If all these events had not transpired the Brazilian bases would have taken on an even greater role in the conflict. As it was, the joint Brazilian and American Naval operations in the South Atlantic were eventually successful in countering the threat of the U-Boats on merchant ships and in capturing or sinking blockade running Axis ships.

The Arsenal of Democracy would have been ineffective if the battles of the North and South Atlantic had not been won. Natal became a vital link for the Army's ATC supply chain to Europe, North Africa and the CBI and Pacific Theatres of war.

Brazil sent troops and a squadron of fighter planes to Italy to fight with Allied forces in that campaign. President Vargas also sent 50,000 workers up into the Amazon jungle to restart the rubber industry to supply that vital material. Unfortunately, about 30,000 of those Brazilian workers perished in that effort.

Those Brazilian casualties exceeded the total number of casualties in the bloody battles of Iwo Jima and Okinawa combined. The "Rubber Soldiers" were an important part of Brazil's war effort.*

* *The Rubber Soldiers - The Forgotten Army That Saved World War II*, by Gary Neeleman.

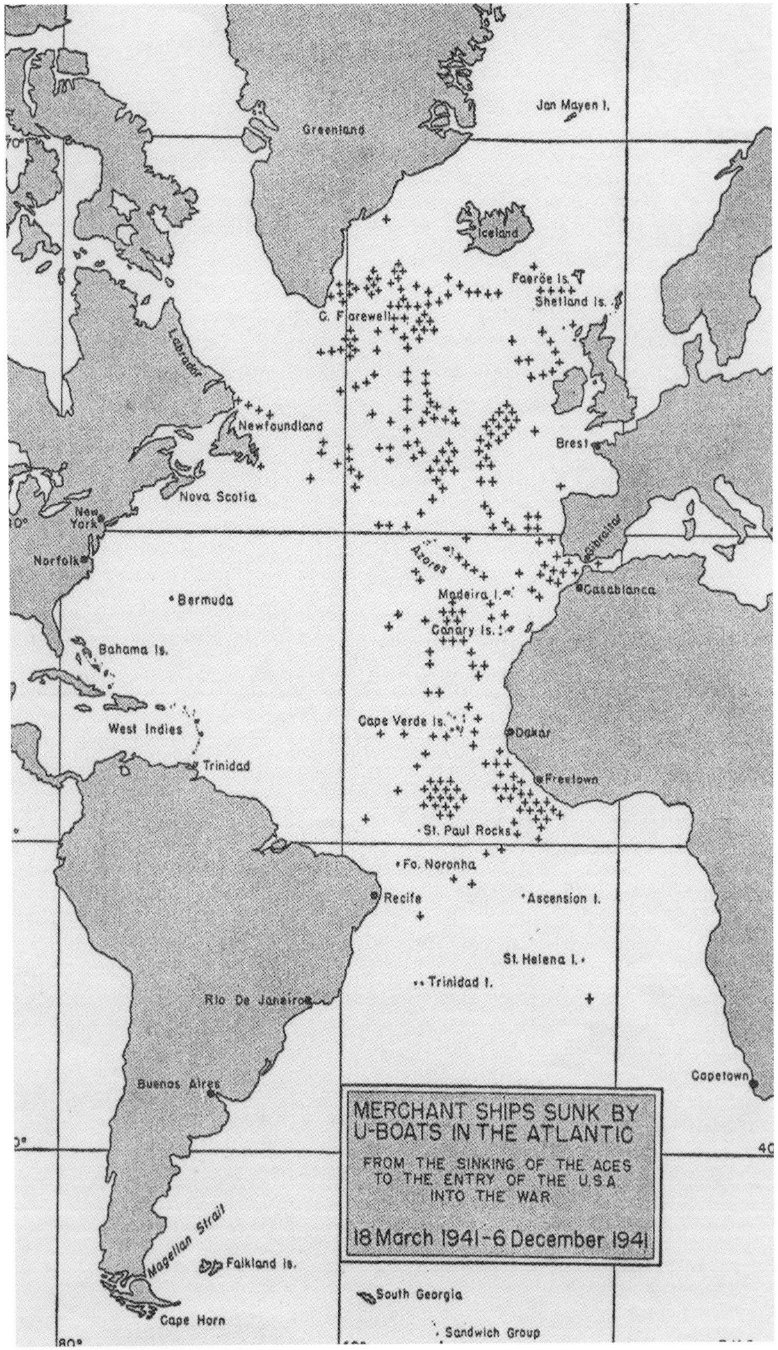

I-7 Map No. 4: From Morison - Reference 5

OVERVIEW OF BATTLE OF THE ATLANTIC

The Allied Powers had to win the Battle of the Atlantic as soon as possible so that the flood of military equipment being produced by the "Arsenal of Democracy" could be transported to the forces of the British and the Soviet Union as well as to our own forces. The battle in the Atlantic both north and south between the combined German and Italian submarine and surface vessel forces and the air and surface forces of the Allied Powers went through four distinct phases as described in Morison's two volumes on the subject.

Phase I

Prior to December 7, 1941, the focus of the Axis Powers was primarily on the North Atlantic convoys to Great Britain, Russia, the Mediterranean, and secondly on the South Atlantic Narrows between Brazil and West Africa. The efforts in the North Atlantic were designed to starve Great Britain and deprive the Russians of supplies via the Archangel-Murmansk terminus. The South Atlantic Narrows area was the best place for the Axis units to decimate British shipping in transit to the Middle East and then the Far East. The Mediterranean Sea was not safe for Allied merchant ships at that time.

The Map No.4 (from Reference 5 – Morison) shows the successful results of Axis submarine efforts during the 18 March to 6 December 1941 period. Since both the USA and Brazil were neutrals during this period (even though the USA was doing everything just short of war to aid Britain and the Soviet Union), there were no sinkings of USA or Brazilian merchant ships. During the period from the start of the European war in September, 1939 until December 6, 1941, the submarines of the Axis Powers were threatening the British Isles with great danger. In 1939 the British had imports of over 60 million tons of goods. In 1940 imports had dropped to 45 million tons and in 1941 they were only 31 million tons. So much for Mr. Blair's comments on the threat of the U-Boats.

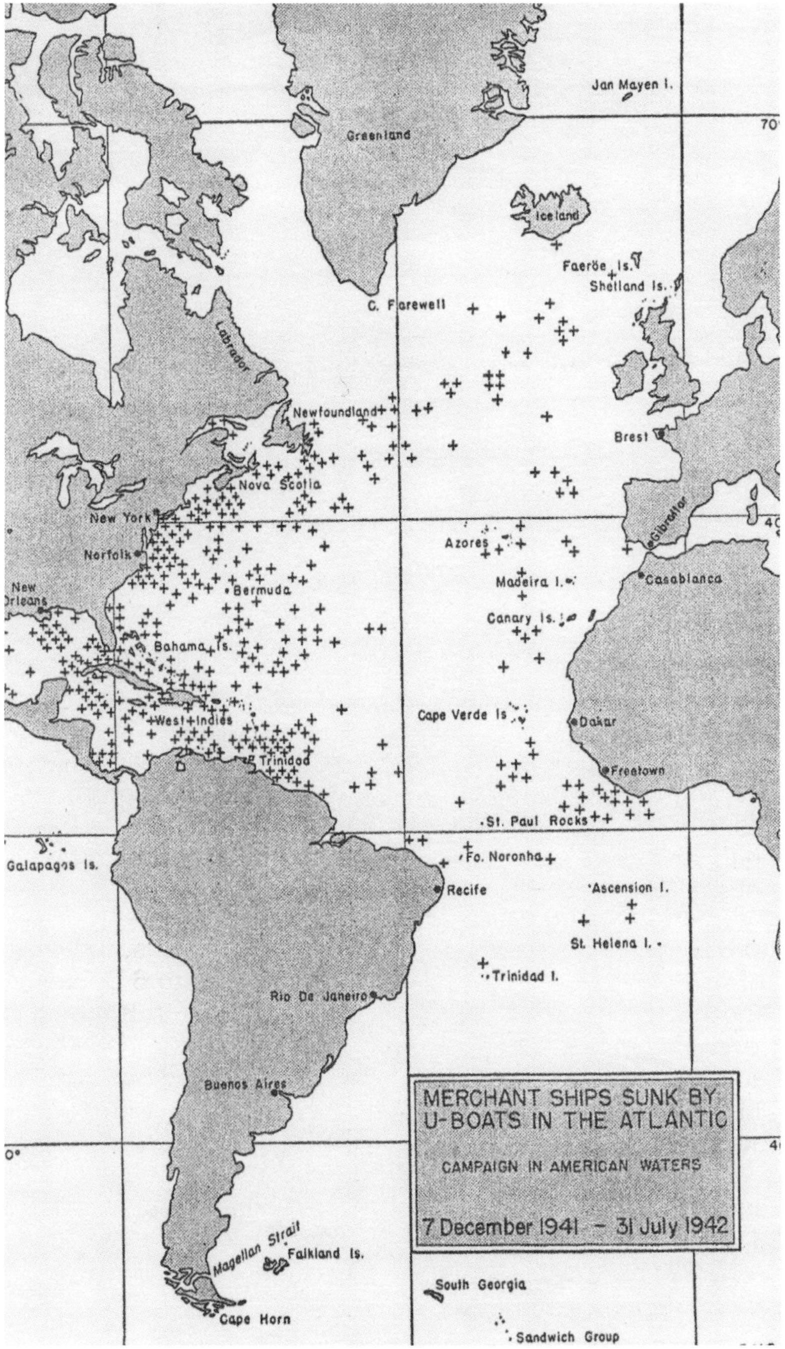

I-8 Map No. 5: From Morison - Reference 5

Phase 2

After Pearl Harbor the emphasis of the U-Boat campaign switched a bit to take advantage of the lack of preparedness of the USA to conduct anti-submarine warfare.

Map No.5 from Morison depicts the drastic impact of the submarine campaign against USA merchant ships in the Gulf of Mexico, the Caribbean, and along the Atlantic seaboard during the 7 December, 1941 through 31 July, 1942 period. The U-Boat forces referred to this period as "their Happy Time". Noting the cluster of sunken merchant ships off Trinidad one can readily ascertain why it was named Torpedo Junction. In the latter portion of this period, the Germans made the mistake of starting to sink Brazilian coastal ships and the Brazilian populace pushed the government into a declaration of war which greatly facilitated our position in obtaining air bases along the Brazilian coast.

Photo I-9 shows a torpedoed ship sinking bow first off the coast of Brazil (U.S. Navy photo).

The attack on American shipping had the code name, Operation Drumbeat. In that period it took a while for our authorities to realize that lights along the coast silhouetted the tankers and greatly aided the U-Boats in targeting them. Spectators used to sit on the beaches watching the huge fires of burning oil tankers. During the first six months after Pearl Harbor, the U-Boats sank 397 ships. Admiral Doenitz wanted to send 12 U-Boats to American coastal waters but Hitler only allowed him to send six of them which was very fortuitous for the Allies.

Once again we were very lucky that Hitler had grossly undervalued the German U-Boats' potential.

I-9: Torpedoed ship hit amidships begins to sink off the coast of Brazil in 1943

Note evidence of fire in stern indicating multiple torpedo strikes.

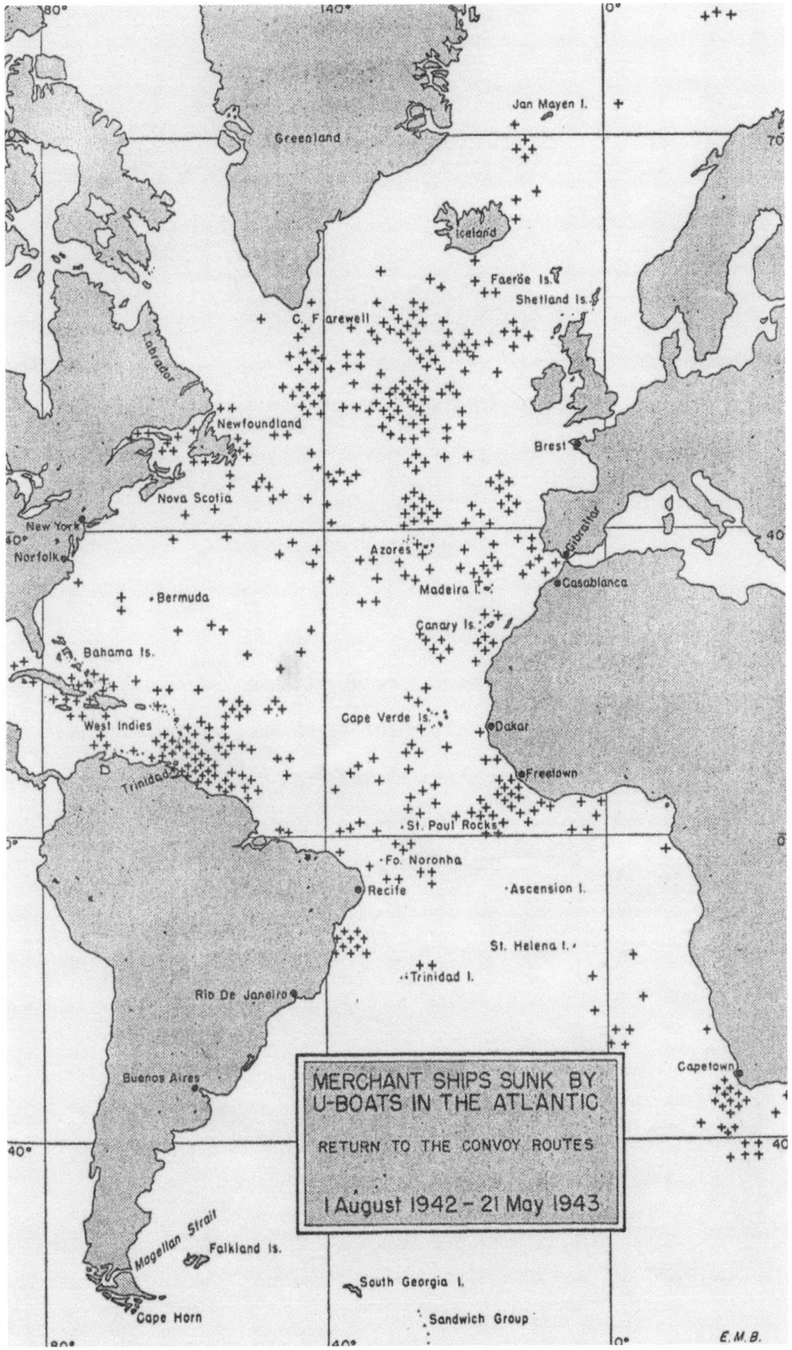

I-10 Map No. 6: From Morison - Reference 5

Phase 3

The third phase (August 1942 to May 1943) saw the emphasis shifting away from U.S. coastal waters to the North Atlantic, Trinidad area (oil shipments), the South Atlantic Narrows and the straits of Gibraltar (as shown in Map no.6 from Morison). Our growing ability to protect the Atlantic Coast of the USA plus Hitler's desire to shut off convoy routes to Russia, and the Mediterranean, were the main causes of the shift in effort. Hitler was a "continentalist" and was understandably oriented toward the German army and its struggle with the Red Army. He blew hot and cold on the U-Boat campaigns. It is amazing that Admiral Doenitz was able to make the efforts he did given the attitudes of Hitler and the German general staff.

Starting in about September 1943, it was apparent that the Allied anti-submarine forces (planes and surface ships plus blimps) were slowly improving performance and that Allied ship building efforts were beginning to outpace losses due to sinkings. The advent of Jeep aircraft carriers in 1944, more long range patrol planes operating off Ascension Island and escort vessels plus dramatic technological achievements in detection and tracking equipment would later turn the tide decisively against the Axis Powers. This does not mean that the sinking of merchant ships stopped in the Atlantic nor that planes stopped being shot down by submarines, but at least those events lessened and the Allied Forces began winning battles.

By early December 1944, the incidence of conflicts in the South Atlantic Narrows with Axis submarines had greatly subsided, not only due to German failures in Europe and Russia, but also due to the SNORKEL breathing device which enabled more prolonged travel beneath the surface by the U-Boats. The SNORKEL was not a perfect device but its use plus the fact that the German submarines no longer chose to stand and fight with their anti-aircraft guns lessened the number of encounters. There was also the fact that the U-Boats were being used to take escaped Nazis and their loot to Argentina and other countries in that area which were still sympathetic to the Axis Powers. Both Japanese and German U-Boats still cruised through the South Atlantic but their emphasis in the last 5 months of the war had shifted more to movement of vital war materials and people.

2

Early Activities of the United States in Brazil

I would dedicate this nation to the policy of the good neighbor – the neighbor who resolutely respects himself, and because he does so, respects others.

Franklin Delano Roosevelt

PERSONAL AND POCKETBOOK DIPLOMACY

The general public's perspective of Brazil was somewhat limited in the 1930's. Mention of that country would evoke thoughts of coffee, Carmen Miranda dancing with a turban bedecked with fruits, and the throbbing musical beat of the Samba. Fortunately we had a president (FDR) who was a life-long student of history and contemporary world affairs.

FDR recognized the need to develop friendships with other nations in the Western Hemisphere, particularly Brazil. During the 1930's he formulated his "Good Neighbor Policy", visited Brazil and developed a personal relationship with the leaders of Brazil. In photo I-11 we see him in conference with President Vargas of Brazil in 1936. FDR had stopped over in Rio de Janeiro on his way back from Buenos Aires and the Pan American conference held in Argentina. These actions were very important and enabled us to quickly enhance our efforts to bring Brazil into the Allied camp within the first 6 to 8 months after Pearl Harbor. Actually, behind the scenes, Brazil allowed us to deploy some minimal surface and Navy air forces at Recife and Natal the week immediately after the attack on Pearl Harbor. None of that would have been possible if FDR had not earlier pursued his "Good Neighbor" policy. FDR's diplomatic efforts supplemented by economic aid included the supply of a complete new steel mill to Brazil.

There were many fuzzy minded elitist people in the USA* who did not agree with FDR's relationship with Vargas who was a dictator. They tended to view the world as they wished it to be rather than assessing conditions as they actually were. Fortunately FDR was a realist and understood that the Brazilian body politic was the reason for the dictatorship at that time. Working with a dictator was the only option available to FDR. Vargas was generally a benevolent dictator.

The Germans and Italians had been working for years to develop close relationships with the people and ruling forces of Brazil. Exchanges of trade and extension of airline capability in Brazil plus a significant flow of European immigrants into Brazil had been fostered. These factors magnified the need for FDR's diplomatic efforts in Brazil.

Getulio Vargas was first designated President in 1930 by the controlling military forces. In 1931 he won an actual election for President. In 1937, in the midst of a Communist scare and supported by the military he abolished the constitutional charter and assumed a dictatorship which lasted until 1945 when he was ousted by the military. During that period he had put through a "New Deal" for Brazilians including a guaranteed minimum wage, a social security system, state schools, medical assistance and maternity leave. Vargas rebounded in 1951 by being elected President again but the political turmoil he encountered caused him to commit suicide in 1954. Today he has a very positive position in the hearts of the Brazilian people.

*See *Time Magazine* article, "Awake at Last", June 20, 1940.

I-11: President Getulio Vargas is bottom left and FDR is bottom right position. This is a 1936 photo - courtesy of FDR Library

The gentleman behind Vargas is U.S. Ambassador to Brazil. The rest are unidentified. Note the friendly smiles.

PREWAR U.S. FACILITIES IN BRAZIL

In the 1930's Pan American Airways, as part of its worldwide growth, had developed small seaplane bases at Belem, Natal, Recife, Bahia, Rio de Janeiro, and south through Florianapolis, Rio Grande do Sul, Montevideo and Buenos Aires. In photo I-12 we see a Pan Am Clipper in the Potengi River at Natal. Pan Am was in competition with the German Condor Line (part of Lufthansa). A German seaplane (Photo I-13) floating in the Potengi in 1941 shows the Nazi emblem on its tail.

Through the summer and autumn of 1941 the Axis Powers appeared to be on the verge of defeating the USSR on the Eastern Front and kicking the British out of North Africa. Had their success continued the fear in U.S. government circles was that the west coast of Africa and the coastline of Brazil would have been their next invasion objectives along with the Middle East oil fields. Accordingly, the U.S. government, in alliance with Pan American Airways began (in 1940-41) an Airport Development Program (ADP) that resulted in starting construction of airfields for land based airplanes at Amapa, Belem, Sao Luiz, Fortaleza, Natal, and Ipitanga (Bahia) in Brazil.

According to Life Magazine's issue of December 15, 1941, it had been officially acknowledged in an announcement made in the first week in December, 1941, that Pan American was flying US-built bombers to the British forces in North Africa via Natal, Brazil. The route from Natal to Bathhurst, which is on the hump of Africa, is a short-cut over the South Atlantic. A plane ferrying activity had been started in October, 1941. Pan American Airways initially flew Douglas commercial aircraft land planes carrying war materials being supplied to the British under the terms of the Lend-Lease program.

Most of the previous commercial flights through cities on the Northeastern coast of Brazil had used seaplanes since adequate airfields for transit of a large volume of land planes did not exist. The seaplane base facilities were also of limited capacity.

Pan American, acting as an unofficial arm of the US government had been working on the project to construct twelve land and land-sea air bases at cities along the Atlantic coast of Brazil for over a year.

By August of 1941, work at least half of these new joint USA-Brazilian air bases was nearly completed.

The use of Pan American, a commercial airline, to carry out these projects gave a certain amount of political cover to the Brazilian government since at that time Brazil was a neutral country.

The extensive work, which was being carried out by hand by a large number of Brazilian workers, was readily apparent to consulate agents of the Axis Powers in the Brazilian cities.

The Italian Lati Airline was still flying planes out of Natal at that time. A photo appearing in referenced issue of Life Magazine showed an Italian airliner flying over Brazilian workers employed by Pan American in building what was obviously to become a US military air base at Natal.

The Lati airline had been active for a number of years at Parnamirim and had their own hanger facilities there. The Italian Consul at Natal was also very active which was unusual for such a small city. Later on the Brazilians confiscated an Italian tri-motor airliner as well as their facilities at Parnamirim, Natal.

Pan American's progress was slow and in 1942 the Army Corp of Engineers (United States Engineering Department or USED) was formally brought in to expedite the work. This sequence of events made the availability of Pan Am's seaplane bases at Natal and other Brazilian cities immediately after Pearl Harbor particularly important to the small contingent of American forces which came to Brazil four days after Pearl Harbor (December 11, 1941).

Fortunately, in addition to the Pan Am seaplane bases we were able to commandeer the German and Italian seaplane and minimal land plane air bases for the use of both the Brazilian and American forces. As can be seen in photo I-15, the former Lufthansa facilities at Natal's RAMPA were extensive and proved to be very helpful.

The attack on Pearl Harbor had found the U.S. Navy (and indeed all our armed forces) woefully unprepared for war. We lacked sufficient quantity and quality of equipment as well as trained manpower to confront the Axis Powers, both in the Atlantic and the Pacific. Fortunately, our moats, the Atlantic and Pacific oceans, afforded us some protection and gave us time to rectify this situation of unpreparedness. Unfortunately this type of mistake was to be repeated shortly after the conclusion of the war. We demobilized too much, too quickly, and paid dearly for that when the Korean War started.

I-12: Pan Am Clipper in Potengi River, Natal, 1942

I-13: Lufthansa seaplane in Potengi River, Natal, 1941

I-14: Italian airliner over Parnamirim, late 1941 (Photo from Life Magazine - December 15, 1941)

This Life article was about the unpublicized program of Pan American Airways who were managing construction of 12 air bases (both land and seaplane) along the northeast coast of Brazil. This program, originally planned in 1940 to serve the Ferry Command, had been greatly expanded. Natal was the linch-pin due to its central position only 1,610 miles from Bathhurst, Africa.

Germany, Italy and France had all been active for more than a decade in airline activities in Brazil and all 3 had airplane facilities at Natal. This photo shows what probably was the last flight out of Natal by an Axis Power airliner.

I-15: PBY's of VP-52 at Natal's RAMPA

The U.S. Navy, Air Force Atlantic fleet made its first effort in the South Atlantic by sending 9 PBY's of VP-52 squadron to Natal on December 11, 1941. The personnel of VP-52 were the first U.S. group to arrive in Natal. Commander Thomas A. Turner, faced the daunting prospect of using his 9 PBY's to patrol the entire 3800 miles of Brazil's coastal area of the South Atlantic Narrows. Turner and his men, living in tents at Natal'sRAMPA (formerly used by German airlines) began to fly up and down the coast, with overnight stops at primitive seaplane bases from Belem to Salvador/Bahia. The small Panair Seaplane Base utilized by VP-52 is on the right side of this photo. Visible to the left near the river mouth are the more extensive German Lufthansa facilities which VP-52 took over. When Lt. Marshall Jamison of the U.S. AAF arrived about December 17, 1941, he had to use the men's room in one of the Pan Am buildings shown on the right side of this photo as his office for several months.

I-16: RAMPA Shore Line - early 1942

This photo, taken from the oceanside looking upstream on the Potengi River shows the tents used by VP-52 personnel which later on would also be used by VP-83 starting in April, 1942. Until late 1942 - early 1943 the facilities at Parnamirim were too limited to accommodate the U.S. Navy squadrons at Natal so the RAMPA was used extensively.

The PBM Martin Mariner squadrons were strictly seaplanes so when they arrived the RAMPA seaplane area was essential. When Parnamirim later was expanded VP-83 and other squadrons which were either land planes or amphibians operated mostly from there.

VP-52 was hampered by the lack of effective U-Boat detection and tracking systems.

Without island advanced bases at Fernando de Noronha and Ascension Island, the coverage range for VP-52's planes was limited. VP-52 did the best they could do given their equipment and circumstances. Both aerial and surface vessel anti-submarine techniques were still in the nascent stage.

Admiral Ingram had a limited surface force based at Recife which augmented the efforts, but it was also not large enough to properly battle the U-Boats and armed surface raiders and blockade runners. As a result, in the period of 6 December, 1941 to 31 July, 1942, the U-Boats sank 39 merchant ships in the South Atlantic Narrows (Morison) with many of the sinkings occurring near the Brazilian coastal area.

Photo I-17; VP-83 crew by FAW-11 PBY-1942: VP-83's first division

VP-83's first division of 6 PBY's arrived at Natal in early April, 1942 to relieve VP-52. The second division personnel went by ship so the squadron was not up to full strength until late June, early July, 1942. This was fortuitous timing because Admiral Doenitz had sent 10 German U-Boats and several Italian submarines into the South Atlantic Narrows in the same time period. When VP-83 was first sent to Natal they were a Fairwing 11 squadron. In photo I-17 we see five air crewmen from VP-83 in front of one of the PBY5A's. In the back row (standing) are: Merrill Hewitt, Bob Seaman, Dick Carper, and Harry Harrelson. In the front row are Rocky Damiano, Chief Mariano, and Dickie Dickinson.

For several reasons, including the fact that the Axis Powers appeared to be winning the war through the summer of 1942, Brazil did not declare war on the Axis until August, 1942. As a result some of the personnel of Condor airlines were still operational at their radio station on the hill back of Natal's Seaplane RAMPA until early 1942. When VP-83's first division of six PBY5A's arrived at Natal on April 7, 1942 they were surprised to hear the German nightly news broadcast note the arrival of the "drunken aviators". It turned out that the Condor Air Line radio personnel up the hill behind the RAMPA had relayed the information to Germany.

In the early months when planes went from Natal to other coastal cities with overnight layovers the facilities were much more primitive and crews actually slept in their planes between missions. As I remember it there were several pipe – canvas bunks amidship in the PBY so there must have been a "sleep in shifts" modus operandi, or some of the crew must have slept on the wings. This would have been exhausting and difficult duty.

I-18: Lieutenant Marshall V. Jamison, USAAF

INITIAL DEPLOYMENT OF U.S. ARMY AIR FORCE AT NATAL

Early Days at Parnamirim Field and the RAMPA

In December 1941, Parnamirim, which was about 12 miles south of Natal, had a modest sort of landing strip, partially asphalt and partially unpaved. Air France and the Italian Lati Airlines both had hangars there and some limited air service. Condor, a German airline flew seaplanes in and out of Natal utilizing the RAMPA Base on the Potengi River. They were still operating there throughout early December 1941.

When the U.S. Navy's PBY squadron 52 arrived at the RAMPA and the early Army Air Force personnel also came on the scene within a week after Pearl Harbor, their living conditions were a bit rough. Navy personnel lived in tents at the RAMPA and Air Force men used tents at Parnamirim or stayed in town.

For a pictorial and narrative description of the early living and working conditions for American service personnel at Parnamirim field the reader is referred to the book entitled "Trampoline to Victory" by Dr. Clyde Smith, Jr., a professor at the University of Rio Grande do Norte at Natal.

A U.S. Air Force second lieutenant, one Marshall Jamison, an Air Force weather officer, arrived in Natal at Parnamirim on December 17, 1941. Photo I-18 is of Marshall Jamison in he 1940's.

Lieutenant Jamison's assignment as Control or Commanding Officer of the Natal base of the newly formed Army Air Corps Ferry Command (AACFC) was both unique and challenging as we note in the following firsthand account of how he got there, what he did, and the subsequent effects on his life.

How I, Marshall Jamison, Ended Up in Natal, Brazil

Professor A. P. Temple, head of the Science and Physics Departments at South West Missouri State Teachers College, Springfield and father of my fiancée, Mary Dell Temple, SAVED me from pumping soap the rest of my life at Proctor & Gamble in St. Louis. He pointed out the first Army Air Corps "Aviation Cadet in Meteorology" course at the University of Chicago. I applied for and then attended the course and eventually became an Army Air Corps Weather Officer- at the imposing rank of 2nd Lieutenant. The Chief of the AAC's Weather Service ordered me, about August 1941 to head the sleepy base weather station at the sleepy base of Losey Field, Ponce, Puerto Rico. By November 1941 I was a brand new 2nd Lieutenant Army weather officer in charge of the Losey Field weather station at Ponce, Puerto Rico.

Mary Dell's parents financed her trip from Springfield, Missouri to San Juan, Puerto Rico (via New Orleans and then by freighter with passenger space and R/T through the Panama Canal). Mary Dell's mother cautioned her to be sure to marry on the first day she arrived in San Juan because "one doesn't know for sure about these military men." My Commanding Officer had given me leave so that I could go over to San Juan on 17 November 1941 to meet my fiancé so we could get married. An Army chaplain married us on the day Mary Dell arrived in the tiny chapel of San Juan's old Morro castle/fortress. Mrs. Temple was pleased.

We had our honeymoon in Puerto Rico's El Yunque forest. Still on leave we travelled to Ponce. I decided to stop in at "my" weather station before going on to our apartment. Upon seeing me, the sergeant-in-charge exclaimed full force, "Where have you been? The C.O. wants to see you!"

I replied that I was on leave, had just gotten married and was still on leave, to which the sergeant urged, "Well, I'm telling you - you'd better go see the C.O. now."

The Commanding Officer grilled me as well and after I explained that I was on leave, newly married and still on leave trying to enjoy my honeymoon, the C.O. responded with an urgency felt during war time.

"You are not on leave now. You are no longer on leave as of this moment. You have received transfer orders. Look. I've never seen anything like this."

> *From the Commanding General, United States Army Air Corps*
> *To the Commanding Officer, Losey Field, Ponce, Puerto Rico*
>
> *You will send 2nd Lieutenant Marshall Verdine Jamison by the first available commercial or military aircraft to Washington, D. C. to report to the Commanding General of the Army Air Corps for assignment to temporary duty outside the Continental limits of the United States.*

My C.O. was perplexed, saying, "You already are outside the continental United States. But orders are orders. I'm requesting a flight for you this afternoon and a car is standing by to take you over to San Juan."

I reminded him that my wife of six days was in my car outside and asked if we couldn't have one more day together. He relented and allowed me to delay my leaving until the following afternoon.

In Washington, D.C., about 25 November 1941, staff of Headquarters, Army Air Corps sent me to the Headquarters of the newly created Air Corps Ferry Command (ACFC). Rommel was advancing steadily on Cairo. Aircraft and crews were needed in Egypt and the Mideast. The ACFC was formed with a South Atlantic Route incorporating the shortest over-water segment (between Brazil and West Africa) to accommodate the shorter-range aircraft of that period.

The new ACFC needed officers for new ACFC bases along that South Atlantic route, any officers, just live persons, even non-pilot officers. The ACFC "stole" five non-pilot officers from the lower-than-ACFC-priority Air weather service. I was taken from Losey Field and now assigned to Freetown, Sierra Leone to take care of ACFC planes coming in there from Natal, northeastern Brazil.

In D.C. I had time to research Sierra Leone in the Library of Congress. Each article I read said "this country is known to be the outsiders' grave", "full of deadly diseases", "grave of the immigrant'. Repeated over and over was the phrase, "white man's grave", "white man's grave". Philosophically I said to myself- 'You are in the service. You are "GI'. You may not survive the diseases and the hazards of Sierra Leone, but perhaps you can have at least a few more days with your new wife, Mary Dell. That's all I ask."

Pearl Harbor, 7 December 1941, occurred while I was in Washington.

Then, about 10 December, ACFC changed my orders from Sierra Leone to Natal, Brazil - from the prospect of fatal disease to one of the world's most pleasant and healthful climates. My former commander at Losey Field had put Mary Dell on a "GI' ship for Panama and New Orleans. On the day she arrived in New Orleans, about 15 December, she flew to Washington. We had a day and night together before I left for my new station in Natal.

Improvisation – The Orders for the Day (and Months) of 1942

About 17 December 1941, I arrived in Natal and became "Control Officer", or Commanding Officer of the immediately-beginning Army Air Corps Ferry Command (ACFC) operations at Natal's Parnamirim airfield. Parnamirim airfield was used by Air France, Panair do Brasil, and Linee Aeree Transcontinentali Italiane (LATI).

I found personal quarters in the Grande Hotel in Natal's Ribeira, or lower city. The Ribeira lies on the broad Potengi River. Pan American's "Clippers" coming in from Africa landed in the Potengi. Panair do Brasil had its offices, communications facilities and Clipper-docking facilities on the Potengi.

Panair do Brasil's men's room became my cryptography office. I would sit on the toilet, take a code device from my Army pilot's leather brief case, and decode just enough of the secret message to learn how many planes were coming in from Belem, Para, Brazil. The Natal Panair do Brasil communications office on the Potengi had received the coded message from Panair do Brasil Belem.

Because of the day's chores confronting me, I would have only enough time to decode that part of the message that gave the number of planes arriving and that I would have to prepare for. Sometimes a person would clamor gently at the men's room door, but I gave the crews' needs a higher priority.

For the security of my pilot's brief case and its secret devices and messages, I used it for my pillow at the Grande Hotel and it was always in hand during the day. A local reporter wrote in a denigrating article: "That unwelcome American officer is always going around Natal with a briefcase at his side. We know for sure that he has secret code devices in that briefcase - and an automatic, deadly hand gun. He has no business being here in Natal."

In the time period December 1941 to February 1942, Brazil was not at war, but conceded to the U.S. the privilege of having 6, but not more than 6, airplanes in Brazilian territory at any one time. For us in ACFC at Natal and Belem, that meant six ACFC aircraft arriving in Natal about noon had to leave for Africa that night (navigating by the stars), so that 6 more aircraft could come into Belem from Trinidad that day.

The manager of all the Air France assets was warmly empathetic to the mission of the United States to defeat Germany and Hitler. He was helpful to me and the needs of the ACFC in every way possible. He placed the Air France hanger at my service and I used it for crew rest. I bought cots and light linen (some 75 cots in the early weeks; later, more). The crews would have gotten up quite early in Belem, would have arrived about noon in Parnamirim, and would be leaving that night for Africa. Rest was important.

About February, I believe, Brazil entered the war and removed the restriction on numbers of U.S. aircraft in Brazil at any given time. More cots were bought for the Air France hanger. We urgently needed more transportation to transfer the crews, purchase supplies, etc. Because I was only a class "B" finance officer, I was not authorized to buy vehicles. The Air France manager had a very large station wagon and small bus he wanted to sell me. I wired the Commanding General, ACFC, in Washington, asking for special permission to buy the Air France vehicles. He replied "no. You are a class 'B' finance officer. Do not buy the vehicles."

I let a week go by and then wired again for permission to buy them. The reply was more ~ "No! Repeat no. You are a class 'B' finance officer. Do not, repeat not, buy vehicles."

The next day, I bought the two Air France vehicles and went to Recife and bought a new medium-size bus. I figured, "These crews are going over into combat; some will never return. We need vehicles. Buying three vehicles here means Detroit has three more for some other Army use. What the heck!"

A few weeks later, the Commanding General, ACFC, and his entourage visited Natal. He took me aside, "Jamison, don't buy any more vehicles. You are going to spend the rest of your life in Fort Leavenworth" (military prison). He didn't put me in Fort Leavenworth; and I didn't buy any more vehicles!

Along with the two vehicles, the Air France manager wanted to sell me a tri-motor Air France passenger plane of that 1930's era. I should have bought that with my own and borrowed money. It would be available now for a NATAL AVIATION MUSEUM! (I wonder what happened to it?)

German Facilities at the RAMPA

In Natal's Ribeira, on the river Potengi, a short distance ocean-ward from the 1942 Panair do Brasil's facility to receive the Pan American Clipper (now the Brazilian Air Force club & restaurant) is a "ramp", or "RAMPA", that gives the spot its name, "RAMPA".

This ramp from the Potengi River to shore made it possible to draw seaplanes (e.g. PBYs) to a dry area for inspection and maintenance. The Germans had such a seaplane which they affectionately nicknamed

"Walfisch" ("Wal" or "whale"). They flew it between Bathurst, Gambia and Natal, Brazil. (Note: In 1973 Bathurst was renamed "Banjul". It is the capitol of The Gambia, West Africa). In 1942 the Germans and Whale were gone, but the building of the German Officers' Club remained at the edge of the "RAMPA's" seaplane parking area. I noted this poem behind the bar of the club:

The Whale

Uber 'm Bach flight der Wal'
Zwischen Bathurst und Natal.
Er ist nicht schnell, doch sehr stabil;
Wer langsam flight kommt auch zum Ziel!

My English translation:

Over the Ocean flies the Whale
Between Bathurst and Natal.
Not so fast, but stable, yes;
Take your time and know success
(or,

Not so fast, but stable, indeed,
Who takes his time will reach his goal!)

My Portuguese translation:

Sobre o mar voa a baleia
Entre Bathurst e Natal.
Veloz nao e; estavel sim;
Sem pressa; certo; vai chegar!

I believe the old German Officers' Club has been torn down; it would have been a nice permanent piece of Natal's history. Perhaps now as part of museum activities an information plaque might be placed at or near the site. Perhaps, also, visitors/tourists would be able to take with them an inexpensive brochure or one-page information sheet with the history of the German Bathurst-Natal operation. UFRN students and/or others might find it interesting to research the history of the German "Walfisch" operation as input for museum pieces at the RAMPA.

Rank – Protocol Versus Practicality

When I was ordered to be "Control Officer" (Commanding Officer) of the ACFC base at Natal I had the rank of 2nd Lieutenant, lowest Army officer rank. In December 1941, a few days after I arrived in Natal, two enlisted persons joined our operation, then several more, and then another 2nd Lieutenant. After some weeks a 1st Lieutenant arrived to be part of the ACFC complement.

I, a 2nd Lieutenant, had a 1st Lieutenant under my command. That is a bit unusual, untoward, illegal in the military. So the Commanding General, ACFC, promoted me to Captain directly from 2nd Lt. I have never been a 1st Lt. (Photo I-10 is a wartime picture of Captain Marshall Jamison).

About April or May 1942 the ACFC sent a Major to work with me, to work under me at Parnamirim. He was an officer who had served in World War I. He was affable and helpful - and there was no problem between us related to a lower ranking officer, myself as Captain, being in charge. ACFC did not choose to promote me to Lt. Colonel!

Meals for Crews

The morning coded message for me via Panair do Brasil at the "RAMPA" would tell me how many planes, B-24's or B-17's, would be coming in that day. In the early days it would usually be the full permitted of six.

I would drive to the Mercado Publico, buy a large basket, handmade in Rio Grande do Norte interior, and for each crew fill it with sweet delicious pineapples, bananas, rolls, a tinned, spherical, delicious cheese from Minas Gerais, and a tinned, cooked ham. This food package served for snacks when the crews came in, but mainly for a meal over the South Atlantic that night.

Later I had the Grande Hotel prepare food dishes that were brought to Parnamirim via taxi, warm, in large containers. A Mrs. Knabb prepared meals for Panair do Brasil crews and passengers, and later also for us. Later, when the base complement grew, meals were prepared at our base.

Size of Parnamirim ACFC Base

In December 1941 initially I was the Commanding Officer of one person - myself. Our number of men and officers grew to about 150 to 200 at the time I was relieved, July 1942, by a Colonel pilot. After I left, aircraft moved through Natal in very large numbers and the base grew to several thousand persons to become the largest, or one of the largest Army Air Corps/USAF bases.

Only Two Engines – A Flying Range, Capacity Problem

B-25s. B-26's and C47s could not make it all the way across unless they carried extra tanks of fuels in their cargo or weapons spaces. These planes came through Parnamirim in ever-increasing numbers. (Editorial Note: Building the air strip on Ascension Island helped later on.)

ACFC Base Relationship with Natal

Natal, in the 1941-1945 period was a city of about 40,000 persons, I believe. The Air Corps Ferry Command/Air Transport Command of several thousand persons represented a significant fraction of the overall population.

I believe I can say that aside from the inevitable alcohol-related incidents, the relationship among Natal and Base persons was exceptionally friendly. The Natal-made cowboy boot became widely famous; dates, marriages, enjoyment of the beaches, purchases in the shops and markets ...

Ups and Downs

In December 1941 the road between Natal and the airfield at Parnamirim was unpaved and moved up and down at intervals that often were very short. A vehicle moving up one of the over-the-dune hills, on reaching the top could not see a vehicle approaching from the other side. Sometimes drivers would enjoy the luxury of driving in the middle instead of in a proper lane of the road. Once, a person with me exclaimed, "You'd think they'd collide sometimes."

Sometimes they do.

The taxi of my Brazilian assistant at the Grande Hotel who prepared containers of hot food for the crews, met another car in such a collision at the hillock. He somehow got the food transferred to another vehicle and arrived two hours late to Parnamirim - in tears. In tears not because of his trauma, but because the food was cold and late for the crews! In the early months of 1942 the hillocks were leveled and the road nicely paved. I believe, but am not sure, that it was ADP, Airport Development Corporation, that did this work.

Onofre, Special Friend

Professor Onofre Lopes da Silva was Reitor (President) of the Federal University of Rio Grande do Norte (UFRN) at that time. One tragic evening one of our B-24's crashed against a dune after takeoff. I knew little about death. Reitor Onofre, a medical doctor and head of a university with its own hospital stepped in. He took over with morgue facilities, arrangements for burial in the Alecrim cemetery, orientation in family notification, and other needs. I, like so many others, am indebted for his help and friendship.

(Decades later, retired from the military and working as a civilian in Natal and living a few doors from Reitor Onofre I was stung by an 8-inch scorpion. In enormous pain and uncertain about my fate, I walked to Onofre's house. When he saw my pain, anguish, and fear, he burst out laughing, saying "Jamison, you are NOT going to die." He treated me and sent me on my way. The memory of his laugh at that time has given ME a hundred personal OUT-LOUD laughs since. My friend Onofre is part of my love for Natal.)

General Cordeiro de Farias

General Cordeiro was in charge of Brazilian Army forces in the Natal - Rio Grande do Norte region. He placed Brazilian Army resources at our service from time to time. Some persons said that he may have had some sympathies with the Germans. I do not know about that. What I know is that he liked me, an almost-over-his-head 2nd Lieutenant and I liked him; he was helpful to our mission. When I was replaced and making my departure courtesy calls, he gave me a powerful both-arm Brazilian abraco; and he was a big man! Another pleasant memory of Natal.

Pobrecito – "Oh You Poor Thing"

I used to swim quite well- competitive in backstroke. Natal has marvelous beaches. Near the old fort at the mouth of the Potengi river is the Praia do Forte, protected by a long reef. I enjoyed swimming there and once, when no one was around, I tied my swim trunks around my ankle, took a 2 1/2 minute breath and floated face-down au naturelle. When my 2 1/2 minutes were up I looked around and was perplexed. Everything was reversed. The reef, instead of appearing oceanward, appeared to be landward.

And sure enough it was. Without my knowing it I had been carried to sea. What happened was this: The tide and wind and waves over the reef were unusually high. The enormous amount of water coming over the reef HAD to return to sea and it did that at high velocity through narrow passages in the reef.

In my 2 1/2 minutes of quiet philosophy I had been swept through a passage to the open ocean enroute to Africa. I was about 50 yards beyond the Praia do Forte reef with its razor-sharp coral stone projections. Enormous waves were breaking into and over the reef.

The fort, the broad Potengi river, and a gentle, smooth beach on the far side of the Potengi were off far to my right. It was late afternoon and night falls fast near the equator. What should I do? Swim to shore directly? Or swim past the fort and across the 3/4 mile wide mouth of the Potengi? I might get to that smooth beach about midnight - if ever (for there were occasionally sharks about)!

I decided to swim straight for shore. If a wave took me into the reef- that would be certain death; if a wave carried me over I might live. Approaching the reef a huge wave caught me and took me into the reef - not on the ocean side and certain death, but onto the reef on its inward.

Not death and broken bones but a hundred cuts of varying depths all over my body. It was an easy 50 yard swim to the beach where I rested in trauma, bleeding into the sand. After about ten minutes I walked to my quarters a block away. I rested again, bleeding, with no concern for the linen.

After perhaps 20 minutes I dressed, paying no attention to blood and clothes. I walked perhaps 3/4 mile away to the Hospital das Clinicas of Reitor Onofre Lopes da Silvas Federal University das Clinicas. At the door I was greeted by an attendant.

They took me in; showered me, bandaged me, put me in hospital pajamas, and put me to bed for a night and day. You can see why my love affair with Natal and Natalenses continues.

Return of Stolen Goods

I, a non-pilot 2nd Lieutenant, was "stolen" in November 1941 from the Army's Weather Service by the desperate, newly-created Army Air Corps Ferry Command. As soon as possible, July 1942, the ACFC replaced me with a Colonel who could fly.

Thoughtfully, they returned me to the Weather Service.
The Weather Service gave me leave to learn to fly and later I became in charge of the 9th Weather Squadron that enjoyed having a weather observing and forecasting station at a military base at - guess where - Parnamirim, Natal-RN, Brazil. Great, good fortune; my love affair with Natal continued!

Quittin' Time

After 21 years in the Army Air Corps, United States Air Force, ACFC, Natal, and direction of the National Hurricane Center in Miami, I decided to retire and try something else. I found myself at Juazeiro do Norte, Ceara, in the "ASIMOW" project, then back in Rio Grande do Norte's Natal and Mossoro and Assu in the "RITA" project. My love affair with Natal and Natalenses continued.

(Editorial Note: Marshall, after retiring as a Lieutenant Colonel decided to further his education. He got involved into two internationally funded projects designed to help development of Northeastern Brazil while working toward his Ph.D. degree at a California University. Over the past decades, Marshall has maintained an apartment in Natal and usually spends a few months there every year).

The Municipal Chamber of Natal

On 11 May 2004 the President of the Municipal Chamber of Natal awarded me the title of Honorary Natal Citizen (for relevant services, and my work at the Parnamirim airbase and my work in the interior).
Natal is now my hometown.

(Editorial Note: After his early experiences at Natal, Marshall went through flight training and became a pilot. Later he became a squadron leader and a U.S. Base Commander.

Additional material about Marshall appears in Chapter 23, Modern Natal.)

Photo I-19; Sam Taylor in hammock at Parnamirim's Tent City - 1942

Photo I-20: Ropa women at laundry day near Parnamirim - 1942

CAMPING OUT AND IMPROVISATION - NATAL - 1942

The U.S. Army Air Force (USAAF) had sufficient air strip available at Parnamirim that they could share their usage with the Navy's VP-83 PBY squadron. However the USED had not yet completed the construction of barracks or other support buildings at Parnamirim, so during 1942 many U.S. servicemen were housed in simple tents; camping out. Mess halls and other facilities were also in tents. A rough time. As a result VP-83 personnel spent considerable time at the RAMPA.

Photo I-19 is of a pilot of VP83 (Sam Taylor) in a hammock in tent city. (Photo courtesy of Richard Wilson) In mid-1942 we note how slender a more normally robust Sam Taylor appears. This was likely due to the meager quality of the food supply at that time. Laundry service was provided by local Brazilian Ropa (clothing) women who used primitive but effective washing methods as shown in this "Laundry Day" (Photo courtesy of Ed Krug).

The Ropa women use a small stream on the periphery of Parnamirim to wash the clothes of U.S. servicemen at Natal. The lack of regular laundry facilities during 1942 was a minor problem in 1942 Natal. Getting sufficient good food to consume on base and to supply the lengthy aerial safaris up an down the coast by first VP-52 and then VP-83 was of greater concern. In Marshall Jamison's write-up he described how he improvised by getting food from the Mercado Publico in town to supply the Ferry Command crews.

The Ropa womens' washing methods on what we called dungarees (blue jeans) resulted in the first "distressed" blue jeans. The young sailors felt that they were "saltier" if their dungarees looked like they had been worn for a long time.

Photo I-21; Parnamirim field in mid-1942

By the middle of 1942, the USED and USACE and their Brazilian counterparts had constructed a few buildings at Parnamirim as we note in this photo. In the foreground, left of the center, are the former Air France buildings and on the right lower side are the cluster of Italian LATI airline buildings which had been built and on the far side of the far new runway one new building, several USAAF planes, and a single PBY of VP-83 are visible, The U.S. planes mentioned and the few new buildings are more visible in Photo I-22 which is an extreme enlargement of Photo I-21.

Photo I-22; American side of Parnamirim field in mid-1942

In this view we note ten B-25 Mitchell Medium Bombers, one PBY, two DC-3's, and two unidentified planes on the tarmac or apron.

The presence of only one PBY (VP-83) indicates that VP-83 was working more out of the RAMPA seaplane base than out of Parnamirim at that time. The Navy had a substantial tent city at the RAMPA plus the German Condor line facilities to utilize.

Near the planes, in the far center of Photo I-22 there is one substantial building. In the lower left a cluster of four buildings is visible.

These planes and buildings appear to be about one kilometer distant from the Air France hanger area and a bit farther from the Italian Lati airline hanger and buildings.

EARLY WORK OF VP-83 FROM PARNAMIRIM

In Photo I-23 (next page), seven of VP-83's pilots and an air crew man are seen in front of a Tent City. (Photo courtesy of Billie Goodell)

When the first division of Patrol Wing 11's VP-83 flying amphibious PBY5A's landed at Natal, Brazil was still publicly a neutral country but was also beginning to be more cooperative with the U.S. Air Forces. The degree of cooperation increased rapidly as the U-Boats began sinking Brazilian ships in the South Atlantic. Within five weeks of arriving at Parnamirim, VP-83 was protecting ships from attacks by Axis Power submarines. Admiral Doenitz had shifted a number of both German and Italian U-Boats into the South Atlantic to intercept the merchant vessels bringing supplies from South America and far Eastern countries to the U.S. and Great Britain. From May 1942 through July 1943 the pace of submarine activities in the South Atlantic was to grow to its maximum level.

VP-83's initial assignment was a very difficult one. They had thousands of miles of coastline and open ocean area to patrol and only 12 PBY's with which to do it. For the first 12 to 18 months they had to operate out of minimal and primitive air base facilities. The following excerpt from reference 10, the Command History of FAW 16 best describes the challenges and how VP-83 managed to cope.

> "The Convoy system for important shipping was established between Trinidad and Bahia starting June 1942 and VP-83 started protecting convoy sweeps at that time. By the year's end all important shipping was convoyed south of Trinidad as far as Bahia. At this time the Doctrine for such coverage was still embryonic and this squadron contributed much to the gradually developing sets of rules which experience and careful experimentation made it wise to establish.
>
> Of interest in this connection was the original procedure adopted for handling the convoy coverages. By Cominch directive marking the geographical areas assigned to the South Atlantic Force (and its successor Fourth Fleet) and the Caribbean Sea Frontier the "Chop Line" for responsibility between the two commands had been established on a line bearing 045 degrees true from the tip of Cape Orange at the northeastern corner of Brazil. This gave VP-83 the area from Cape Orange all the way some 2200 miles to Bahia as the zone of their responsibility. It was no small assignment for a squadron of 12 Catalinas.
>
> The problem was solved in a unique sort of way. While the squadron headquarters were at Natal, by the summer of 1942 the Army had competed the runways for its fields at Amapa, Belem, Sao Luiz, Fortaleza, Natal and had a good start on Recife. Ipitanga then had one old runway used by Pan American Airways and the other foreign lines. With these bare facilities VP-83 would then send a detachment of two or three planes north to Belem and Amapa or south to Ipitanga outside Salvador-Bahia when word was received from Fourth Fleet that a convoy was about to cross the Chop or was starting out from Bahia, at that time the southern terminus of the convoy runs. On arrival at Belem or Amapa, a camp of tents for the plane crews would then be set up adjacent to the runways or the landing area, if a water landing had been made, and all hands would cook their own meals and spend the night.
>
> The following day one or two planes would go out and cover the convoy, while the third plane broke camp, packed up the tents and mess gear and proceeded to the next nights stopping point where they would have the camp established for the two planes out covering the convoy by the time they returned in the evening.
>
> The following day the plane that had made the camp would take the coverage and so forth until the convoy had reached Bahia or was taken over by Caribbean Sea Frontier planes. When day and night coverage was required, four planes instead of the usual two or three would be sent".

Please note Paul Richter's story titled, "A Perilous Adventure in a Rugged Airplane" in Chapter 6 for a first hand account of typical perils faced by VP-83 personnel during their forays up and down the coasts of Brazil in those early days.

Photo I-23; Seven VP-83 pilots and a crewman in a Tent City in Natal in April, 1942.

Sam Taylor is on the right end of the back row and Vance Dawkins is on the right end of the front row. The others are unidentified at the moment.

Because their were several Naval Aviation Pilots (NAP's) in VP-83, enlisted men who served as pilots without having the rank of commissioned officers, the sailor in dungarees could also have been an NAP. This photo was probably taken at the RAMPA seaplane base on the Potengi River in Natal.

The tent behind the group looks like the kind used at the RAMPA and behind the tent a hillside is visible.

There were hillsides at the RAMPA but Parnamirim was mostly flat.

Note the lightweight summer flying suits on the seven pilots. These were very different from what we wore flying out of Quonset Point in the winter.

Photo I-24 (next page) shows a PBY5A (the amphibious version of the Consolidated PBY) on the tarmac at Natal.

For the first 18 months of the U.S. Navy's aerial efforts to protect the convoys in the South Atlantic Narrows the PBY was indispensable due to its amphibious abilities. None of the other available aircraft had the capability to operate from both the limited land air strips and the primitive seaplane water landing spots along the coast of Brazil. The activities described in the excerpt from the Command History of the Fleet Air Wing 16 would have been impossible without the PBY. The PBY was one of the most significant and useful planes of World War II in other theatres of war as well. Over 2,000 Consolidated PBY's were built and used by the USA, Great Britain, the Canadians, and the Soviet Union during the war.

A PBY (the British called them Catalinas) of British Coastal Command Squadron 209 rediscovered the Bismarck in the Atlantic after the British Navy had lost contact and enabled the destruction of that German super battleship.

It was an air crewman in a Navy PBY on a patrol sweep that spotted the Japanese fleet off Midway. This sighting allowed the U.S. carriers to strike first resulting in a major U.S. victory which turned back the offensive tide of the Japanese Imperial Fleet, saved Midway, and potentially the Hawaiian Islands from invasion. The Japanese lost not only 4 aircraft carriers but also the best of its carrier air crews at Midway. The very long cruising range of the PBY was crucial for long range reconnaissance flights.

At the end of July 1945, a PBY of VPB-23, piloted by Adrian Marks, was courageously landed in the ocean despite a heavy sea (12 foot swells) and thereby rescued 56 sailors from the Indianapolis which had been torpedoed and sunk by a Japanese submarine off Peleliu. The full story of Marks and his crew's heroic sacrifice of their PBY and all events surrounding the loss of the Indianapolis is spelled out in Reference 9, "Abandon Ship". The Indianapolis saga was a personal loss because one of my high school classmates, Harry Hickey, was lost in that disaster.

From start to finish, the PBY proved to be one of the best airplanes of World War II. It was also the first plane I ever flew in. The PBY (and also the PBM) had a safety advantage in long patrols over water due to their ability to land and take off from the ocean. As long as the hulls of those airplanes were reasonably sound they could float.

Land planes like the PB4Y and PV-1 Ventura could not land well in water and stay afloat. I know of no cases where there were any survivors from ocean landings of such planes. I do remember crewmen who parachuted out of a PV-1 Ventura and managed to survive. In particular an air crewman who had been a horse race jockey in civilian life safely parachuted out of a Ventura. His first name was Sal.

PBY with Nose Wheel Problem

Fortunately accidents with PBY5A's were not particularly frequent because it was a well designed and sturdy airplane. In this case something very basic happened to the nose wheel assembly in this side view of a PBY (photo I-25). One can clearly see some structural features of the aircraft. "The Blisters" on either side forward of the tail assembly contained jump seats and single 50 caliber machine guns on each side.

Between the Blisters and the wing area, there was a section with several bunks (the plane could fly for 20 hours or more at a time), a galley, and a rack of parachutes.

It was a good thing that I never had to take a parachute off the rack in a PBY and put it on. Indeed during my first few flights at Quonset Point I had not been trained to either fit a parachute on me or told how to use it. I did know enough not to pick up a parachute by the red handle since that would open and deploy the chute. The parachute riggers would not like that.

Forward of the main cabin was a section for the navigator and radioman and in the pylon connecting the fuselage to the wing was an area for the flight engineer's space. Two pilots sat behind the windshield of the cockpit and a gunner/bombardier had a seat in the nose area which had one or two 30 caliber machine guns. In making attacks on U-Boats the accuracy and timeliness of suppressing fire from the Blisters and nose gun were critical in determining whether the attacking airplane or the U-Boat and its ack-ack 20 and 40 millimeter cannons would win the battle.

I-24; PBY on tarmac - Parnamirim, 1943

I took this photo in Natal in October, 1943.This means that this PBY was not from VP-83 which had converted to PB4Y's by then.

I-25; PBY with nose wheel problem

PBY's always had tendencies to rock back and forth on the nose wheel particularly when brakes were engaged.

IMPROVEMENTS IN FACILITIES AT NATAL

Both the U.S. Army Air Force (USAAF), the U.S. Navy, and their Brazilian counterparts began to provide better base facilities at Parnamirim during 1942 and 1943. The following series of photos illustrates this construction activity.

Photo I-26; Typical barracks under construction at Parnamirim

The combination of an overhang and ventilation louvers along the bottom of the walls kept these barracks comfortable. I do not remember any problem with the warmth of the days and nights at Parnamirim and I am sensitive to too much heat. (Photo I-26 from National Archives). The construction at Parnamirim was a great boon to local workers from the area.

I-27: Officers Quarters Parnamirim - USAAF

In front of this building constructed in 1942, we see a “woody” station wagon. When Marshall Jamison came to Natal he needed transport to bring food and supplies to the air crews which were in transit through Parnamirim (Photo I-27 from National Archives). At first he rented the station wagon from the Air France manager but later he bought it even though the Army’s bureaucratic chain of command would not authorize him to buy capital equipment since he was only a Class B Finance Officer. One had to be a Class A Finance Officer to purchase capital equipment. Clearly some in the chain of Command had not yet adjusted to wartime exigencies. Protocol still sometimes took precedence over common sense. Marshall successfully ignored protocol in this case thereby negating a snafu. No wonder the acronym snafu was widely used in all branches of the Armed Forces.

I-28; Outdoor showers and lavatories at Parnamirim

It took a while to get used to the cold water showers that airbase personnel would have available in the roofless shower enclosures attached to the left hand end of the lavatories as shown in photo I-28 from National Archives. The fact that these cold showers were the norm at our Brazilian coastal bases is evidence of the benign climate there.

Further evidence of the fine climate is noted in this following quote from a relevant reference; "The Northeast Coast gets about as hot as Rio during the summer, but due to a wonderful tropical breeze and less humidity it is rarely stifling." "all in all, it is hard to imagine a better climate." This applies as far north as Fortaleza.

I-29; U.S. Navy Barracks - Parnamirim: by early 1943

By early 1943 the U.S. Engineering Department (USED) and their Brazilian workers and colleagues had completed much of the necessary construction at Parnamirim and no permanent base personnel had to live in tents anymore. I do not recall having to use mosquito netting either. A "Tent City" was still used to accommodate the many hundreds of transient servicemen just passing through Natal. Shortly after this photo I-29 was taken, both a Ship's Store (Navy version of Post Exchange or PX) and a theater with a roof (open at the sides) and a stage were constructed.

The U.S. Navy portion of Parnamirim was small compared to the size of the USAAF area which was a reflection of the huge traffic of Air Force personnel and equipment through Natal. The Army Post Exchange was very large and it did a booming business.

I-30; Nose hanger a noite - Parnamirim

Further evidence of the favorable climate at Natal is apparent from the use of Nose Hangers rather than enclosed buildings for aircraft repair work. This photo I-30 was taken at dusk in late 1943. The Nose Hanger had originally been used by the U.S. Army Air Force but when the first land based Navy squadron VP-83 (PBY's) arrived in April, 1942, the facility was turned over to the Navy. This photo shows a Lockheed Ventura PV-1 with its nose in the hanger.

I-31; U.S. Navy Theatre - Natal - Parnamirim

By late 1943 the recently constructed open air theatre (with a roof) became busy with movies, entertainment by touring USO shows, and boxing matches. The USAAF also had a movie theatre but it did not have a roof. Photo I-31 shows the U.S. Navy theatre and a large audience.

I-32; Panair Pier and Terminal - Natal

Panair facilities at the Potengi shore were greatly improved by November, 1943 and are seen in photo I-32. The "Archway Building" with the control tower on the top is still there today. Hopefully the Archway Building will be refurbished and preserved as a museum.

I-33; RAMPA from Potengi River - December 1943

Here we see a Consolidated Coronado in December 1943 to the right of the Panair dock. The Coronado had flown non-stop from Patuxent River, Maryland NAS in 28 ½ hours. To the left of the cabin cruiser an inspection party has gathered to be taken to see the new seaplane.

I-34; New type seaplanes at the RAMPA - Natal

By early 1943, long range PBM's were in service in Brazil. Two of these Martin Mariners are shown here at the RAMPA.

Two OS2U (King Fisher) float planes are on the apron near the Potengi River.

3

Natal – Brazil

You lads are going to a very hot place.

Chief Photographers Mate E. O. Sanders to the author and
four shipmates being transferred to Brazil in June, 1943

LOCATION OF NATAL

Natal is a coastal city at the mouth of the Potengi River in the northeastern state of Rio Grande Do Norte. It is the capital of that state. Though most Americans of today do not have significant knowledge about this mid-size city, such was not the case during World War II, when many thousands of American servicemen served in or passed through Natal. Natal is about 200 miles north of Recife (which is the more well known capital city of the State of Pernambuco), and about 300 miles south of Fortaleza, the beautiful fast growing capital coastal city of the neighboring state of Ceara. Map No.7 is from the 5th Edition of The Rough Guide to Brazil, published by Rough Guides LTD. In 2003, reproduced with permission of the publisher and it shows the location of Natal in the northeast section of Brazil. This is a modern day map and the current system of highways did not exist in the 1940's.

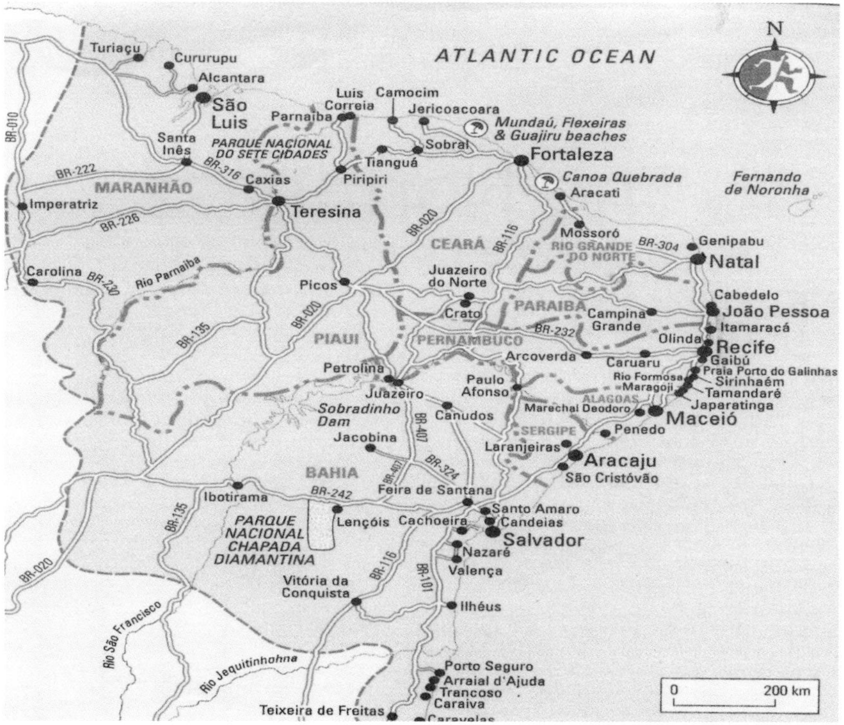

I-35; Map No. 7: Northeast Brazil - 5th Edition of Rough Guide to Brazil, published by Rough Guides LTD in 2003. Reproduced by permission of the publisher.

The reason Natal became so important during World War II is its location on the easterly hump of Brazil which made it a close jumping-off port for air traffic to Africa. This location had also prompted the attention of the European airline companies of Italy, Germany, and France prior to World War II. They all had some limited airline services stopping at Natal. Natal is relatively remote from the southern Brazilian power axis of Brasilia, Rio de Janeiro, Santos and Sao Paulo so it is not in the news much now either in Brazil, the USA, or the world press. However, its favorable climate and outstanding beaches are making it a more prominent tourist area today. Even though Natal is only about 400 miles south of the Equator it has a sub-tropical and temperate climate due to prevailing ocean breezes. It was one of the better places for U.S. personnel to serve in World War II.

In the 1500's the French who came to secure Brazil wood trees to make red dye had set up trading posts in the Natal area. The Portuguese, who were the principal colonizers of Brazil and conquerors of its native Indian tribes, drove out the French in 1597 and built the fortress of Os Reis Magos (the Three Wise Kings) at the mouth of the Potengi River at Natal.

Map no.8 of modern day Natal shows the location of this colonial era fort at the end of the peninsula of Natal. This map is from the 5th Edition of The Rough Guide to Brazil published by Rough Guides LTD. In 2003, reproduced with the permission of the publisher.

Subsequently, in 1633, the Dutch, who had originally constructed Recife about 200 miles south of Natal by applying their renowned land reclamation capabilities to a swampy area, arrived in Natal and drove out the Portuguese. However, the Portuguese regrouped and came back and retook the town of Natal, the peninsula on which it was built, and the fort in the latter 1600's.

Like most of their European colonizer counterparts the Portuguese developed an agricultural economy (largely sugar cane). To do the work they brought about 12 million African slaves to the coast cities of Brazil (mostly to the Salvador/Bahia and Recife areas) over a period of many decades. They had initially enslaved the native Indians for this purpose but many of them revolted and or fled to the interior necessitating the importation of the African slaves. Natal was at the northern fringe of the area where slavery of Africans prevailed, so the African racial heritage is much smaller than in Recife and Bahia.

The Portuguese, including the clergy, promoted promiscuity and procreation with, first, the Indians, and later with the African slaves to produce more workers. Celibacy was not practiced at that time by the clergy, nor was marriage. Progeny of Portuguese white men and native Indians were called "mamelucos". Mixtures of Indians and Africans were labeled "cafusos", and African and European offspring were called "mulattos". Overt racial discrimination did not appear to be prevalent among Brazilians during our time in that country.

The following seven photos provide an overall perspective of Natal and its people during the war years.

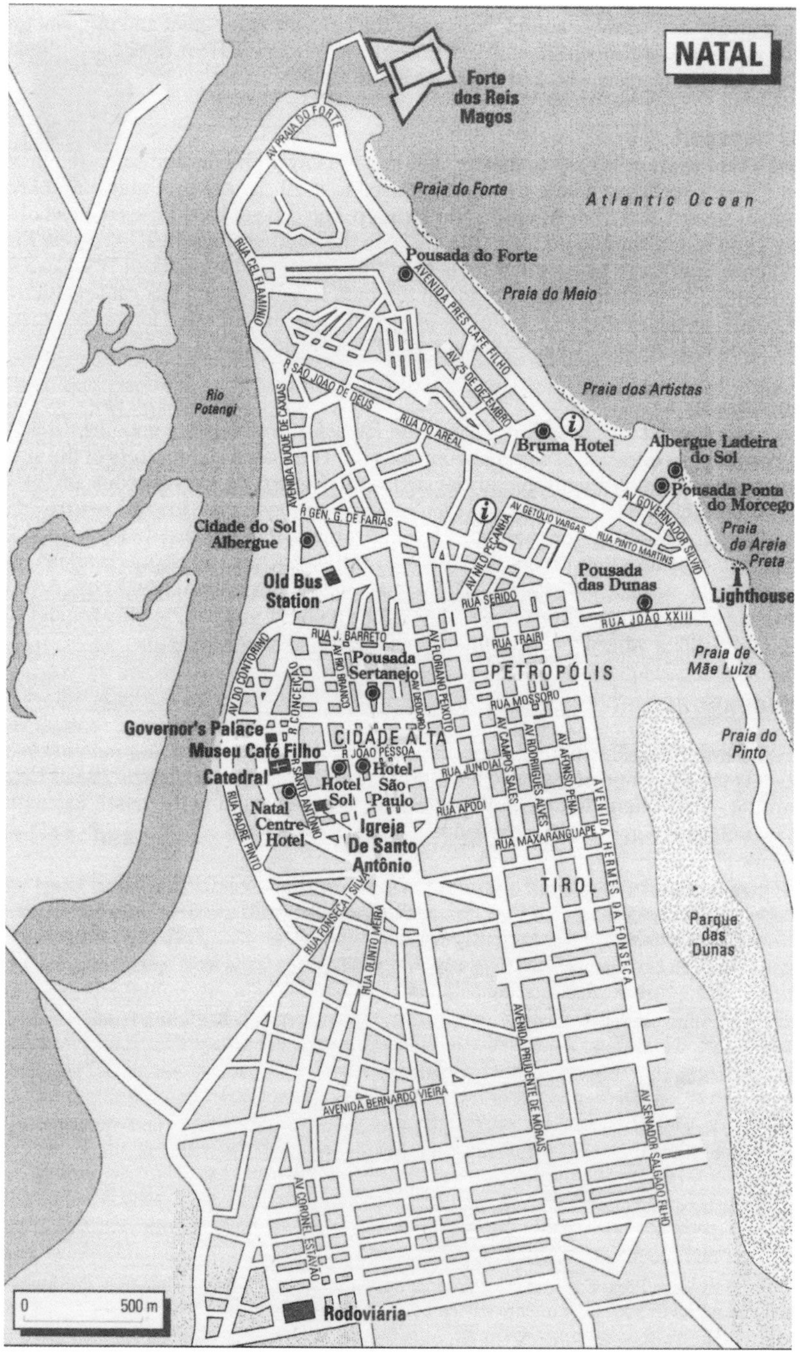

I-36; Map No. 8: Peninsular Section of Natal; from 5th Edition of Rough Guide to Brazil. Published by Rough Guides LTD.

I-37; A Boatload of Brasileiros (Natalenses)

Photo I-37 was taken during a ride from Natal across the Potengi River to the beaches of Redinha on its north side. A look at the faces of the Brasileros in the boat shows how various mixtures of the different ethnic and racial groups have melded in modern day northeastern Brazil. Brazil is as much or more of a “melting pot” than the USA. Brazil en toto at that time was estimated to be 30% white, 5% pure Indian, 12% pure black, with the balance mixed. Regions varied as to racial makeup.

I-38; Downtown Natal from Cidade Alta - December, 1943

Photo I-38 was taken from a church steeple (the Igreja Presbyteriana do Natal) up the hill looking down toward the lower section of Natal known as the Ribeira area. Further up the hill was Cidade Alta or Upper City where many residents of Natal had their homes. Floating on the Potengi River in the center left of the photo are 3 PBM Martin Mariners of VP-74 squadron of Fairwing 16. Just visible in the upper right center of the photo one can see the overhead roof of nose hanger facilities at the RAMPA seaplane base near where the Potengi met the South Atlantic ocean. A large seaplane – a Coronado, is noted floating in the Potengi.

I-39; Natal as a Seaport in the 1940's

While Natal did have some connection between inner portions of the state of Rio Grande do Norte state and the South Atlantic it had not emerged as a significant trans-oceanic port. Some coastal traffic did utilize Natal as a port as evidenced by the small ships shown in the left portion of photo I-39. Like most Brazilian coastal cities of that era the land-based transportation system connecting Natal to Fortaleza in the North or Recife in the south was relatively slow and not widely used. Lieutenant Sam Taylor of VP-83 noted that when a convoy of aviation fuel bearing trucks was sent overland from Recife to Natal in 1942, they had to utilize a large winch equipped tow truck frequently during the torturous journey because there were gaps in the road system. Coastal shipping was the principal way of moving goods.

I-40; Ribeira Dockside Close-up – 1943

In this photo the fifth building from the right which has a balcony with a canopy and is in front of a 3 story building showing five protusions from corners of its roof is the famous Wonderbar saloon and brothel.
A subsequent photo (I-99) shows a soldier and sailor on that balcony. The ability to get from that balcony to a boat on the river is a feature of a subsequent anecdote about an escapade at the Wonderbar. Behind the Wonderbar is the ornate building which housed a business of the Italian Consul.
One could get to the Wonderbar through that building. The Wonderbar building has been demolished but the 3 story building is still in use.

I-41; Natal Beaches: Praia do Melo; Praia do Forte

In photo I-41 taken from the 1943 USO Beach Club on a hill looking northward toward the Ribeira, the RAMPA, and Forte dos Reis Magos areas, one sees a broad expanse of open beach. Note how all the palm trees are bent inland due to the prevailing ocean breezes which make the climate so favorable. The sandy northern banks of the Potengi in the Redinha area are visible in the distance. The many small windowless thatched roof dwellings were typical beach side homes in the 1940's. As will be seen in recent photos of this beach, the small dwellings have been replaced by much more modern buildings. Much of the open beach area has been built up since the war.

I-42; Southeast View of Beachside and Ocean from USO Beach Club – 1943

Photo I-42 shows that the size and complexity of beachside homes increased in the more southerly area of Natal's beaches in 1943. The hill from the Beach Club was steep and servicemen and their friends from Natal normally went farther south to enjoy the beaches nearer Ponta Negra.

I-43; Café Sao Luiz and Restaurante, Beachside, 1943

Photo I-43 shows a 100% pure café at beachside, Natal. I don't believe I went into the café at that time. The gentleman clearly has four responsive burros since he is driving them without any harness leads. Natal was a small rather pastoral city in the early 1940's. The benign climate of Natal and the development of adequate amenities made it a reasonable place for U.S. servicemen. However, the factors which made it "good duty" were the friendliness of the local Natalenses toward the Americans and the small town atmosphere. Additional photos of people, places and buildings of Natal in 1943-44 appear in Chapter 13.

4

Natal's Parnamirim Air Base
"Crossroads of the World"

Natal had, as everyone knows, a decisive influence on the war, offering to the United Nations the major facilities for obtaining its objective.

General Eisenhower at Natal on August 3, 1946

ALLIED FORCES AT PARNAMIRIM

In earlier times the (1920's and 1930's) Natal had already become a gateway to South America for airplane travel but the facilities were minimal and the number of planes involved were miniscule compared to what happened in World War II years. The U.S. Army Air Force Ferry Command and Air Transport Command (ATC) collaborated with Brazilian forces in expanding capability at Parnamirim by adding barracks, mess halls, a Post Exchange (PX), medical buildings, and the other accoutrements necessary to accommodate the thousands of air crews transiting via Natal to Freetown-Accra area of West Africa. Prior to these construction efforts Parnamirim was mostly an open field with sandy soil, a couple of radio towers and a small air strip.

The Brazilian Air Force, whose plane complement had been augmented by transfer of some U.S. built aircraft, also trained and flew anti-submarine missions from Parnamirim. The U.S. Navy worked jointly with its Brazilian counterparts in augmenting their facilities at Parnamirim. The U.S. Engineering Department (USED), working with Brazilian help, enlarged the runway and control tower facilities at Parnamirim. U.S.E.D. had female American employees which made for a lot of bad jokes about USED girls.

By April 1943 the newly formed Fleet Air Wing Sixteen had the PBY 5A's of VP-83 and VP-94 plus the PV-1 (Ventura) squadron VB-129 all operating out of Parnamirim. VP-74, with PBM's (Martin Mariners) operated out of the RAMPA at Natal.

ATC and Ferry Command Routes and Activities

The USAAF air transport operations had two main routes across the Atlantic in an easterly direction as previously shown in Map no.2 (from reference 3, Dmitri). The Northern route via Maine – Labrador – Greenland and Iceland was rather perilous for a good part of the year. The Southern route shows why Natal's Parnamirim field became the largest U.S. – Allied air base outside the continental United States in terms of air traffic. The weather was much more suitable on the Southern Route across the Atlantic.

Large amounts of war materials and a great number of personnel were needed in the Mediterranean, European, China-Burma-India, and Western Pacific theatres of war.

The Map No.9 (from reference 5, Dmitri), shows the routes followed across Africa through the Middle East to India and then over the Himalaya Mountains (The HUMP) to Kunming, China. Reference 3, "The Flight to Everywhere" by Ivan Dmitri, a photo journalist, is a splendid pictorial history of the Air Transport Commands' bases, personnel, equipment, and efforts during the war.

It is apparent in Ivan Dmitri's book that once the USAAF planes left the friendly confines of Natal they were headed to much more primitive areas in Africa, the Middle East and Asia.

Photo I-44 shows a USED lady receiving an award.

The U.S. Engineering Department had a number of civilian employees.

The men and women of the ATC endured very primitive living and working conditions all the way from ACCRA on the Gold Coast of Africa to ASSAM in India and then flew the extremely perilous journeys "over the HUMP" to keep the Chinese supplied.

In addition to the routes across Africa through the Middle East to India and then over the Himalaya Mountains to Kunming, China, a very important route for the European war was that through the Gulf of Arabia and Persia (Iran) to the Soviet Union. Particularly during the first two years after Hitler invaded the Soviet Union the route via Natal ending up in the Soviet Republics bordering Persia was critically important. The Northern Atlantic route was extremely perilous for both ATC planes and Allied merchant ships not only from the U-Boats but from German aircraft in Norway and daunting weather conditions. Ivan Dmitri must have had a good reason not to include the ATC route through Persia to the Soviet Union in his itinerary.

To learn just how perilous the North Atlantic route to Russia was the reader is referred to an outstanding book (Reference 21) authored by a U.S. Naval officer, Commander William Carter who served in the Armed Guard on a U.S. merchant ship on the Murmansk run. In his book Commander (then a Lieutenant) Carter tells the story of Allied convoys, sometimes within the Arctic Circle, attempting to elude German U-Boats and surface naval units as well as aircraft, with minimal escort protection.

The Russians were in desperate condition in 1941 and 1942 for supplies of explosives, tanks, artillery and trucks and the availability of the Southern supply route with convoys sailing through the South Atlantic off Brazil to Africa and beyond was a lifesaver for their defensive efforts. This scenario illustrated the importance of Parnamirim.

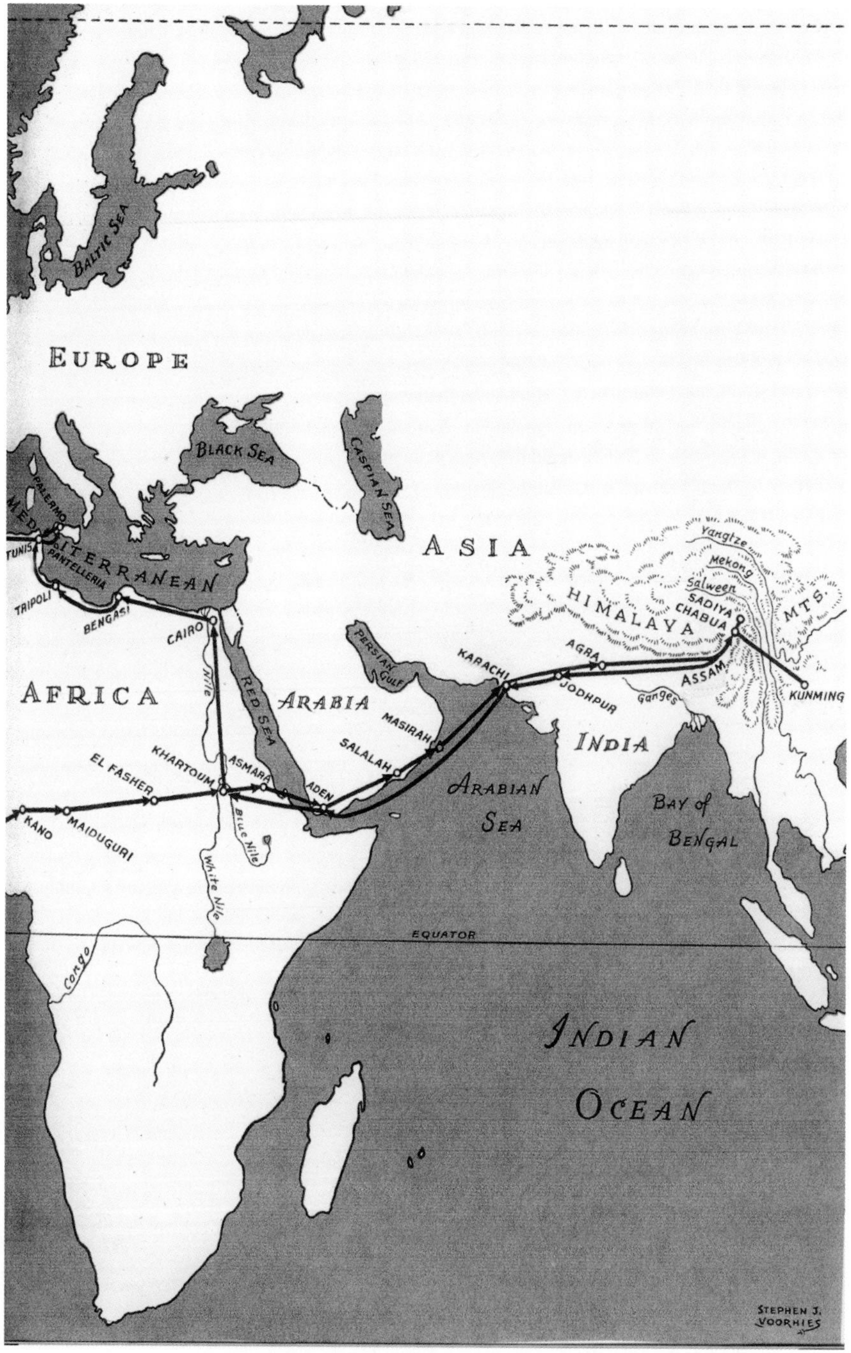

I-45; Map No. 9: ATC routes to theatres of war from Dmitri's - Flight to Everywhwere - McGraw Hill

ARMY AIRFORCE ACTIVITIES AT NATAL

From 1942 until nearly the end of the war, the USAAF expanded facilities at Parnamirim. The next four photos show typical plane traffic at Natal. In addtion to Ferry Command and regular USAAF pilots many foreign flight personnel came to Natal while ferrying planes to both the European and Pacific theaters. The fifth photo shows Parnamirim in 1944.

I-46: C-87 cargo plane of the Air Transport Command

In addition to use as a principal stopover for the Ferry Command sending planes to all the theatres of war, the ATC, into which Ferry Command later incorporated, sent hundreds of cargo planes through Parnamirim with all kinds of war related material and personnel. In this photo we see a C-87 (the freighter version of the B-24) being fueled from barrels. Later a gasoline pipeline was built from Natal's dock to Parnamirim.

The gasoline pipeline and a rail line were installed alongside the road from Natal to Parnamirim.

The road from Parnamirim to Natal was rough and unpaved for the first year or so. Marshall Jamison tells of some adventurous episodes on that road in early 1942.

I-47; A B-25 Mitchell Medium Bomber

The Army Air Force Ferry Command was very busy routing planes south from Miami to Natal and on to Africa, Europe, and the Middle and Far East theatres of war. As can be seen the Air Force also painted nicknames and drawing on their planes. In the nose of this B-25 is a 75 mm cannon for use against Japanese merchant vessels. However, due to heavy smoke inside the plane created on firing the 75 mm cannon they were soon removed and replaced with multiple 50 mm machine guns. The Navy (Marine Corps) version of the B-25 was designated PBJ.

I-48; B-17 Flying Fortress at Parnamirim – 1943

Hundreds of B-17's flew via Natal, primarily to the European theatre, with many of them ending up operating out of England. The B-17 was a rugged heavily armed plane and carried the brunt of the U.S. Eighth Air Force raids on Germany. Despite having multiple machine gun turrets above, below, forward, and to the rear, until the advent of long range escort fighters, the casualty rate was tremendous. More American Flyers lives were lost over Europe than were lost in all the heroic land battles in the Pacific.

I-49; B-24's on Tarmac at Natal

Prior to early 1944 the B-17 and B-24 (or the Navy's version designated PB4Y) were the largest bombers frequenting Natal. In photo I-49 we see two B-24's on the tarmac.

Very early in 1944, one of my shipmates came running excitedly into the Photo Lab shouting come on lets go up to the flight line. You won't believe the size of the airplanes now arriving. It was the advent of the first of the B-29's on their way to the Pacific. At that time the B-29 had not been publicized so we were not permitted to take any photographs of it. Some of these early B-29's were going to India and Western China to engage in early USAAF bombing campaigns against Japan. This was prior to our capture of Tinian or Saipan Islands which were later used as B-29 bases. The use of B-29's from India or Western China was apparently not effective and the really successful raids on Japan occurred later from the other bases in the Western Pacific.

I-50; Parnamirim After Full Construction - 1944

Photo I-50 shows most of the expanded Parnamirim Air Base. Note that in addition to over one hundred permanent buildings it was still necessary to employ over two hundred tents to house the many thousands of military personnel passing through Natal.

The Brazilian side is to the right and the far side and is only partly visible.

The Fairwing 16 portion of Parnamirim was relatively small compared to the USAAF section and the Brazilian area.

By 1943, the combined efforts of the Brazilians and U.S.E.D had made Parnamirim a pleasant place for service personnel and Natal was a good "liberty town". This was particularly a boon to the USAAF and transient personnel that faced the prospect of the journeys through Africa, The Middle East, and India to China which made for rugged duty. The following three photos show some typical on base off-duty activities at Parnamirim.

I-51; USO Dancer on Stage Navy Theatre

This photo of a USO dancer is reminiscent of a famous photo of Carmen Miranda which showed her with skirt twirling horizontally whilst she was sans underwear in a full frontal perspective. That particular photo of Carmen Miranda was more prevalent than any other one in Brazil.

I-52; Boots at Parnamirim - 1943

This photo shows a sailor polishing a pair of the "Natal Boots" which many air force personnel purchased as they passed through Parnamirim. The boots were not necessary at Natal because the joint efforts of Brazilian and U.S. health officials had eliminated the mosquito problem but such was not the case in Africa, the Middle East, India, and the Pacific where the Air Force personnel were headed.

I-53; Opening of Ships Store at Parnamirim

In late 1943, the U.S. Navy opened a new Ships store complete with Cerveja (Beer), soft drinks (Guarana), an ice cream bar and other goodies. Shown here iare left to right: Dale E. Wright; Connery (with cigar); R. Bronner (Standing); Eugene Webb (with bottle); Unknown; Bailey (Chief Aerographer) and Arthur J. Sykes. All these individuals were in Headquarters Squadron (HEDRON) Fairwing 16.

I-54; Kelley at Bat

Regular softball games provided exercise for personnel at Parnamirim. The catcher's name was Whiteside. Note the ventilation ports along the bottoms of the walls of the barracks in the background of this photo.. The combination of those lower ventilation ports and the open window shutters helped keep the barracks relatively cool.

IMPACT OF PARNAMIRIM'S GROWTH ON NATAL

As would be expected, the growth of Parnamirim airfield and the concurrent arrival of several thousand U.S. service and engineering personnel at Natal starting in December 1941 had a profound effect on the economy and populace of Natal.

Parnamirim air base grew to encompass 3,301 acres and employed 2,800 Brazilians. The city of Natal had a total population of only about 50,000 at that time. The average Brazilian laborer considered the pay of 3 cruzeiros (or milreis) per day to be very good wages. The exchange rate was 20 cruzeiros per dollar and a wage of 15 cents (U.S) per day was greeted with enthusiasm by local workers. The American service men also liked the price of the local cerveja (beer) which was 3 cruzeiros (15 cents) per bottle. At that time an American service man (Photographer's Mate Third Class – equivalent to a sergeant in the U.S. Air Force) had base wages of 93 dollars per month plus a 20% add-on increment for overseas pay. Also those on flight duty got an additional added pay increment of 50% of base pay.

Houses in Natal could originally be rented at a rate of $20 per month. As would be expected, some of the favorable prices tended to increase as demand increased and locals realized that they could increase prices to Americans.

Quite naturally when a large group of virile young men find themselves far from home and bereft of the normal contact with and conviviality of female companionship experienced back home, they seek local liaisons. In Natal male/female relations took several forms as will be noted in some of the anecdotal stories which subsequently appear. The U.S. Armed Forces medical contingent attempted to indoctrinate service men about the danger of frequenting brothels but the effort was only partially successful.

Natal had several small cafe/bars where servicemen could enjoy beverage, light food, and the companionship of the female waitresses, some of who were susceptible to persuasion and advances and some who were not.

I cannot remember the name of the small cafe/bar which we of the photo lab gang used to frequent for libations and light food. It was on Rua Dr. Barata which was the heart of the business district which was in the Ribeira at that time.

I do remember well two of the waitresses who were very friendly and even tempered. The prettiest one was Louisenette whom numerous sailors tried to date but she did not comply with their wishes. The other one was the ever smiling Irasuda. She also was a "Good Girl" and did not accept any of the many entreaties of the sailors.

Discreet and controlled female companionship was also available (though chaperoned) at the two USO clubs in Natal. One of the USO's was downtown and the other was at a beach club.

There were marriages of U.S. servicemen and Brazilian women. One other notable marriage was that of an American Army nurse (Thelma Tamlyn) and a U.S. trained Brazilian pilot (Fernando de Mendoca).

Natal also had three brothels: the Maria Boa; the Wonderbar; and, the Goodyear. Since I had been raised in a home where Victorian attitudes prevailed and the Navy's medical orientation films had scared the daylights out of me, I was never in any of the brothels. With the thousands of U.S. service personnel based or passing through Natal, the Brothels did a thriving business. The medical reports in the History of Fleet Air Wing 16 show that the amount of venereal disease cases got to be a growing problem. During the early months of increased presence of U.S. service personnel in Natal there was only one significant hotel in town. Unfortunately for the venereal disease problem military authorities were booking personnel into the Hotel International not realizing that it was actually part of the Wonderbar brothel enterprise. The military later began to control and supervise testing of brothel personnel and also regulated the activities to some degree. They also did so at Recife.

In addition to the economic stimulus, the growth of Parnamirim resulted in improved roads and added many buildings at the air field. At the end of the war all the facilities and most of the equipment was turned over to the Brazilians. Today Parnamirim is a significant city in its own right and Natal is now a metropolis rather than a small town.

Those reading this book can get a perspective of the post-war growth of Natal by comparing pohtos in Chapter 22 (Modern Natal) with those photos I took in 1943-44.

5

Battles in the South Atlantic

Thus the Battle of the Atlantic was second to none in its influence on the outcome of the war.

Samuel Eliot Morison, historian

AXIS POWER NAVAL FORCES DOMINATE IN 1942

Prior to mid 1943, the combined forces of German U-boats and Italian submarines were having significant success in sinking merchant ships in the South Atlantic Narrows between Brazil and Africa. Further, they were not being effectively challenged or deterred by Allied efforts. All too often, trans-oceanic ships were being sunk.

In addition, blockade runners were slipping by in mid-ocean to carry vital materials from the Japanese occupied territories to Europe. It took us nearly 18 months to build up forces and procedures to begin to turn the tide.

While there can be little doubt that VP-83's valiant efforts in the latter half of 1942 protected some of the coastal area convoys, the squadron's coverage range and relatively small number of planes prevented them from destroying Axis submarines in that year. Because there were no U-Boat losses in 1942, Admiral Doenitz decided, in early 1943, to send more U-Boats to the South Atlantic to capitalize on the relatively small number of Allied planes and surface vessels previously noted in that sector. Fortunately, Admiral Ingram had been receiving reinforcements, both surface units and airplanes in anticipation of increased U-Boat activity.

During the December 1942, January 1943 period two new squadrons: VP-74 with Martin Mariners (PBM's) and VP-94 with PBY5A's arrived to aid VP-83 in countering the Axis Power submarine and surface vessel offensive. In addition, the Brazilian Air Force (FAB) built up and diversified its aircraft squadrons so that by August 1942, when Brazil declared war on the Axis Powers, they began to carry out joint activities against the Axis Power units. Admiral Ingram also received additional surface vessels to build-up Fourth Fleet capabilities.

This build-up of Allied air power began to have some effect in the first 6 months of 1943. With the availability of the additional squadrons Fairwing 16 was formed and the various squadrons were dispatched full time to other newly improved and expanded air bases all the way from Belem in the North to Florianopolis in the southernmost area of the Brazilian coast.

In all of 1942 VP-83 did not routinely have an advanced base on Ascension Island for land or seaplanes. This limited the range and scope of anti-submarine flights.

In order to protect a particularly important convoy sailing to Africa carrying vital supply of artillery shells and tanks to General Montgomery at Alexandria, VP-83 temporarily sent three PBY's to Ascension Island so they could shadow and protect this most important convoy, which they did. After that convoy got through the Atlantic Narrows safely, the detachment of PBY's flew back to Natal. Montgomery received his supplies and proceeded to win the Battle of El Alamein.

Apparently the availability of fuel and supplies at Ascension Island was so limited in 1942 and until September, 1943 that it was impossible to consider basing of Fourth Fleet land planes on Ascension.

I-55; Doomed Allied Merchant Ship Off Brazilian Coast

This ship in photo I-55 has obviously been torpedoed amidship and would soon join the metal scrap pile in the South Atlantic seabed. This scene would be repeated dozens of times in the South Atlantic from 1941 through much of 1943. Note the circular gun emplacements both on the bow and the stern of the ship. This indicates the presence of an Armed Guard contingent on board.

ALLIED FORCES COUNTER ATTACK

Now more up to strength, the combined forces of Fairwing 16, Fourth Fleet and their Brazilian counterparts begin to effectively engage the Axis naval units in the South Atlantic Narrows during 1943.

VP-83 Strikes Back

Between 6 January and 15 April, 1943, PBY's from VP-83 destroyed the U-164, the U-507, and the Archimedes (an Italian U-Boat). These were the first 3 U-Boats sunk by FAW 16 planes.

The story of the "First Kill" of U-164 on 6 January, 1943 is best told by a key participant, the air crew chief of Bill Fords 83-P-2, one Billie Goodell, who recently sent the author the following description:

First Kill – Destruction of U-164

You have read different accounts about the squadrons' first kill. Well, since it was my plane, here is the way it was. We were covering a northbound convoy of about fifty ships, when we got off the coast of Belem. We were relieved by another squadron so we went into Belem for gas and spent the night. The pilot was Lt. Ford and the copilot was Lt. (jg) Dawkins.

We met at the plane the next morning and Mr. Ford asked us if we wanted to fly back over the jungles or the ocean. No one knew so he said he would flip a coin. The results were that we would go the ocean route.

We took off and headed south. The crew was tired from all of the hours we had spent in the air the days before so we told them to sleep and get some rest. Meanwhile, I was alone in the after station seated next to the port fifty caliber. We were flying about three thousand feet out at sea. I had a pair of binoculars and was seeing if I could make out where the water and sky met.

There were quite a few clouds but I could see patches of blue water every so often. In one of the openings I spotted a white wake and a U-Boat off the port side. I called Lt. Ford and told him there was a sub about eleven o'clock. He told me that he hadn't spotted it yet. I had already unstrapped the port gun when we made a sharp left bank and put old 83-P-2 in a steep dive. He had spotted it and was going in for the kill. I began to strafe the sub and tracers were flying under the port wing. We could see the crew on deck, most in bathing trunks. They tried to pull covers off their deck guns, but never made it. Lt. Ford straddled it with two depth charges on each side. I continued firing as the bombs exploded and the sub rose and broke in half. We made a sharp turn to the port and I kept on firing; all of a sudden a hand on my shoulder pulled me back and said, "Bill, you are killing all the survivors".

Mr. Ford went down to about a hundred feet and began to circle. One guy was straddled on a tank of some sort and another was swimming toward him. There were a few bodies in the water and lots of oil and debris. The water began to get rough. We made a pass and I threw a life raft over the side. The currents carried it away from them, so we went upwind and threw our last raft out. It inflated and both men got aboard. I took a canister of water, wrapped a life vest around it, and threw it to them. It got rough and we lost sight of the raft. We radioed their position and headed for Fortaleza.

We landed with about eighty gallons of gas left. I had shot the antenna off under the port wing and we had to fix it. Lt. Ford made reservations in town and we all checked in. We were all seated at a large table eating a victory dinner. About the end of the meal I looked up and never saw so much brass. I hollered "attention" and we all stood up. "At ease and please be seated." It was Admiral Ingram and his staff that got the word and flew all the way to Fortaleza. First thing he said was, "which one of you is Goodell and Ford". After shaking hands with everyone they left.

We took off real early the next morning for Natal. The men were still in their tents. Lt. Ford said, "Let's wake them up". He called the tower and got permission to make a victory run. He came down to fifty feet, poured on the coal, and went over the tents wiggling his wings. Boy what a thrill. Guys ran out in skivvies wondering what in the world was going on. We found out later the two survivors were picked up and were in Fortaleza. We sent a plane up and brought them back to Natal. The next photo shows the two German prisoners from U-164 arriving at Natal. U-Boat 164 would not sink any more Allied ships.

Editorial Note: Billie Goodell would later receive the Distinguished Flying Cross for his key role in spotting and helping to destroy the U-164. He would go on to serve 33 months in VP-83/VB-107 in Brazil.

Chapter 7 has more information on Billie Goodell, Plane Captain.

I-56; German Prisoners from U-164 at Parnamirim

This photo shows shows Bootsman Gerhard Schonfelder and Matrosengereuter Alfred Jadike being led to prisoner of war quarters at Natal. They would spend the rest of the war in a POW camp. Four depth charges can be seen under the wing of the PBY5A Catalina of VP-83.

VP-83 no.10 Destroys the U-507

Lieutenant Lloyd Ludwig's' PBY, flying convoy coverage out of Fortaleza, caught the U-507 on the surface on January 13, 1943. Ludwig then made a prompt and accurate depth charge attack with no. 10 in which the bombs scored a perfect straddle on the U-Boat. Ludwig and copilot, Lieutenant Mearl Taylor, quickly flew back to alert the convoy they had been covering so they did not witness the final death throes of the U-507. At first no. 10 was not credited with a definite kill but post-war records show that the U-Boat did sink and the crew perished. Reference 4 includes a detailed account of this battle action.

While the destruction of the U-507 was a real feather in the cap of VP-83-10 and Fairwing 16, it is unfortunate that it was not a Brazilian plane that did the job.

On August 15th of 1942, prior to Brazil's entry into the war, the U-507 had torpedoed and sunk two Brazilian coastal passenger ships near Bahia and 400 Brazilians perished. The next day the U-507 sunk another Brazilian ship (the Annibal Benevolo) and 150 Brazilians drowned. Korvetten Kapitan Harro Schact, in command of the U-507, followed up by sinking the Itagiba and Arara, two more Brazilian ships in the evening of August 17, 1942 with several hundred more Brazilians being lost at sea.

In all, the U-Boats in August, 1942, had sunk 6 Brazilian ships with a total casualty count of over 800 people.

The actions by Herr Schact were the primary reason that President Vargas lead Brazil to then declare war on the Axis powers. Vargas was prompted by significant Anti-Axis street demonstrations which occurred throughout Brazil after the August rampage by the U-507.

One wonders whether the U-507 had returned to Europe after its August 1942 successes and before Lloyd Ludwig in P-10 had despatched it to the bottom of the sea in January, 1943. Perhaps Admiral Doenitz had "milch cow" U-Boats deployed in the South Atlantic in the latter part of 1942. We do know that in 1942 Doenitz, in response to the easy pickings at that time had sent 10 U-Boats and several Italian submarines into the Atlantic Narrows off Brazil.

Barrier Sweep Tactics Meet Success

On the way back from a 5 plane barrier sweep looking for Axis submarines on April 15, 1943, one of Thurmond Robertson's' crew (Seaman Second Class Earl J. Kloss) in a PBY of VP-83 spotted a submarine. It turned out to be the Archimedes of the Italian Navy. Robertson attacked the sub by dropping depth bombs which severely damaged the Achimedes. Now out of bombs, Robertson called in Lieutenant Gerald Bradford who had been flying second PBY on the same Barrier Sweep. Bradford homed in and dropped four depth bombs from fifty feet altitude which destroyed the submarine. Only two survivors were later rescued and brought to shore.

Unlike the U-507 case, Lieutenant Robertson who made the first attack which crippled the Archimedes so that it could not submerge, and Lieutenant Bradford whose depth bomb attack sank the submarine, did receive prompt credit for the kill. Their crews actually saw the submarine sink and the 30 survivors of the crew in the water.

Thurmond Robertson would stay in the Navy after the war ended. As noted by Ed Krug in his section of this book, Thurmond perished in a crash while piloting a plane during the post-war Berlin Airlift.

I-57; VP-74 PBM's bombing the U-128

The fourth U-Boat to be destroyed (the U-128) was the first win for the PBM's of VP-74 and the destroyers Moffett and Jouett. On May 17, 1943, the two PBM's, 74-P-6 (Lieutenant Davis), and 74-P-5 (Lieutenant Carey and Ensign Smolsnik) carried out successful depth bomb attacks on the U-128 which caused the submarine's crew to begin abandoning ship. Shortly thereafter, the destroyers arrived, shelled the U-128, and it soon sank beneath the surface. Fifty one Germans survived and were picked up by the destroyers. Two months later, Lieutenant Cary, his crew and plane were all lost at sea after being shot down during an attack on the U-199. In photo I-57, Depth Bomb Drop on U-128, we see one of the PBM's approaching the U-128 on a bombing run and the splashes from the suppressing fire from the PBM as it approaches the U-Boat. Beneath the PBM we note several depth bombs which have been released from the plane. This is a graphic illustration of the difficulty in accurately dropping bombs from a moving airplane onto a moving submarine. Bomb sights which were designed for bombing stationary targets from high altitudes, were no help. The bombs, due to momentum, fall in an arc like path from the plane so it is a "seat of the pants" proposition to gauge when to release the bombs so that the ocean end of the arc path of the bombs is on or very near the U-Boat. Practice bombing exercises were extensively utilized in Brazil so the pilots could gain experience in the art of releasing the depth bombs at the right moment.

As the build-up of forces on both sides of the conflict in the South Atlantic was occurring the author, in early July 1943, was included in a 120 sailor contingent being assembled at Norfolk Naval Air Station for transfer to Fairwing 16 in Recife, Brazil.

The last leg of the transit to Recife was aboard the USS William Evarts (an army transport) from Trinidad to Recife. Due to a 10 day delay in Trinidad it was mid August by the time the USS William Evarts left a convoy off the coast of Surinam and steamed by itself, unprotected, for several days before arriving in Recife.

Fortunately for the author and the other passengers and crew on the Evarts, Fairwing 16 and Fourth Fleet ships had blunted the mid-1943 blitz by destroying six U-Boats in July and one in early August. Even though the Axis Powers sent additional U-Boats to replenish losses, the Allies had countered the Blitz.

As we will note further on, the success of the Allied Forces was hard-won and quite a few brave men lost their lives prematurely as a result of the battles. We were materially assisted by interception and decoding of radio traffic between the U-Boats and Germany.

The July 1943 U-Boat Blitz

We now know that at most times at least seven German submarines were prowling the South Atlantic off Brazil in the middle of 1943 looking for Allied ships passing that way.

Sometime in late June, 1943 the U-662, U-591, and U-598 left St. Nazaires' heavily fortified U-Boat pens and sailed toward the South Atlantic. They managed to proceed unscathed through the Bay of Biscay despite the Allied air patrols. They were joined by the U-604 shortly after leaving the French coastal area. For the U-602 this would be the fourth patrol which indicated they had previously enjoyed significant success.

These U-Boats would be joining the U-172, U-185, U-199, U-510, U-513, and U-590 which had already been active off the Brazilian coast when the aforementioned four U-Boats were scheduled to arrive at their assigned stations in July. When memories of the havoc created off the U.S. Atlantic seaboard by six U-Boats right after Pearl Harbor were recalled one can imagine the alarm at Fourth Fleet Headquarters in Recife when the probable presence of about ten U-Boats off Brazil was noted.

Despite the destruction of the 4 U-Boats in January to June, 1943 period, the Axis Powers, for strategic reasons, decided to step up U-Boat and other naval unit activity in the South Atlantic Narrows. They dispatched several more U-Boats into the South Atlantic.

FAW 16 planes still were not able to fully patrol the broad expanse of the Narrows well away from the Brazilian Coast. The result was the "July Blitz" by the many U-Boats in the South Atlantic Narrows.
Admiral Ingram anticipated the Blitz and both FAW 16 and the Fourth Fleet were reinforced and started an aggressive response to the efforts of the U-Boats. Naturally more battles at sea took place. We won some and we lost some.

A key element in the build-up of Fairwing 16 capability was the dispatch of VP-83 personnel in June 1943 back to the USA to be re-equipped with PB4Y (B-24) Liberators which were faster and could carry more armament than the PBY's. The change over to the Liberators as VB-107 squadron took about five weeks due to training needs. The other Fairwing 16 squadrons kept very active during the absence of the VP-83 personnel.

VP-94 Sinks U-Boat 662

On July 21, 1943, Lieutenant (jg) R. H. Rowlands' successfully depth charged the U-Boat U-662 off Belem. U-662 had been stalking a convoy and had survived unscathed from a previous attack by another PBY5A piloted by Lieutenant (jg) S. E. Auslander on July 20th.

Rowlands' PBY number P-4 won the typical gun battle between his gunners firing their machine guns and the U-Boats crew firing their 20mm and 37mm cannon. Rowlands' crew won because they were accurate in their gunfire while one of U662's dual 20mm gun sets jammed. P-4's rudder and one of its crew men were hit but then the P-4's guns wiped out the U-Boats ack-ack crew and a successful drop of depth charges destroyed U-662.

I-58; 94-P-4 Above German U-Boat 662

I-59; Survivors from the U-662

No doubt Kapitan Lieutenant Heinz - Eberhard Muller felt relatively safe when 94-P-4 approached since he had already withstood three attacks from U.S. planes within the previous few days and escaped damage. Stan Auslander in a PBY had made an attack on U-662 on July 20, 1943 with no damage inflicted on the U-Boat. His running gun battle with U-662 and his depth bomb attack did not harm the U-Boat at all.

Auslander had also called in the ships escorting the convoy he was protecting but they also were unable to mount a successful attack.The following day Eberhard-Mullers' luck ran out.

This shows the forward half and conning tower of the U-662 is a further illustration of how close and attacking plane had to get to its target U-Boat in order to directly hit the submarine.

There had been a fourth survivor of the U-662 but he had died on the life raft before the remaining three men were fortunate enough to be picked out of the sea by the crew of the USS Siren (PC 494).

The full names of the other three survivors were Matrose Noberge Freiters, Herman Grauff, and Ferdinand Marx. Kapitan Leutant Muller ad his crew had put up a spirited battle with Rolland and his PBY crew but in the end he and the other members of his crew lost the battle, the U-Boat and their lives.

These three men, Muller, Grauff, and Marx were to be 16 days adrift before being picked up by a U.S. ship. A full description of the battles with U-662 appears in Reference 4.

Triumph Follows Tragedy for VP-94 Crews - July 9, 1943

The following verbatim excerpt from the "Command History of Fleet Air Wing Sixteen" (February 18, 1943 – December 31, 1944) described two engagements between VP-94 PBY's and the German U-590:

"The Amazon and Fortaleza area also came in for their share of activity and a series of attacks were made by VP-94 planes in the vicinity of 03-22N, 48-28Y, on July 9th which resulted in the sinking of the submarine, but also the death of one of VP-94's pilots, Lt. (jg) Hare. The best recital of the attacks is the story written up by Lt. Cutler from conversations with some of the pilots that were engaged in the action.

The Triumph

Lieutenant Dick Rowland's mention of Lt. Stan Auslander's attack referred to the action of July 9, 1943, when a (VP-94) PBY with Auslander as first pilot, Lt. (jg) John M. Elliot as second pilot and Lt. (jg) Frank McMackin as navigator, took off from Belem at 0700 Peter. In the plane's crew were six men, all whom had received the air medal twice. One of them had also received the Purple Heart.

Two hundred miles off Amapa, northeast of Belem, they sighted a submarine about 15 miles away just submerging. It remained surfaced about three minutes during which time the crew wondered whether it was a submarine or just another surface ship. But as they closed in they saw the conning tower just going down. They turned on all switches and got set. They noticed a slight oil slick on the smooth sea. Having no green (dye) marker, they dropped a bronze slick to mark the spot, they circled for about five minutes about 1700 feet above the clouds then started using gambit tactics.

They flew the first leg of their (square gambit) course a distance of 25 miles at 1000 feet, then went up to 3800 feet for the next three and were away from the spot about an hour and ten minutes.

Just as they made the last turn, they saw the sub dead ahead. Auslander took the yoke from Elliott who went back aft for the camera, while McMakin plotted the position. The bow gunner had trouble getting his guns to bear as they swung down in, but finally got on and rattled off a burst which splashed about the conning tower. Auslander made a good run as Elliott dropped the bombs. The plane crossed the sub at about 200 knots (plenty for a PBY) missing the water at the end by a bare ten feet. The surfaced U-Boat probably never knew what had hit them. When the plane swung back they saw five men in the water, three of whom disappeared at once.

The plane had been flying just above the tops of the clouds at about 3700 feet when the bow gunner, an enlisted man named Smith, sighted the sub immediately below. They dove down through the clouds breaking out at 1200 feet about a half mile astern of the sub. When they had dropped their bombs and turned to pull out of the dive, all hands were violently thrown into the bilges, and the starboard waist hatch gunner, who had been trying to get in a shot at the sub, perforated the plane's wing with his next burst. By the time the plume of the explosions had subsided, nothing could be seen but the five men, kicking and struggling in the water and some debris consisting of deck planking, casks, boxes and timber. "We couldn't hear what the Heinies were saying", said McMackin, "but we saw their open mouths". They dropped one inflated life raft to them which disappeared in the swells. The other was out of commission. Two uninflated Mae West's which were dropped, sank. Then Elliott dropped two inflated ones which the survivors seized.

The crew stayed in the vicinity for an hour taking pictures. They watched a small oil slick spread sharply from its apex into a ribbon about a mile long. They sighted a convoy, blinked to it that they had just sunk a submarine. Meanwhile the two remaining members of the quintet who had been on the conning tower when they dropped for the run were waving their arms and shouting, begging to be rescued. "But it was too risky to land in those swells", observed McMackin. "It wasn't worth it".

All hands, who incidentally, had not been shot at, felt exuberant. They felt they had evened the score for Frank Hare. This was the first of the three subs VP-94 sank. (Edit. Note – Auslander's crew did not know that they had sunk the U-590 which had earlier killed Frank Hare)

An Army private named Smith was aboard, having come along for the ride. During the excitement he remained in his bunk to keep out of the way. When the plane landed, he disappeared, as Lt. Don Stapp, squadron, ACI Officer, interviewed the crew.

On the same day earlier in the morning another submarine (Edit. Note – Actually it was the U-590) had been sighted and attacked but with less success. Lt. Banta and Lt. (jg) Armenaki of VP-94 in 94-P-7 on an anti-sub sweep northeast of Belem had sighted a sub at 0920Z at 03-22N, 4838W. They sent in a contact report and Lt. (jg) Hare, Lt. (jg) Phelps and Lt. Argento took off in the ready plane 94-P-10 to go to the contact. While flying at 4500 feet above the clouds, they spotted this same submarine at 1250Z at 03-43N, 48-43W. Since Argento had taken a sunsight only a few minutes before, they knew their position was fairly accurate. A few minutes later Price Phelps exclaimed, "Look", there it was. Hare went in to a steep dive while Argento got the camera ready and saw that all hands were at battle stations.

Just then some 20MM shot tore a gaping hole in the port wing only four inches from the bombs. About ten seconds before the plane straddled the submarine, a second burst hit Hare, and he crumpled in the smoke-filled cockpit. A shrapnel burst that missed the bow gunner by three inches shattered the instrument panel. The radioman put out the fire that had broken out while the plane's 30 caliber guns were blazing away at the sub. "Ah" sighed Mike Argento later, "if we had only had twin .50's".

Phelps opened the windows to get rid of the smoke, then as the plane started into a steep bank about 75 feet, he noticed Hare slumped in his seat, the first realization that he had been hit. Phelps took the yoke and turned sharply to starboard, circling widely, while Argento and the plane captain moved Hare from his seat to a bunk. The Plane Captain, De Lorenzo, broke down at the sight of Hare's condition for he, like his shipmates, was devoted to him. When Argento sent him to release the remaining bombs, he saw that the cable was cut and in a frenzy of anger, seized the yoke in an effort to make another run on the sub. Phelps, however, knew this was futile as the bombs could no longer be released because of the damage to the mechanism. Meanwhile the U-Boat which was still circling, possibly because of damage, continued firing at the plane.

Argento gave Phelps the course home and sat beside him. They had cut Hare's shirt off with scissors and had sprinkled sulfa powder on the wounds in his throat and head. It took the plane 2.5 hours to reach the base instead of appreciably less since they had no instruments, accordingly their landing was doubly dangerous. Two doctors, and ambulance and a crash truck awaited them at the field. The crew, Price Phelps who had been nicked in the stomach and shoulder and Hare were taken to the Army hospital, where Dr. Davis did all he could to fix them up. Lt. (jg) Hare had already died of his wounds, any one of which would have been mortal. He had gone to his death gallantly and was awarded the Purple Heart and the Distinguished Service Cross posthumously. The attack on the submarine was given a G assessment, as there was no definite evidence that it had been damaged."

An Epic Battle: VB-107 Versus the U-848

The U848 was one of the 29 newer IXD2 submarines in the Kreigsmarine force. At 87.6 meters (287 feet) in length and 7.5 meters (29.5 feet) abeam it was a large vessel displacing 1,616 tons.

Korvettenkapitan Wilhelm Rollman was commanding officer of the 57 man crew of this U-Boat which was designed to have a range of 23,700 nautical miles on the surface. This type of U-Boat was designed to allow the U-Boat fleet to range into the South Atlantic and cruise on via the Indian Ocean all the way to the Japanese held submarine bases in Indonesia (Penang, Jakarta, and Sabang).

Anti-aircraft guns included twin 20 millimeter and twin 3.7 centimeter cannons. A 10.5 centimeter deck gun was provided to allow shelling of merchant ships. Thus the U-848 had significant defensive weaponry to use against low flying aircraft.

In November of 1943 the U-848, on its way to the Japanese bases, was passing within two hours flying time from Ascension Island. Rollman's orders were to join the Monsoon wolf pack which was operating out of the Japanese bases.

Korvettenkapitan Rollman hoped to use the 24 torpedoes he carried on a few Allied ships as he voyaged to Indonesia. I wonder if the Japanese had shared the design of their excellent Long Lance torpedoes with the Germans?

On November 2nd, 1943, the U-848 sank the British Steamer (the Baron Semple) so Rollman's voyage included at least one victory.

On November 5th, 1943, the U-848 was going past Ascension Island when Lieutenant Charles Baldwin, flying 107-B-12 out of Ascension first spotted the U-848 at 1125 running on the surface.

Baldwin took 3 attacking runs on the U-848. On the first run he dropped 6 depth charges from an altitude of 75 feet, one of which struck a bit forward of the conning tower and obviously damaged the U-Boat because it started to leak a lot of oil. On the second run the U-Boat eluded the airplane successfully. On the third run the 3 remaining depth charges were dropped but they fell short of the U-Boat.

Now out of depth charges, Lieutenant Baldwin contacted Lieutenant Bill Ford flying 107-B-4 who then arrived on the battle scene at 1245. Ford quickly made an attack run at an altitude of 25 feet but his depth charges fell short of U-848. Ford promptly made a second run and dropped his last 3 depth charges but they still fell 30 feet short of the U-Boat. Lieutenant Ford then headed B-4 back to Ascension which Lieutenant William E. Hill flying 107-B-8 had previously left at 1209 to join in the battle. When B-8 made a run on U-848 at 1235 the PB4Y's No.2 engine was hit by anti-aircraft fire from the U-848. With only 3 engines Lieutenant Hill could not risk another bombing run so he returned to Ascension.

He knew that 2 Army B-25's were on their way and that B-4 was being refueled and reloaded so it could rejoin the battle.

The 2 B-25's could not hit the U-Boat and one of them got its hydraulic system shot out.

Lieutenant Sam Taylor flying 107-B-4 with B-4's regular crew arrived at 1650 at the large oil slick and then found the U-848 at 1655. He immediately made a bombing run dropping 5 depth charges across the bow of U-848 from an altitude of 70 feet.

Lieutenant Taylor whipped B-4 around in a tight turn and made a second run dropping his 4 remaining depth charges at an altitude of 50 feet.

The combined effect of the two bomb drops by Sam Taylor was to cause a huge explosion with the U-848 being ripped apart. About 25-30 men and 3 life rafts and a piece of the U-Boat were seen in the middle of the oil slick with much debris.

B-4's crew dropped a life raft and an Army PBY dropped 3 more to the survivors. Lieutenant Taylor signalled HMS Fort Cumberland and asked them to pick up the survivors but they did not do so. One survivor was picked up by a U.S. Cruiser 30 days later but he only lasted 3 days in a Recife hospital. He was buried in Recife with full military honors.

This battle and subsequent ones graphically illustrated the importance of the presence of VB-107 on Ascension Island.

I-60; Close-up of U-848 Under Attack

During Charles Baldwin's morning attack in 107-B-12 the photo I-60 was taken by a member of B-12's crew. We see that the depth bombs dropped during this run were dropped too soon as they can be seen exploding well short of the target. As the PB4Y sped away from over the U-848 this excellent photo shows four German crewmen who were manning the two dual sets of anti-aircraft guns crouching to avoid the gunfire from 107-B-12. Two crewmen on the right are shirtless, the soles of the shoes of a third crewman are visible, and a fourth AA gunner is crouched over the 37mm guns on the left. Charley Baldwin's other run on U-848 was more successful.

Photo I-61; Depth Bomb Above U-848

Between 1700 and 1800 hours Lieutenant Samuel K. Taylor, Jr. made two climactic bombing runs on the U-848. There are two photos of the totally successful second bombing run. The first photo of the second bombing run photo (I-61) shows some depth bombs have already struck a mortal blow on U-848 and another depth bomb is still suspended in the air just above and to the right of the stern of the U-848.

Photo I-62; Coup de Grace for U-848

The second photo from the second bombing run shows the U-848 in the middle of several exploding depth bombs. Finally the coup de grace had been inflicted by Lieutenant Taylor and the crew of B-4. The events occurring in this lengthy battle again illustrated two characteristics of encouters between allied planes and U-Boats. First, good anti-aircraft fire from U-Boats could be effective and secondly, USAAF planes tactics of higher altitude bombing were largely ineffective since the target UBoat was moving.

Failure of HMS Cumberland to rescue the U-Boat survivors may be attributed to hardened attitudes sparked by earlier incidents on survivor rescue opportunities.

Reverence 4 by Alan Carey, contains a multi-page and detailed running account of the battle with the U-848: His narrative includes several paragraph length recollections of the battle by 5 men of VB-107 who participated in the attacks.

I-63; Destruction of U-849

This is an original photo of depth charges hitting U-849 on November 25, 1943. The PB4Y of VB-107 piloted by Marion Dawkins carried out this attack on U-849 which exploded after being hit by the depth charges. Lt. Dawkins had come so close to the submarine that pieces of debris from the bombs flew up and did some damage to the PB4Y, but he was able to return to his base on Ascension Island after the battle. One portion of the depth charge bounced off this U-Boat and lodged in the PB4Y tail, Lt. Dawkins retrieved this piece of metal and still has it as a souvenir. As can be seen, the air crew member made good usage of a K-20 camera to record this action.

I-64; Crew of VB-107-B-10 (The Subduer)

Lt. Dawkins and his air crew of the VB-107-P-10 are shown in this photo in front of their plane, the "Subduer". They are: Back Row; Preston, Jack McCabe, Lee Bergstrom, Peterson, Grocki, Richard Wilson, Russell, and Fyffe. Front Row: Richard Riggs, Marion Dawkins, Deibler, Jean Cook, and Blauvelt.

Lt. Dawkins later became Admiral Ingram's' pilot on the Southern Cross. He remained in the U.S. Navy after the war and finished his career as a Rear Admiral.

Today Vance Dawkins lives in Atlanta, Georgia.

I-65; Crash at Sea of VB 107-B-12

Unfortunately, the U.S. Navy planes were not always successful in avoiding crashes at sea which, in the case of the PB4Y (B-24) Liberators, meant certain death for the crews since PB4Y's did not land well in water, particularly when they lost power.

In photo I-65 taken on January 2, 1944, we see the huge splashes resulting from the crash of VB 107-B-12 (PB4Y piloted by Lieutenant R.T. Johnson) at sea about 71 miles short of a safe return to Ascension from a battle with a German blockade runner, the Wesserland.

The pilot, Lieutenant Robert T. Johnson and his crew had their planes wing tank hit by anti-aircraft fire while they were engaging the blockade runner in battle. The other nine brave men lost in this action were, Eugene Bowers, John Cowan, James Wells (all Ensigns), and Donald Carpenter, Edward Fisher, Russell Hamilton, George Roper, Joslyn Simpson, and William Winter (all air crew men). The destroyer USS Somers later that day, shelled and sank the Wesserland. The full story of this battle is spelled out in Reference 2. Lieutenant Robert Johnson was post-humously awarded the Navy Cross.

Much has been written about the on again, off again level of cooperation between British and American forces during World War II. In the battles in the South Atlantic the degree of cooperation between the Brazilian and American forces was consistent and effective. The same cannot be said about the earlier efforts of the British and American units to work together.

In August of 1943 the Brazilian Navy minister (Vice Admiral Henrique Aristides Guilhem) flew in a Brazilian PV-1 from Rio to Salvador and on to Parnamirim, Natal to hold conversations at all these joint bases with his local commanders and the U.S. commanders. Captain Walter S. Macauly (American Naval Mission in Brazil) and Captain Gastao Brasil Carmo Junion accompanied the Vice Admiral: on the way back they stopped at Ibura field in Recife (photo I-66) where they were greeted by Colonel Aurelio Lira Tavares of the Brazilian Army. These visits were typical of the close cooperation between top Brazilian and American officers.

It wasn't until September, 1943 that active direct cooperation between the American/Brazilian allies and the British began to become as effective as possible. It remains a mystery why it took 20 months of war after Pearl Harbor before the U.S. and Britain began to cooperate fully in the South Atlantic.

At the end of September, 1943, the decision was made to put a detachment from VB-107 on Ascension Island. Just as importantly, the flow of information on U-Boat and blockade runners between the British and U.S./Brazilian forces increased resulting in more effective tracking and interdiction of Axis Power U-Boats and blockade runners. The extent of the success of the Allied Forces is reflected in Map No.10 (from Morison – Ref. 4) showing the sinkings of Axis U-Boats which took place in 1943-1944. Morison's map was not totally accurate since it was later learned that 17 U-Boats had been destroyed rather than the 14 shown on Map no.10.

The destruction of 17 U-Boats by the Allied Powers during 1943-44 was significant when one remembers the havoc created by only 6 U-Boats off the U.S. and Caribbean coast in the 1941-42 period.

Joint Attack - Brazilian Forces and Fairwing 16 on U-199

One of the best examples of cooperative efforts resulted in the destruction of U-Boat 199. That German submarine was first attacked by a Fairwing 16 PBM of VP-74 out of Rio de Janeiro piloted by Lieutenant (jg) Walter F. Smith. While 74-P-7's depth charges heavily damaged U-199, the German boat was not sunk. Smith kept his PBM near the crippled, but still moving U-Boat, until a Brazilian PBY, piloted by Cadet Alberto Martins Torres arrived and dropped depth charges sinking the U-Boat. This engagement is more fully described in Reference 4 and in the subsequent portion of this work which describes the Brazilian 350th Fighter Squadron, Lieutenant John Buyers, and Alberto Martins Torres. In addition to joint attacks on Axis Power naval units, the Brazilian forces and Fairwing 16 carried out combined training maneuvers. In photo No. I-67 we see a large Brazilian submarine during a joint training exercise.

I-66; Brazilian and American Officers

Vice Admiral H.A. Guilhem (hand to chin) - Brazilian Navy Minister talking to General Cordeiro de Farias- Brazilian Army with Captain W. Macauly (in center - head of Navy mission in Brazil) at Ibura Field - Recife, August, 1943. Captain G.B. Junion of U.S. Navy is behind the Vice Admiral. Other officers unidentified.

I-67 Large Italian built Brazilian sub in joint training exercise

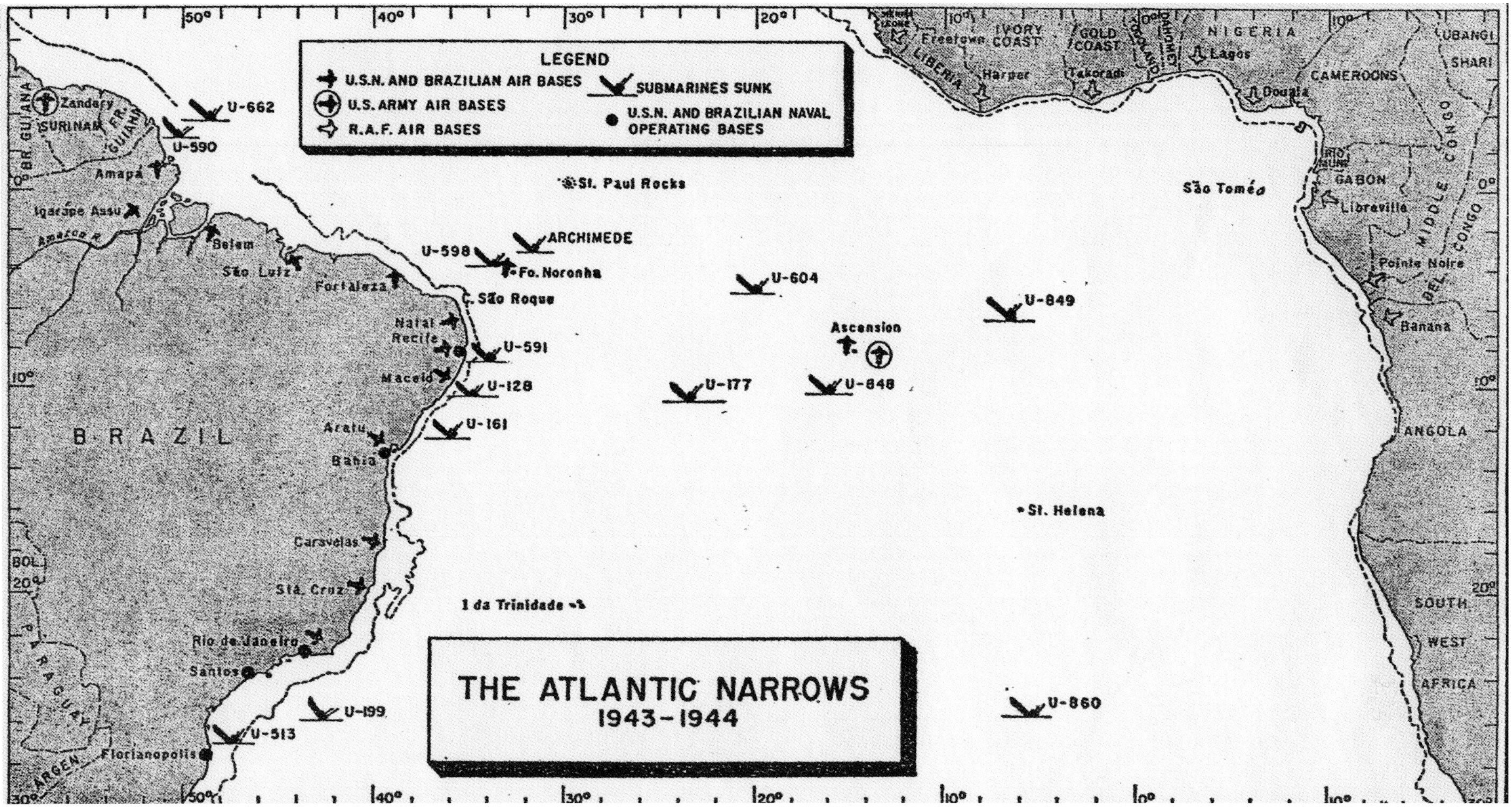

I-68; Map No. 10: Location of some sinkings of U-Boats in the Atlantic Narrows in 1943-44 per Reference 5 (Morison).

Later information, some from German Admiralty records, shows that 17 U-Boats were sunk in the Atlantic Narrows, rather than the 14 shown.

Jeep Carrier Task Group – Fourth Fleet

By mid-1944, the Fourth Fleet and Fairwing 16's efforts against both U-Boats and armed surface raiders was augmented by arrival of Carrier Task Group 41.6 (CTG 41.6). This force centered around the Jeep or escort carrier USS Solomons (CVE 67).

Jeep carriers were made by putting a flight deck on a Liberty ship to permit operations of a small number of fighter bombers (F4F Wildcats) and torpedo bombers (TBF Avengers) from their flight decks.

CTG 41.6 also had accompanying destroyer escort ships (D.E.'s) to protect themselves from U-Boat attacks. Many of these CTG's were used in the North Atlantic and Pacific battles.

The planes off the Solomons (Squadron VC-9) had previously destroyed 5 U-Boats in the North Atlantic so it was an experienced squadron. However, battles with U-Boats were still hard fought and deadly engagements as we note in the following summary story of the destruction of U-860.

VC-9 versus U-860

On June 15th, 1944, a Grumman Avenger (TBF) piloted by Ensign George E. Edwards located the U-860 at about 10:21 in the morning proceeding southward in the South Atlantic on its way to Penang, a joint German-Japanese submarine base in the Indian ocean. Fregattenkapitan Paul Buchel, commander of the U-860 was apparently a very confident skipper because he traveled on the surface 24 hours a day. For a while his luck held, for when Edward's attacked the U-860, the U-Boat shot the TBF down and Edwards, his radioman, and rear gunner perished.

The same day in the afternoon, two more torpedo bombers and two F4F Wildcats relocated the U-860, once again proceeding on the surface despite the fact that the U-Boat's skipper must have known that more planes from the carrier would be hunting his U-Boat.

The four U.S. planes carried out machine gun strafing and rocket attacks on the U-860 which damaged the submarine and suppressed its anti-aircraft fire, but did not sink it. Two more torpedo bombers joined the fray, one being piloted by Lieutenant (jg) W. F. Chamberlain.

Two more rocket attacks slowed the U-Boat to about 3 knots but it still took a depth bomb drop from 50 feet altitude by Chamberlain's TBF to finally sink the U-Boat as dusk arrived. Unfortunately Chamberlain's plane was caught in the large explosion on the submarine caused by the depth bombs and Chamberlain and his two man crew perished in the ocean.

Ironically the two German submariners who survived the battle and were rescued by the USS Straub (a D.E.) were the somewhat over-confident Fregattenkapitan Paul Buchel and his executive officer. A more detailed account of this battle is contained in reference 4.

6

VP-83/VB-107
The Bellwether Squadron of Fairwing 16

For extraordinary heroism in action
against enemy forces in Atlantic Waters

Presidential Unit Citation to VP-83/VB-107

Eventually, Fleet Air Wing 16, which was commissioned at Norfolk in February of 1943 would, at various times, deploy a total of 15 different heavier than air squadrons and two lighter than air squadrons (blimps) in Brazil. These would include squadrons equipped with PBY's, PBM Martin Mariners, PV-1 Lockheed Venturas, and PB4Y-1 (B-24) Liberator planes. All of these aviation units would perform well in the Battles of the South Atlantic.

VP-83 personnel had the honor of destroying the first U-Boat sunk in the South Atlantic. Subsequently, as VP-83 in PBY's, and later as VB-107 in PB4Y Liberators, they would go on to sink 9 U-Boats and aid in the destruction of armed Axis surface raiders. VP-83/VB-107 would become the leading squadron of Fairwing 16. VP-83/VB-107 also had the longest tour of duty (33 months) in Brazil and lead the way in devising convoy coverage and anti-submarine tactics. Indeed, when several of their pilots were later sent to the Air Anti-Submarine Development (AIRASDEVLANT) program at Quonset Point Rhode Island Air Base for training it was apparent that they were more knowledgeable than the "trainers".

VP-83 Personnel Transition to VB-107

The officers and air crew men of VP-83 rotated back to Norfolk, Virginia early in June 1943 to pick up and begin a very brief training period in the twelve Consolidated B-24D's (PB4Y-1's) that they were initially to fly in as VB-107. The training period was a mere 10 days so the pilots and crew were only partially trained in their new 4 engine planes when they returned to Brazil in late June. Nonetheless, they began anti-submarine sweeps from Natal, Recife, etc. starting on July 5, 1943. One of the reasons for the great haste and shortening of the projected 30 day training period was the knowledge at Fairwing 16 headquarters that more U-Boats and blockade runners had begun to become active in the South Atlantic. (the July Blitz)

LOSS OF A GREAT SQUADRON LEADER

The story of a brave leader of VP-83/VB-107 was compiled by reference to the words of his fellow pilot's since that storied officer, gentleman, and leader lost his life in an heroic effort to destroy 3 German U-Boats in the South Atlantic on a fateful day, August 11, 1943. On the next page we see Bertram Prueher as a Lieutenant when VP-83 was formed at Norfolk in 1941. The second photograph I-70 was taken in Brazil in 1943 and it is apparent that the rigors of two years of combat duty had been endured by the then skipper of VB-107.

In the period from August 3, 1943 through August 11, 1943, Commander Prueher in VB-107-B-1, the Spirit of 83, carried out four attacks on U-Boats 604, 185, and 172. His first attack on August 3rd on U-604 severely damaged that vessel. U-185 was also attacked later on the same day. As a result of the August 3 attack, U-Boat 604 was ordered by U-Boat command to rendezvous with two other U-Boats so that U-604 could be prepared for scuttling after removal of the crew (including the wounded from 107-B-1's attack) and other essential material. The rendezvous of the 3 U-Boats occurred on August 11, 1943 and surveillance means allowed Fairwing 16 to be aware of where and when it was taking place.

I-69; Lieutenant Bertram Prueher in 1941

When this photo was taken Bert Prueher was a pilot in VP-83 which was commissioned on September 15, 1941 at Naval Air Station Norfolk, VA. He was one of a number of pilot plane commanders who had flown out to California to pick up one of the new PBY5A's with which the squadron was being equipped. At that time VP-83 was part of the patrol wing structure of the Air Force, Atlantic Fleet. Lieutenant Commander Ralph Sperry Clarke was the commanding officer of VP-83 at that time. From mid-September 1941 until mid-March 1942, VP-83 provided convoy coverage from the east coast.

I-70; Lieutenant Commander Prueher as skipper of VB-107 in 1943

Bert Prueher had previously assumed command of VP-83 in January, 1943 replacing Lieutenant Commander Almon Loomis who had succeeded R. Sperry Clarke in September, 1942. Commander Prueher spent almost 17 months in Brazil; first flying in VP-83's PBY's, and then VB-107's PB4Y's as that squadron fought Axis naval forces in the Battle of the South Atlantic. He was extremely well liked by the pilots and air crews of VP-83/VB-107 as he proved to be an inspirational and brave leader. His passing which occurred in a last epic battle with 3 U-Boats at once was a blow to all his comrades in arms.

Commander Prueher, by putting an unprecedented and risky amount of gasoline in 107-B-1, was able to reach the point of rendezvous at the extreme limits of VB-107-B-1's operating range. Lieutenant Ed Krug remembers standing on the tarmac at Parnamirim along with other VB-107 personnel and watching Prueher's plane struggle to become airborne with the heavy load of gasoline. 107-B-1 got off alright but unfortunately when it located the U-Boats, the combined anti-aircraft fire from the U-Boats shot down VB-107-B-1 as it pressed its attack on U-172. All hands aboard the Spirit of 83 lost their lives in this action.

U-604 was scuttled; U-185 had been damaged in an earlier attack by 107-B-1 and was later destroyed as it limped back toward the U-Boat pens in Lorient, France; but U-172 survived. A more detailed description of this battle between Commander Prueher's PB4Y and the three U-Boats appears in Reference 2.

VB-107's other planes searched the area for several weeks in August and September but were not able to locate any survivors of the Spirit of 83. I was puzzled by why only one PB4Y was sent to tackle 3 U-Boats? Ed Krug of VB-107 informed me that Commander Prueher would not allow any of the other pilots and their planes to accompany him on this most perilous mission. This episode showed that as of August, 1943 there was a still a "Black Hole" in the South Atlantic Narrows which was beyond effective operating range of VB-107's PB4Y's. The search planes carried extra fuel instead of full armament load.

Work had been underway for some time to construct additional facilities at Ascension Island so that Fairwing 16 might be able to use it as an advance base to facilitate better coverage of the Atlantic Narrows and southward. The loss of 107-B-1 pointed up the urgent need for use of Ascension Island. At the time of Commander Prueher's death his wife Jean and their small children were at her grandmother's home in Wisconsin. Their son, Joseph Wilson, followed his father's footsteps with a notable Navy career, culminating as a Vice Admiral and later Ambassador to China. Commander Prueher's grandson also is an Annapolis graduate and he continues the proud tradition of naval service by the Prueher family.

Presidential Unit Citation – VP-83/VB-107

Because of the actions of all the pilots and air crews of this venerable squadron, the unit citation I-71 which appears next was awarded. The men of VP-83/VB-107 would stay in Brazil until January, 1945 before they completed their 33 month tour of duty. Some men and planes went to England from Brazil, others either went to the Pacific in other squadrons or served as instructors at Hutchinson, Kansas.

VP-83/VB-107 PERSONNEL AND PLANES

The following section includes brief descriptions of the lives of several of the pilots and air crewmen of VP-83/VB-107 and photographs of the planes and crews. In viewing some of the photos of crews and their plane the reader will note that while originally various planes were assigned to specific pilot plane commanders (PPC's) and their crews, the needs of combat necessitated flexibility and variation in PPC and air crew assignments. Thus, for instance, you will note that while Passarola (B-3) was Sam Taylor's plane, Lieutenant Carrell I (Zoom) Pinnell would later fly Sam's Passarola in carrying out an attack on a U-Boat off Ascension Island. Likewise, Sam Taylor had flown Bill Ford's 107-B-4, the Macahyba Maiden, with Ford's crew when Sam applied the coup de grace to U-848 off Ascension.

As the months of combat passed there would be different PB4Y's labeled B-1 through B-12. As the photos show there were two B-1s, B-5's, etc., some having different nicknames as well. In addition, VB-107 employed two versions of the B-24 (PB4Y). The original planes were B-24D's which had a fixed forward nose compartment containing a 50 caliber machine gun. Later on the squadron had B-24J's which had ball turrets in the nose. The photo I-72 shows a newly arrived B-24J version of the PB4Y on a tarmac at Parnamirim.

PB4Y (B-24) PASSAROLA: VB-107 B-3

In PHOTO I-73 we see two aviation machinists' mates working on an engine of one of VB-107's PB4Y's. These were dependable planes which were faster than PBY's and had longer operating range than the PV-1 Ventura's which were also used by Fairwing 16. However, they could not land safely at sea, so if disabled and forced to ditch at sea, their crews would perish, and unfortunately this happened several times. Their major advantage, in addition to speed, was their larger bomb carrying capacity.

The cartoon characters and names on the planes were mostly painted on by a squadron crew member who obviously had real artistic ability. The name Ridgerunner beneath the pilots window was the nickname of Lieutenant Samuel K. Taylor, Jr., who was normally the Pilot Plane Commander of Passarola (B-3). The name Sno-Wyte refers to Ensign Ed White, Second Pilot.

The name Passarola, which was chosen by Charles Wells, the Air Crew Captain has some interesting history. A Brazilian priest, one Bartolomeu de Gusmao built a device which has been alternately described either as a strange aircraft with elements of a flying boat, parachute, and ornithopter (the Passarola or Great Bird) or more likely a small hot air balloon which Gusmao demonstrated unsuccessfully to the King and Queen of Portugal in 1607. To put some modern context to the name Passarola the crew had a painting of Jose (Zé for short) Carioca a Disney character from a 1944 film entitled "Saludos Amigos and the Three Caballeros" painted on B-3 to represent the so called Great Bird. This Passarola certainly proved to be a Great Bird.

THE SECRETARY OF THE NAVY
WASHINGTON

The President of the United States takes pleasure in presenting the PRESIDENTIAL UNIT CITATION to

PATROL SQUADRON EIGHTY THREE
later BOMBING SQUADRON ONE HUNDRED SEVEN

for service as set forth in the following

CITATION:

"For extraordinary heroism in action against enemy forces in Atlantic Waters during the periods January through April 1943; July 1943 through February 1944; and the month of September 1944. Engaged in convoy escort operations and ocean sweeps against enemy commerce raiders and blockade runners off South America, Patrol Squadron EIGHTY THREE (renamed Bombing Squadron ONE HUNDRED SEVEN on May 15, 1943) pressed home numerous attacks and, despite heavy antiaircraft fire, sank one enemy Italian and six German submarines. These courageous officers and men further played a major role in sinking a seventh German submarine and an armed German Blockade runner, and assisted in destroying an eighth German U-boat. Through its tactical resourcefulness and outstanding functional efficiency, this squadron contributed greatly to the development of effective aerial anti-submarine doctrine and tactics and pioneered in the operational application of 'Barrier Patrol' techniques. The superb aerial teamwork attained by these pilots and aircrewmen and their record of heroism in action reflect the highest credit upon Patrol Squadron EIGHTY THREE and upon the United States Naval Service."

For the President,

Francis P. Matthews
Secretary of the Navy

I-71; Unit Citation to VP-83

I-72; PBY4 (B-24 J) on tarmac at Parnamirim - 1943

Several VB-107 pilots flew older B-24 D's back to the USA (with some adventures along the way) to pick up the new improved B-24 J's.

I-73; VB-107-B3 (Passarola) at the nose hanger.

It is unknown as to how Charlie Wells came across the name Passarola.
Did he know the legend of Bartolomeu de Gusmao?

Commander Samuel K. Taylor, Jr.

Sam Taylor was born on a farm in the hills of Tennessee in 1917. The physical rigors of farm life gave Sam excellent physical condition. That and his better than average eyesight (20/10) would prove beneficial in his subsequent career as a US Navy flyer. After completing his own schooling, Sam spent a year and a half as a high school teacher with summers being occupied by working on the Norris Dam project of the Tennessee Valley Authority (TVA). In late 1940 one of Sam's friends suggested they take the physical and flight aptitude tests being offered by the US Navy. Sam passed the tests but his friend failed the physical. The services were still being quite selective at that time but later on Sam's friend was accepted into the Army Air Corps and Sam met him later in Belem, Brazil during the war.

On January 14, 1941 Sam was sworn into the navy and sent to Opalocka Naval Air Station (NAS) for "Elimination Training". There he had to demonstrate proficiency in landing within circles, qualifying for carrier duty and solo flying. He then was sent to NAS Jacksonville for final flight training and received his wings and commission in August, 1941. In photo I-74 we see Sam Taylor (on the left) and two of his aviation cadet friends in front of a Stearman (Yellow Peril) training plane.

Sam joined VP-83 at Norfolk later in August when that PBY squadron was being formed. In April of 1942, after further training in PBY5A's, some ferrying of planes from San Diego, and convoy patrol out of Norfolk, Sam flew into Natal, Brazil with the first division of VP-83. Sam remembers well the first 15 months flying patrol out of Natal and the other cities of northeast Brazil when the basing and support facilities were rather primitive and the squadron was developing the skills and techniques necessary to effectively challenge and defeat the Axis Power naval units.

By the time VP-83 had returned to the USA in July, 1943 to switch over to PB4Y's, Sam had become a pilot plane commander and was assigned VB107-B-3 (the Passarola). His most notable victory was when he finished off U-848 with a perfect straddle of bombs. He was awarded the Distinguished Flying Cross (DFC) which was pinned on by Mrs. Eleanor Roosevelt at Natal in 1943. An additional very significant accomplishment at Natal came when he courted and then married his wife, Pattie, who was a Red Cross girl at Natal. Pattie had also been a school teacher before the war. She was originally from Colorado but obviously after 63 years of marriage has adapted to the beautiful state of Tennessee. After spending a total of over 30 months in Brazil, Sam and his squadron were rotated out. He went to Hutchinson, Kansas NAS to serve as an instructor as did some of his squadron mates. The rest of VB-107 squadron was sent to England.

Back in Tennessee, Sam went back to teaching high school and also flew executive planes for David Lilienthal (the Director of TVA). Sam and Pattie's first child had been born while they were at Hutchinson, Kansas and they subsequently had 3 more children. Sam stayed in the US Navy's Organized Reserve after World War II and was in the Ready Reserve during the Korean War. He reached the rank of Commander during his many years in the organized reserve before retiring from naval service. After serving at the Principal level in school Sam retired from teaching and continued operation of his dairy farm. One of Sam and Pattie's sons is now the primary operator of the farm where they reside today, not too far from his place of birth.*

Sam Taylor richly deserved the Distinguished Flying Cross pinned on his uniform by Eleanor Roosevelt at Natal in 1943. (See photo no.118 in Chapter 10.)

Lieutenant Carrell I. Pinnell (Zoom)

On February 16, 1944, Passarola (107-B-3) piloted by Lt. (jg) Pinnell, while patrolling off Ascension Island attacked and sank a U-Boat by making a perfect straddle with depth charges. Photo I-75 Lt. (jg) Pinnell and his crew just after they returned to base after sinking U-Boat 177. From left to right; J.D. Cook, R.S. Swanson, "Zoom" Pinnell, J.M. Leonard, S.S. Shedaker, W.R. Zudrell, Anderson, R.L. McKernan, and W. Phelps.

Zoom was born in Newman, Missouri in 1914. He enlisted in the Navy in September 1936 in the midst of the Great Depression. He went through boot camp at Norfolk, VA. In 1938 he was sent to aviation machinist mates school in San Diego. By 1939 he was serving on the aircraft carrier, the USS Ranger, in the Caribbean Sea. Zoom married his 3rd grade sweetheart in 1940. In 1941 Zoom, who by that time was an Aviation Machinists Mate first class, was sent to Pensacola Naval Air Station for flight training to become a Naval Aviation Pilot (NAP). The concept of training experienced enlisted men to become enlisted men pilots was an effort to produce many much needed pilots as quickly as possible. This clearly was easier to do since the experienced enlisted man would already have become familiar with naval duties and in most cases, also had knowledge of the workings of airplanes and carriers.

* Editorial Note: See Appendix B for a news article on Sam's postwar life.

Photo I-74; Sam Taylor and friends in front of Stearman training plane

These 3 aviation cadets in training were, at the time of this photo, in the early days of flight training. This flight training would have been preceded by ground studies to acquaint cadets with U.S. Navy procedures as will as mechanical aspects of aircraft and pilot techniques.

I-75; Passarola and crew at Ascension

Here we see Lt. (JG) Zoom Pinnell and his 8 man crew bck at their base on "The Rock" after sinking the U-177 Reference (4) has an excellent description of this battle and its aftermath assembled from talks with U.S. crew and from German records.

After graduating from Pensacola flight school and being promoted to Chief Naval Aviation Pilot (NAP), Zoom joined VP-83 as it was being formed at Norfolk in September of 1941. VP-83 had quite a number of enlisted NAP's when it was formed. NAP's were junior pilots and while they, at first, could fly twin engine patrol planes they were not pilot plane commanders and were usually not assigned to particular planes. Eventually the NAP's of VP-83 did receive commissions as officers and were allowed to be pilot plane commanders on four engine airplanes (PB4Y's). Zoom Pinnell was second pilot on a VP-83 piloted by Ensign Thurmond Robinson on April 15, 1943 when it attacked and disabled the Italian submarine Archimede off Natal. Since Robertson was out of bombs he called in a second VP-83 PBY piloted by Lieutenant Bradford who proceeded to complete the destruction of the Archimede with an accurate drop of bombs.

When VP-83 morphed into VB-107 by switching from PBY's to PB4Y Liberators, Zoom had become a commissioned officer and a pilot plane commander. As noted, Zoom was the PPC when he led Sam Taylor's crew in Passarola as they sank the U-177 in February, 1944.

Zoom stayed in the Navy for 20 years and retired as a Lieutenant and located his family in Pensacola. He was a successful realtor for 40 years, retiring in 1986. He continues to reside in Pensacola. Another successful Mustang and a patriot.

The Macahyba Maiden Crew: 107-B-4

When Lieutenant Bill Ford came back to Natal in mid-1943 after picking up the PB4Y subsequently labeled the Macahyba Maiden, he gained some new crew members and lost some of his VP-83 PBY crew: Frank Burgess and Paul Richter had been with him in VP-83. Frank was now an Ensign (he had been an NAP in VP-83) and Paul Richter was now an Aviation Chief Radioman. Richard (Dick) Wilson, ARM 3/C was one of the new members of Bill Ford's crew at that time.

In photo I-76 (courtesy of Richard Wilson) we see the 13 men who happened to be in the crew of the Macahyba Maiden on the day the photo was taken. The PBY's of VP-83 had featured an 8 man crew including the pilots.

In the back row of this photo are; left to right, Frank Burgess, Rocky Daimano, Butler, Bill Ford, Burton, and Feckory. In the front row are Bohron, Rackly, Paul Richter, Meyer, Dupree, and Carpenter.

After the "Maiden" sank her first U-Boat, the crew renamed her the "Madam". Macahyba was a very small village near to Parnamirim at that time. Since it was off the beaten path and featured a small bar serving whisky and wine and was frequented by nubile young ladies of Macahyba it became a target of opportunity for navy men who did not have passes or transportation to Natal. On one particular evening the Shore Patrol (the Navy's military police) rode into Macahyba unexpectedly to check if any miscreants were there since the village was off limits. Frank Burgess, among others had to hide in a pig pen to elude the Shore Patrol.

When VP-83/VB-107 personnel had their annual reunion in Natal in 1997, the mayor of Macahyba was an honored guest. Macahyba, like Natal, has grown quite a bit since the war. Parnamirim is also now a city of significant size.

Lieutenant Frank Burgess: Yeoman 2/C – Enlisted Naval Aviation Pilot – Ensign – Lieutenant

The career of Frank Burgess in the peace-time and war-time navy was a most interesting one. His early lifetime was a reflection of the state of things in the USA before the war, and during the Depression. Frank, born in 1918, was an orphan on a farm in Oklahoma and experienced all the problems of the dust bowl years. He proudly called himself an Okie. He was raised by relatives and did have some inheritance from his grandmother but clearly did not experience an affluent childhood. After graduating from high school in 1937 he enlisted in the US Navy in 1938. We should note that getting into the military service in the late 1930's, indeed even in 1940, was not easy because many young men sought the security and regular pay check offered by military service. We were not greatly expanding our military until late in 1940.

Remember that FDR, in one of his famous fireside radio chats, said: "I look out at a nation which is ill fed, ill housed, and ill clothed." "I wish to see a chicken in every pot and a car in every garage." One wonders what he would say about our current life styles. I am certain he would be amazed by the current "Era of Conspicuous Consumption". In any event, Frank Burgess was a resilient young man who made a productive career for himself starting in the US Navy, Air Force, Atlantic Fleet.

After boot camp, Frank became a yeoman on the USS Perkins. When the war started there became an urgent need for aviation pilots and Frank, as a Yeoman 2/C was allowed to take flight training at Pensacola during 1941. The navy had realized that it was easier and quicker to train seasoned enlisted men experienced in naval procedures than it was to bring new recruits from civilian life directly into pilot training programs. Frank, after graduating as a Naval Aviation Pilot (NAP) but still wearing his Yeoman Second Class insignia was greeted with skepticism upon

I-76; Macahyba Maiden (B-4) and crew at Natal.

This photo must have been taken before B-4 under command of Lt. Sam Taylor had applied the Coup de Grace to the U848 on November 3, 1943 since the Maiden in the emblem had not been changed to Madam.

transfer to a new aviation unit. His squadron mates could not reconcile the idea that a yeoman could be an NAP. He would occasionally wear an Aviation Machinists Mate (AMM) rating badge to squelch some of the skepticism.

After completing flight training he joined VP-83 and was in Bill Ford's crew when VP-83 transferred to Brazil in April 1942. Frank continued in Ford's crew after it switched to PB4Y's and became VB-107. The decision to name Ford's B-4 the Macahyba Maiden was a unanimous decision by all of the crew but one suspects Frank was a key player in that decision. According to Frank Burgess the planes name, Macahyba Maiden, was based on a group of young ladies and not on any individual one.

As a member of Bill Ford's crew, Frank was a pilot in 107-B-4 during both attacks on U-848 in that memorable battle. While Bill Ford was piloting Macahyba Maiden earlier in the day for an early attack on the U-848, Sam Taylor had later taken B-4 out for the final decisive attack. Subsequently Frank Burgess received orders to return to the USA while he was still at Ascension Island. He needed to get back to Natal to catch a naval air transport (NATS) flight back to the states but his own plane was not scheduled to rotate back to Natal. Fortunately Zoom Pinnell offered Frank a ride back to Natal on his plane so Frank was able to catch the NATS flight. The next day, the VB-107 plane on which Frank was serving at the time was lost at sea with no survivors so Frank was always grateful to Zoom Pinnell and credited him with saving his life.

Frank stayed in the navy for 20 years retiring in 1958 as a lieutenant. After the service he opened a restaurant but that was not a successful venture. He then worked for 7 ½ years at Ryan Aircraft company before joining his wife in the real estate business. Frank and his wife had two sons, one of whom lives in Chula Vista. Frank was very active in establishing a Naval Aviation Museum in San Diego.

I received a letter from Frank dated January 10, 2007 in which he stated that he was going into hospital on January 15 for a dangerous operation. Sadly, he died the day after the operation at the age of 89. He had led a full life and one can reasonably conclude that as a youngster in the Dust Bowl in the 1930's there was no way he could have imagined how eventful his life would be nor how he would be able to be of such great service to his country.

Requiescat in Pacem.

Lieutenant Commander Paul Richter

Paul Richter was born on a farm near Billings, Montana in 1921. His father was 13 years old when Paul's grandparents came with their children to the United States from southern Russia. The young lady who would become Paul's mother also came along with her family on the same ship from Russia. Their families were part of a group known as "Volga Germans".

Both families had come from German populated villages around the lower Volga River, near the city of Saratov. There were hundreds of thousands of ethnic Germans in a large enclave in that area. The Richter family ancestors had migrated to Russia under the aegis of Catherine the Great, Empress of Russia from 1762 until 1796.

Catherine, a German princess born in Stettin, Germany, had married Peter who had become emperor of Russia in 1762. Catherine, shortly after her weak and ineffective husband had become the new Czar, had him deposed and executed. Catherine was a gifted and westward oriented leader who modernized Russia to some degree. She had encouraged families from Germany and other central European countries to migrate into Russia and the Ukraine. She also expanded Russia's empire by successfully warring against Poland, Turkey, and the Siberian tribes. As a result she made the southern Ukraine, the Crimea, and Siberia part of her empire. For all her accomplishments, Catherine remained aristocratic and did not improve the economic or social status of the plebian and lower classes. In effect, Catherine started the Russians on their "Continental Imperialist Journey" which eventually resulted about 122 years later in the creation of the Soviet Union. She was also a notorious female version of Casanova. One of her lovers was the King of Poland.

In subsequent decades, the Russian emperors began to draft many villagers into the Russian army to serve as cannon fodder. There was also significant religious discrimination. As a result, when migration to America became possible, many ethnic German families left Russia and came to the United States. Paul Richter's grandparents and their children were among a group of such migrants in 1903. The story of their migration and eventual settlement is an interesting one.

When the ship carrying the grandparents and parents of Paul Richter as well as his mother and her family arrived in 1903 in New York Harbor, the group was denied entrance to Ellis Island because there had been some diseases among the people on the ship. Paul's future mother, who was 16 at the time and her family, got onto another ship which went to Galveston, Texas where they gained admittance. Paul's grandparents and family went by ship to Canada and from there slipped across the border from Sarnia, Ontario into Port Huron, Michigan where they resided for a few years.

Paul Richter's father subsequently moved his family to Montana where he bought a farm and took to growing sugar beets. Paul's mother and her family also ended up on a farm near Billings and subsequently the families renewed contact and Paul's father and mother married.

Many of the Volga Germans had brought along seeds of a weather resistant strain of wheat so they became wheat farmers in Nebraska and the Dakotas. In so doing they were key players in developing the wheat industry. Mixed in with the wheat seeds were seeds of the tumbleweed (the Russian Thistle). In 1920 it was estimated that there were 300,000 Volga Germans (as they were called) in the USA, mostly in Nebraska and the Dakotas.

Paul Richter was born in 1921. After high school graduation he left the farm to join the Navy in 1939. While life on a Montana farm has some good points, one can also empathize with many 18 year olds, particularly during the depression, deciding to join what was then a peacetime US Navy so as to see more of the world. He had two older brothers who also had joined the navy which probably influenced him. One of his brothers, John Richter, became a navy photographer and achieved the rank of Chief Warrant officer. John would later participate in "Operation Crossroads", The Bikini Atoll Tests.

After training as a radioman, Paul was sent to Pearl Harbor into a PBY-3 squadron where he stayed until October, 1941. He was one of 25 men from his squadron at Pearl who were sent to Norfolk to serve in the newly commissioned VP-83, a PBY5A squadron. On December 7, 1941, Paul's two brothers were still at Pearl Harbor but they survived the attack. There had been five PBY squadrons at Pearl Harbor. At the time of Pearl Harbor, Paul was a Radioman 2/c who was on the list to go to flight school and become a pilot. Perhaps unfortunately for him, Lieutenant Prueher, the pilot of his flight crew at the time decided that experienced radiomen were too scarce and Paul was not allowed to go to flight school. Radiomen were indeed scarce at that time. It took quite awhile for them to become more plentiful because in the months after Pearl Harbor the fatality rate for radiomen in the Pacific fleet combat was very high.

In April, 1942, Paul flew with the first division of VP-83 to Parnamirim field at Natal. For most of his time in VP-83 and later VB-107 Paul was a member of Bill Ford's crew and was in on several successful attacks on U Boats. When VP-83 transitioned into VB-107, Paul, by then a Radioman 1/c was assigned as 1st Radioman/Turret Gunner on flight crew 107-B-4. In photo I-77 we see Aviation Chief Radioman Paul Richter at a table in the Wonder Bar in Natal in 1944. There is a bottle of scotch whiskey on the table; a sign that Scotland must still have been able to export whiskey during that wartime. The Chief Petty Officer with his elbow on the table is Rocky Daimano.

One of the most memorable battles with U Boats was the attack on U-598 on July 22, 1943 by several PB4Y's from VB-107. Paul was in Bill Ford's B-8 when they finished off the U Boat. This battle is described in Reference 4, including several quotes from Paul Richter. The perils associated with having to get within 50 feet or so of a U Boat to ensure an accurate drop of bombs was all too apparent to Ford's crew who saw Lieutenant Waugh's B-6 plunge into the ocean after making a bomb drop. Waugh's plane was caught in the detonation of its own bombs. Lieutenant Waugh and his crew had only just arrived in Brazil. All hands on B-6 were lost in this battle in which the U-598, which ironically had also just arrived off the coast of Brazil, was destroyed with only two crew members surviving.

Paul Richter completed a 30 year navy career in 1969, retiring as a Lieutenant Commander. He had served at various places around the world including stints off the coast of Korea, Japan, and in Northern Europe. He and his wife were stationed in England in 1960-63 where he was assigned to a unit that provided logistic support to our submarine facilities in Scotland and Bergen, Norway and also to our communication station at Londonderry, Ireland. After leaving the service he worked for 12 years with a defense contractor. Today he resides in La Mesa, California with his wife of many years, Anna Mae.

Paul Richter sent me the following description of an eventful journey in a damaged PBY from Natal to the USA in 1942 to facilitate major repairs to the airplane.

A Perilous Adventure in a Rugged Airplane (A PBY) by Paul Richter

When we still had the PBY's (1942 & part of 1943), our plane received major structural damage when we tangled with a thunderhead coming out of Belem on the way out to cover a convoy. We made it back to the airport there and eventually back to the home base at Natal. There, the maintenance experts decided that we could ferry the plane back to the States for overhaul, provided we flew short hops (minimum fuel load) and flew in good weather only. How we were supposed to get through the permanent equatorial front around Belem in good weather, no one was able to tell us. But we decided to have a go at it.

We went from Natal to Fortaleza, from there to San Luiz, then to Belem,

I-77; Paul Richter and Rocky Damiano in bar, 1944.

Here we see two aviation chief radiomen of VB-107 enjoying liquid refreshments in the Wonderbar in Natal's Ribeira area. By this time both sailors had been in Brazil for 2 years. Paul Richter is on the right.

When this photo was made, four Richter brothers were in the U.S. Navy, John, the oldest was on the USS Sumner in the South Pacific surveying coastlines of islands prior to invasions. Richard was in a PBY squadron operating out of Perth, Australia while Bill, the youngest was in training in the Navy.

Paul Richter would serve for 30 years, ending up as a Lieutenant Commander. John would serve for 24 years and Richard would become a 20 year man before retiring as a Chief Petty Officer. Bill left the Navy after the war and became a dentist.

Clearly the Richter family had done their share.

Rocky Damiano returned to New Jersey after the war. Paul Richter and Rocky remained lifetime friends.

then to Amapa - all approximately three hour flights. From Amapa we were trying for Georgetown, British Guiana which should have been about another three hours but as it turned out we were immediately in a severe storm (mucho shuva); and I think we were lost as soon as we lifted off the runway. We fought this storm for six hours, right on the deck in almost zero visibility. We were getting low on fuel when we spotted the mouth of a large river, so we turned in looking for a place to land. We immediately spotted a good sized city, which turned out to be Paramaribo, Dutch Guiana. We put down in the river but due to the storm the water was so rough that as we hauled back to stop the plane, a large wave smacked the bottom, popping rivets and causing us to take on water. But the scary part was smoke coming out of the tunnel hatch compartment in the tail of the plane. I thought, this can't be - there is nothing back there that can burn. But when I looked I remembered this is where the IFF transponder was located. At the time, that equipment was so classified that it came with an explosive device built in so that it could be detonated in case the plane came down in enemy territory. The shock of the wave hitting us caused it to blow - no more IFF! But no further damage.

In the meantime, the pilot was taxiing as fast as he could go due to us taking on water, and heading for what looked like a ramp, which was probably left over when Pan American ran flights down that way. The ramp was covered with mud but there was a black gentleman guiding us to it. We lowered the landing gear and started up the ramp which was fine except that our guide led us off the side and the port gear promptly sank almost out of sight. So we were stuck in the mud!

All of us were in the muck all the rest of that day, and the next, trying to dig our way out. But the more we dug, the further the plane sank. We didn't know what to do next, when we looked up and saw about four American soldiers watching us. It turned out that they were members of a unit that was based in the area to guard the bauxite mines. Their old sergeant allowed as to how he had access to a crane that could probably lift us out of there. We said, "Bring it on!" He said, "I'll tell you what. We will lift you out if you will give us a ride in your airplane." Naturally, we agreed.

The next day he and his crew showed up with a giant truck equipped with a crane. And sure enough, they hooked up and lifted us out with no problems. It took us the rest of that day to pull the wheel and clean everything out and the next day, with the soldiers aboard we taxied back into the river for a water takeoff and flew back to the airport which was called Zandrey Field at that time - about a fifteen minute hop. The soldiers were happy, and so were we. Good example of Army/ Navy cooperation during those trying times. We did make it back to the overhaul facility in Norfolk after many more stops on the way. They gave us another PBY, and it was back to Natal. Bill Ford was the plane commander on this jaunt.

Richard A. Wilson – Aviation Radioman

Dick Wilson was born and grew up in northwestern Pennsylvania in a small town near Jamestown, New York. He enlisted in the US Navy in September 1942 and after boot camp at Great Lakes, he received training as a radioman and aerial gunner at Jacksonville, Florida. In May of 1943 he joined VB-107 at Norfolk, Virginia just as they were being equipped with new PB4Y (B-24D) airplanes. At first Dick was a member of Dan Diebler's crew in 107-B-10 (the Subduer). Later he served primarily on 107-B-8 piloted by Ed Hill.

On November 5, 1943, Dick Wilson was aboard when Ed Hill piloted B-8 to the area off Ascension Island where U-848 had been previously attacked earlier in the day by Charley Baldwin in B-12, and subsequently would be sunk by Bill Ford in B-4. While U-848 had been damaged by two earlier attacks and could not submerge, its anti-aircraft gun crews were still in good shape. Ed Hill made a bomb run over the U Boat but his bombs fell short (not an uncommon occurrence). During the run the German gunners scored a direct hit on the number 2 engine of B-8 setting it afire. Ed Hill, knowing that B-4 was soon to arrive back at the scene of battle and that the U-848 could not escape, got B-8 safely back to Ascension. When B-4 piloted by Sam Taylor got there it finished off the U-848.

Dick Wilson was to continue flying in Dan Diebler's B-8 crew for several more months both off Ascension Island and out of Natal when the planes were rotated. While on leave in Rio de Janeiro, Dick also enjoyed wearing "civvies" for a few days as we see in photo I-77. Lee Bergstrom, Aviation Chief Radioman is on the right.

On January 1, 1944, to his surprise, Dick Wilson's request to go to flight school to become a navy pilot was approved and he left VB-107 to go to Connecticut for preparation prior to further training. After completing that phase he proceeded to be trained in flying small planes (Aeroncas and Piper Cubs) and was sent to Chapel Hill, North Carolina for final pre-flight schooling about July 1944. In photo I-79 we note Dick Wilson, Aviation Cadet, marching just prior to being presented with the Navy Air Medal for participating in an attack on a U-Boat in the South Atlantic.

At this time, the US Navy decided that it had too many pilots in training and was not going to need all of them. This decision was probably sparked by what had happened at the Battle of the Philippine Sea

I-78; R. Wilson and L. Bergstrom in Rio - 1943.

Here we see 2 air crewmen of VB-107 on a brief R & R leave in Rio in October, 1943. They were there after having served over 100 hours of flight time on anti-sub patrol off the "Rock" (Ascension Island). The deployment to the Rock had been ordered shortly after VB-107 had lost its skipper (Bertram Prueher) in a battle with 3 U-Boats in an area at the outer limits of the range of PB4Y's from Natal.

Dick and Lee were part of an air crew that had flown a PV-1 to Rio for a short leave. These were well deserved respites from combat patrol off the Rock. Per Dick Wilson, "There was not much to do on Ascension, no women, no bars, no grass, and very little fresh water, rough duty."

I-79; R. Wilson receiving his medal 1944.

The wide spread need to provide pre flight training for many thousands of "officers in training" meant that many university campus facilities had to be utilized by the armed forces. This photo was taken on one such campus being used for that purpose. Dick Wilson got to see several universities and naval facilities as the rapid changes in fortunes of war effected the plans of the Navy training programs. Had Dick been allowed to complete his pilot training and become a commissioned officer the chance of his remaining in the service like Frank Burgess and Zoom Pinnell would probably have increased.

(among other things). During that famous lop-sided battle, Marc Mitscher's Task Force 58 with its 15 aircraft carriers had sunk 3 of Japan's remaining carriers. The Task Forces' fighters and anti aircraft gunners had in a short time span shot down 373 Japanese planes which were obviously being flown by woefully untrained Japanese pilots. This was the famous "Marianas Turkey Shoot" which showed we were well on our way to destroying Japanese naval air power and any residual strong naval resistance. The Navy at that time was operating 947 training schools for various military disciplines with over 300,000 people in training. As a result many of those in pilot training (including Dick Wilson) were told they could either resign and go back to their enlisted ratings and duties or they would be flunked out.

Dick Wilson chose to resign his officer in training status and went to Hutchinson, Kansas Naval Facility as a radioman to train new flight crews. There he was reunited with a number of the pilots and air crew men formerly of VB-107 who were also there to serve as trainers. The balance of VB-107 squadron personnel and planes had been transferred to Great Britain in January of 1945.

In the spring of 1945 the Navy reversed course and recalled Dick Wilson into the pilot training program and sent him to the University of Iowa to finish his pre-flight training. Next he was sent for primary flight training at Memphis Naval Air Facility and flew in the "Yellow Peril", Stearman trainers. The navy had probably changed their course because of what had happened at Iwo Jima and particularly because of the extensive damages caused by the Kamikazes at Okinawa. While naval air power and naval surface vessels of the Japanese had been dealt with, the threat of the Kamikazes in the Far East land invasion of Japan had prompted the navy to decide they would need many more trained pilots than envisioned after the Marianas Turkey Shot. At that time we did not know that the subsequent use of the atomic bombs at Hiroshima and Nagasaki would result in the surrender by the Japanese. When that did occur, the renewed pilot training program was curtailed again. Dick Wilson would then serve as a Radioman in New Orleans, San Diego, Guam, and in a Carrier Aircraft Service Unit (CASU) in the Philippines before leaving the service in February 1946.

After the war, Dick returned to upstate Pennsylvania where his parents, brothers and sisters resided. Subsequently he spent 30 years in electronics related business and became vice president of sales for a small company in that area. The camaraderie that Dick Wilson experienced in being with his VB-107 squadron mates in combat had led him to be a key participant in some of the many reunions that personnel of that squadron had held annually over the course of the years since 1966. In 1997, the squadron reunion was held in Natal. It apparently was a memorable occasion and Dick Wilson was a primary host.

Those wartime experiences also prompted him, in 1993, to write two editions (References 11, 12) of an illustrated history of VP-83 and VB-107. He became the squadron historian and continues to collect information about the squadron and Fairwing 16. He has kindly helped the author of this book by supplying information and photographs. Dick and his wife Billie now live in Elkton, Florida.

Wallace Richard (Dick) Carper – Aviation Chief Radioman

Dick Carper (as he preferred to be called), was born in 1919 in a small community called Beaver which is near Beckley, West Virginia, which in turn is about 70 miles south of Charleston, West Virginia. He enlisted for navy reserve training in 1939 and continued to live in South Charleston with his aunt and uncle while receiving some training. In photo I-80, we see him as an apprentice seaman. No doubt economic conditions were not propitious in 1938 when he graduated from high school. In 1940 he was called to active duty and was sent to Charleston, South Carolina for radioman training. He graduated in April 1941 as a Radioman 3/C.

Dick Carper was then posted into VP-56, a PBM Mariner squadron at Charleston, but very shortly thereafter he was transferred into VP-83 (a PBY squadron) as it was being formed at Norfolk in September 1941. In April, 1942, VP-83 was sent to Brazil and Radioman Carper proceeded to see many of the coastal cities of northeast Brazil and a lot of the South Atlantic Ocean over the following months. Dick Carper came home on leave in November 1942 and was married to a Miss Patton who was from his home town of Beaver, West Virginia.

In photo I-81, we see Dick Carper with a pet Saguin monkey on his shoulder. We do not know whether or not this was his pet or the simian belonged to one of his squadron mates. Nor do we know whether or not this is the monkey which later tragically fell out of the side hatch of a plane into the ocean as described in one of Billie Goodell's anecdotes.

I-80; Dick Carper, Apprentice Seaman

This photo would have been made in 1940 when Dick Carper and four of his friends were home for a visit. He would shortly be in training to be an aviation radioman, one of the most perilous jobs in the Navy. Fortunately for Dick, he was assigned to the Atlantic Fleet Air Force which still could be perilous but a bit safer than his counterparts in the Pacific Fleet Air Force.

In the first 18 months of the war in the Pacific the life span of aviation radio man could be brief.

Frequently a pilot would land on a carrier to refuel in a battle and his cry would be "give me ammo, fuel, and another radioman to replace the dead one in the rear seat".

I-81; Dick Carper with pet saguin monkey - 1943

More often than not pet monkeys would be acquired while the new owner was not fully in control of his faculties. This may not have been the case for Dick Carper.

In the mid-April through mid-May period of 1943, VP83 personnel and some of their PBY's went back to Norfolk Naval Air Station to acquire and do limited training in PB4Y (B-24D) aircraft prior to a prompt and hurried return to Natal. At this time Aviation Radioman Dick Carper was assigned to the crew of 107-B-7. The full crew of this first 107-B-7 (a B-24D) appears in photo I-82. In the back row, left to right are: George Wilson – ARM 2/c; D.B. Watson – AMM 2/c; Merril Hewitt – AMM 2/c; Dick Carper – ARM 1/c; Walter Gilchrist – AMM 1/c; Stevens – S 2/c; Jesse Singer – AOM 2/c. In the front row, left to right are J.L. Norris; Ensign Hallmark; Lieutenant Josh Tobin (PPC) Ensign Brenner (Navigator); Lt. (jg) Zoom Pinnell (1st Pilot).

VB-107-B-7 and its crew were involved in attacks on U-Boats. In one of those engagements a 40 mm shot from the U-Boat struck the wing of B-7. The shot punctured an oil reservoir and caused an engine problem to develop. However, the pilot, Josh Tobin, was able to bring the plane back to Ascension Island safely. As the reader will note there was a second 107-B-7 called Brown Baggers Retreat. It was a B-24J version of the PB4Y and it also had a different crew.

After his tour of duty in VB-107, Dick Carper was promoted to Aviation Chief Radioman and became flight engineer on Admiral Ingram's PB4Y, the Southern Cross, on November 1, 1944. The Admiral had been promoted to Commander in Chief of the Atlantic Fleet. He took Vance Dawkins, a pilot from VB-107, and Dick Carper as key personnel on the Southern Cross. In the next photo I-83 we see the Admiral congratulating Dick Carper and presenting him with a personal citation for meritorious service in August, 1945. Shortly thereafter, (August 1945), Dick Carper mustered out of the active duty with the navy and went home to West Virginia. He stayed in the Naval Reserve and occasionally went through brief periods of follow up service.

Dick Carper moved to Danville, Virginia to work in the insurance industry where he and his wife raised their family. His son, Thomas Carper, was in naval aviation during the Vietnam war. Tom Carper moved to Delaware and successively served as a Congressman, Governor of Delaware, and currently as a US Senator from Delaware. Dick Carper and his wife also were blessed by the birth of a daughter who they named Sheila.

Sheila Carper Adkins graduated from Marshall College and lives with her husband in Kentucky. Sheila describes her father, Dick Carper, as a very intelligent man and a good father. Sheila kindly loaned me her father's photo album so that I could reproduce photos relative to his service.

While war is a terrible thing, the experience of being involved can have character building results. Dick Carper passed away in 1992.

I-82; Crew of 107-B-7

This photo was taken in late 1943 or early 1944, by this time Dick Carper was an Aviation Radioman 1/c and Zoom Pinnell was 1st pilot. Zoom is at right end kneeling and Dick Carper is in the middle of the back row.

I-83; Dick Carper with Admiral Ingram - 1944

In I-83 we see the Admiral congratulating Dick Carper and presenting him with a personal citation for meritorious service in August, 1945. At this juncture Aviation Chief Radioman Carper was crew chief for the Admiral on Ingram's PB4Y, the Southern Cross.

I-84; Crew of the Virgin Sturgeon (107-B-1)

In photo I-84 (courtesy of Billie Goodell) of the Virgin Sturgeon's crew, we see Billie Goodell (third from right, bottom row). No doubt Billie needed a new billet after the crash of the "Ghost". The original 107-B-1 was Lieutenant Commander Prueher's plane (The Spirit of 83) which was lost in combat.

I-85; Crew of 107-B-2

Shown in this photo is the first crew of B-2. Ed Krug is first on the left of the back row and Charlie Walker is third from the right on the back row. Later on, after personnel rotations occurred, Ed Krug became Pilot Plane Commander of B-2, at which time he named the plane the "Maggie", in honor of his wife.

I-86; VB-107-B-5

Presumably, the B-5 shown is not Admiral Ingram's plane, even though it is named the Southern Cross, which later became the Admiral's plane.

The crew members' identities are unknown.

I-87; VB-107-B-6

This photo is of VB-107-B-6, the Sea Beasts, which was originally piloted by Phil Haverty and later by Marion (Vance) Dawkins. Dawkins was piloting B-6 when he attacked and sank the U-849 on 25 November, 1943. In this photo in the back row, third from left is Phil Haverty; next to him on the right is Morgan. The second from left in the front row is W.L. Spree fifth from left is George Brownlee and last (on the right) is Alfred Parker.

I-88; VB-107-B-7

I-88; The crew of the second PB4Y to be labeled VB-107-B-7 (Brown Baggers Retreat) appears in front of their plane in this photo. Note that this no.7 is a B-24J version of the PB4Y. Another later B-7 was labeled Bounce Drill. This means that VB-107 had 3 successive PB4Y's which were labeled 107-B-7 during its 33 month tour of duty in Brazil.

I-89; VB-107-B-9

This photo shows nine of the crew members of 107-B-9 (The Passionate Pilgrim). They were just back from participating in the destruction of U-863. We can identify the PPC (Jack Burton) who is second from the left in the back row, and Pete Gallagher who is second from the right in the back row. Bob Riley, another pilot is probably in the center in the back row.

I-90; Crew of the Gallopin Ghost of the Brazilian Coast (107-B-11)

This is the crew of the Ghost when this photo was made. (Courtesy of Billie Goodell). On the left in back row are Billie Goodell, Swartz, Giombi, Wallace, Gamble, Maul, Smothers, and Leftwich. In the front row are, left to right, unknown, Grimm, Shirley (PPC), and Fritz. It is clear that the makeup of crews varied from time to time.

I-91; Crew of the Gallopin Ghost of the Brazilian Coast (107-B-11) on wings of plane

Billie Goodell is the first one on the right end in the row of enlisted air crewmen, while the five officer pilots are on the right in the photo.

7

Billie Goodell – Plane Captain

For heroism and extraordinary achievement as Gunner of Patrol Plane Two attached to Patrol Squadron 83 during an engagement with an enemy submarine…

From the Distinguished Flying Cross
Letter of Commendation to Billie Goodell

The spirit and skill of the enlisted air crewmen of VP-83/VB-107 is typified by the story of Billie Goodell, Aviation Machinists Mate and Air Crew Chief.

THE DEFINING MOMENT OF BILLIE GOODELL'S LIFE

On January 6, 1943, Billie, who was scanning the ocean from a jump seat in the "blister" on the side of 83-P-2, spotted the German U-Boat U-164 off the coast of Fortaleza, Brazil. The pilot Bill Ford quickly dove the PBY toward the surfaced U-Boat. Billie sprayed the German sailors on the deck with machine gun fire. This action enabled 83-P-2 to straddle the U-164 with depth charges and destroyed it by breaking it apart. Two of the 54 German crew members survived and became prisoners of war. In photo I-92 we see Billie manning his machine gun in the blister of PBY 83-P-2. This battle is more fully described in Billie's own words in the preceding Chapter 5. For this first sinking of a U-Boat by 83-P-2, Lieutenant Ford and Billie Goodell were both awarded the Distinguished Flying Cross (DFC) by Admiral Ingram. Photo I-93 shows Admiral Ingram pinning the DFC on Billie Goodell at Natal. A copy of the DFC awards letter I-94 also follows.

Billie Goodell went on to serve as an air crew chief in various squadrons of the U.S. Navy Air Force and completed 22 years of such service.

After his formal naval service, he worked for a number of years at U.S. air bases as a civilian employee. Billie and his companion, Jean, reside in Alabama.

FROM ALABAMA TO BRAZIL

From what he has told me in many phone conversations over the past five years, Billie's early life in Alabama was not "a bed of roses". He also knew, as most everyone else of our generation knew, that service in the U.S. Armed Forces most certainly loomed in his immediate future. His decision to enlist in the Navy was very understandable. In photo I-95 we see Billie as a very young looking apprentice seaman just as he entered "boot camp" at Norfolk, Virginia in February 1941. Billie had enlisted for a "minority cruise" at age 17. After receiving training as an Aviation Machinists Mate and aerial gunner, he joined VP-83 at Norfolk. By early 1943 Billie had matured significantly as we note in photo I-96 of him in flight gear. People do tend to grow up very rapidly during wartime military service.

In the following paragraphs Billie describes his early days of training:

After Boot Camp (Basic Training) at Norfolk, Virginia in February, 1941, several of us from our company were assigned to Aviation Machinist Mate School at the Naval Air Station. At school we learned a lot about aircraft. Next we went to Assembly and Repair where they overhauled aircraft. We spent a lot of time in different departments there. I hung around the test pilots ready room and they would let me go up with them, what a thrill! After graduation we had a choice of assignments. Mine

I-92: Billie Goodell in 83-P-2 in 1942

This shows the location from which Billie spotted the U-164 on January 6 of 1943. As can be seen the 50 caliber machine gun mounted on a swivel gave wide latitude for directing the fire from the weapon to the target below. Note the summer flying suit Billie is wearing. The crews of VP-83 routinely carried out aerial gunnery practice and a good deal of skill was needed to hit a moving target whilst the plane carrying the gunner was also moving. Obviously Billie had developed considerable skill firing the machine gun.

I-93: DFC Award to Billie Goodell - 1943

Here we see Admiral Jonas Ingram pinning the DFC on the uniform of Billie Goodell at Parnamirim Field. To the right stands Lieutenant William Ford who just previously had been similarly decorated. Bertram Prueher, Commander of VP-83 is arranging items on the stand.

THE SECRETARY OF THE NAVY
WASHINGTON

The President of the United States takes pleasure in presenting the DISTINGUISHED FLYING CROSS to

BILLIE GOODELL, AVIATION MACHINIST'S MATE SECOND CLASS
UNITED STATES NAVY

for service as set forth in the following

CITATION:

"For heroism and extraordinary achievement as Gunner of Patrol Plane TWO attached to Patrol Squadron EIGHTY-THREE during an engagement with an enemy submarine in the Atlantic Ocean on January 6, 1943. With remarkable alertness, GOODELL sighted a hostile submarine surfaced at a considerable distance and after reporting it to the pilot promptly manned his gun for the attack. Climbing partly out of the plane for the most effective fire of his port waist fifty caliber gun, he raked the enemy submarine, accurately timing his fire with the launching of a severe depth charge attack. By his exceptional vigilance which had enabled him to sight submarines at great range on several occasions, and by his courageous and skillful devotion to duty, he contributed to the complete destruction of an important enemy vessel."

For the President,

James Forrestal

Acting Secretary of the Navy.

I-94: DFC Award letter to Billie Goodell

Numerous German U-Boats, as well as Italian submarines, during the latter half of 1942, had been sinking dozens of Allied ships while not suffering any losses themselves. This made Goodell and Ford's efforts in sinking the U-164 so important to the Allied cause.

I-95; Billie Goodell Apprentice Seaman - 1941

I-96; Billie Goodell Plane Captain - 1943

This is what a 17 year old fresh out of basic training (boot camp) looks like. The "Boot" name derives from the canvas leggings worn over ones trousers while in basic training. His next billet would be in sea or outgoing unit - awaiting a new assignment.

After over two years of service including: formal training in a particular discipline; practice in aircraft maintenance and operation; and, actual patrol and combat, this image shows significant maturation has taken place. Also his hair has regrown from his boot camp buzz cut.

were either to go on the USS Wasp or become an air crewmen on the USS Hornet, or Patrol Squadron VP-83. I chose the Patrol Squadron rather than the newly commissioned aircraft carriers. (Editorial Note: The Wasp was sunk on September 15, 1942 during the Battle for Guadalcanal).

At first we had no planes, so we did a lot of training. Soon the planes (PBY's) began arriving from San Diego. We were formed into crews and began patrols off the East Coast. We had a couple of incidents before we eventually left for Natal:

An Unscheduled Stop at Jacksonville, Florida

One time we had been with a convoy and were getting low on fuel so we decided to go into Jacksonville, Florida Naval Air Station for the night. The East Coast was in a blackout at the time. The pilot kept calling the Control Tower to turn on the landing lights, but got no response. Finally we spotted two rows of red lights. We put our gear down and started an approach. As we got closer I noticed the pilot was pulling up and putting on the power and then we saw the red lights were on the Mathews Bride over the St. Johns River and not the landing strip. Having located the bridge the pilot knew then where the air field was located.

He then said to us. "I will wake that bunch up" (they still had not turned on the landing lights); he got over the river, went down to a hundred feet and zoomed right over the Control Tower. Let me tell you, the place then lit up like a Christmas tree. The pilot pulled off the runway in front of the Tower, jumped out of the plane and did some chewing out of the Control Tower personnel. The M.P.'s came out with the Office of the Day, who said, "If you keep this plane here overnight, you will have to unload those four depth charges from beneath the wing". We were getting madder all the time. They came out with a bomb cart and a couple of mattresses. They laid the mattresses on the ground under the wing and dropped the bombs on them. I gassed up the plane and we headed back to Norfolk the next day.

A Near Disaster at Charleston, South Carolina

Before patrol squadron eighty three deployed to Natal, Brazil, we were doing anti submarine duty off the Atlantic Coast. That was when the Germans were sinking many ships off the coast. We picked up a convoy going south for a while and later since we were so far out and short on gas we went in to Charleston, South Carolina for the night. It had a small airfield called Hawthorn. A jeep met us and parked us in a grove of pine trees. We deplaned and the pilot asked for one of us to remain and guard the plane. I had to gas and get the plane ready for the next day so I told him I would remain with the plane. He said fine and he would send a gas truck out for me.

Well, about thirty minutes later an army fuel truck arrived. They had begun an army base there and when the men got word about our plane they begun to mass around. They had never seen a plane like this PBY-5A. Questions began pouring in while I was gassing up. After I finished the men wanted to know if they could look inside. I told them I would take five at a time so it would not be crowded. It went well until one of the guys asked me how the gun worked. I had both blisters open at the time. It's easy I said. You undo the strap holding the fifty caliber in place, swing it out the blister which I did, just pull the slide back and press the trigger. I did and all I could see was a line of tracers floating over the pines. Well let me tell you, the guys in the plane liked to have killed themselves getting out. The gas truck drivers and all ground personnel disappeared leaving the truck behind. The ordnance man forgot to unload the gun when we came in from patrol. Well, I was scared to death. I hid the few rounds that had fired and waited for them to come and take me away. About thirty minutes later I saw two army men coming. All they said was, "we came to get our truck." Never saw anyone else until the crew arrived the next morning. To this day I have never told anyone. Lucky me the gun was pointed upward.

A Pollywog Becomes a Shellback

In early April, 1942, VP-83, then part of Patrol Wing 11, was ordered to get underway to Natal, Brazil, to join the forces of Admiral Ingram in that theater of war. The first division of six planes flew there first and the second division personnel went by ship. Herein Billie describes his most notable experience during his first episode of sea duty:

In 1942, the second section of Patrol Squadron 83 boarded the USS Albemarle, (The Able Mabel), an aircraft tender bound for Trinidad. When we arrived at Trinidad they off loaded us to wait for further transportation to Natal, Brazil where the other half of the squadron had already arrived and set up the tents. We were at Trinidad for nearly a week before they loaded us aboard the USS Somers-DD 381. We then headed south for Brazil. We were all pollywogs. In the navy everyone is considered a pollywog until they cross the equator. Then after a brutal initiation you become a shellback. Well, here we were a bunch of airdales aboard a blackshoe ship, so we all knew what to expect. They prepare for this initiation for days in advance.

We were all charged for some stupid reason for punishment. My charge was bunk time over running and trying to get flat feet for a medical discharge. They saved garbage, put eggs in the sun to rot, mixed jello with hair and red hot pepper and sauce etc. They had everything set up for the day when we reached the equator, the ship stopped, lowered the colors and ran up a large black and white flag with a skull and crossbones on it. Everyone dishing out punishment was a royal something or other. Royal King was a large fat black seated with a mixture of stale grease and oil around his belly button. We had to kneel and kiss his belly button while someone pushed your head into his belly. Then the royal doctor would lay you on a steel spring bed and shock you with electric prongs. Remember we were naked and sprayed down with salt water. Royal barber shaved your head, while seated with your back to a pool of salt water. Before you knew it you were in the pool being beat until you could climb out. Then the royal cook fed you the jello, forced you to open your mouth, and slapped the rotten egg in while socking you on the chin. Most of the men threw up. Then you had to crawl through a long canvas chute filled with this rotten garbage while being beat from both sides. After all of this was over you were officially a shellback. I became one on May 5, 1942 aboard the USS Somers DD381. Editorial Note: After becoming a "shellback" each sailor is given an I.D. card and certificate. These are carefully retained to prevent an encore initiation. A copy of Billie's Shellback ID card (I-97) follows.

IMPERIVM NEPTVNI REGIS
THIS CERTIFIES THAT
BILLIE GOODELL
CROSSED THE EQUATOR ABOARD THE
U.S.S. SOMERS DD381 ON 5/25/4
SIGNED
COMMANDING OFFICER

I-97; Billie Goodell's Shellback Certificate - 1942

Since Billie Goodell came across the equator on a U.S. Navy Destroyer he was subjected to an extensive and harrowing shelback initiation as were the other sailors in the "Airdale" group. His description of the proceedings in King Neptunes Court makes me thankful that I crossed the equator in Mid-1943 on a U.S. Army transport ship. That vessel, the USS William Evarts was manned by merchant marine sailors and the only U.S. Navy crew memeers were the few gunners in the armed guard contingent on board to operate the ship's guns. Thus our initiation was much milder on the Evarts. At least Billie and his mates were not keel hauled.

OFF DUTY EXPERIENCES AT NATAL

The first year of anti-submarine patrol duty at Natal and the makeshift small bases up and down the Brazilian coast was difficult as described previously. However, time spent at the friendly small town of Natal offered some more pleasurable diversions as described by Billie Goodell in the following four personal anecdotes:

Duty at the RAMPA and a Dangerous Liaison

During my tour of duty at the ramp in Natal, Brazil we were mostly on our own. We lived in tents and did most of our cooking with supplies from the main base. We had to have sentry duty for we had a shack where we stored torpedoes. We hardly ever used them, for the Catalinas carried two depth charges under each wing. If they did need torpedoes, the plane would land in the river, taxi up to the ramp, and we would load them.

The first night that I was there I was sound asleep when the sky lit up like it was daytime. I heard the drone of aircraft engines and went outside to see a Pan Am Clipper land in the river. They would drop flares at night to see how to land. It taxied up to the pier, which was very close to our ramp, and unloaded its passengers and mail. Then it would anchor out in the river until the next day. The Pan American Clipper was the only airline flying between the states and Rio. It also made stops at some of the large cities along the Brazilian coast.

The Wonderbar had a competitor called the Goodyear bar. It was located not far from the ramp but inland. It had a large bar and tables under cover with a large patio in the open with an adobe wall around it. Doors led off from the bar where the girls lived or whatever. The girls also waited on tables and hustled drinks. We would sit there, eat peanuts, and drink their lager beer. When I would go in I kept noticing that this same red head named Cymara Britto would always come to the table. I never led her on, but chatted and bought her drinks. One day she disappeared for awhile and came to the table with a Whitman chocolate box. "Is that for me, I asked"? She opened the box, and in there was a fully loaded pearl handled thirty eight revolver. "Yes, it is for you if I ever see you messing around with any of the other girls". I told my buddy to grab his hat and we got the hell out of there. Someone told me later that she went back to Recife.

They had sailboats that picked up passengers at the main street pier near the ramp to take them across the river to swim. One day I put on my swim trunks and waited on the sailboat to come by. He saw me and pulled in close. I jumped in and swam out and he took me aboard. He let us off at the beach and went back for another load. I walked up the beach, met two pretty girls, and sat down and talked for awhile. I saw the sail boat returning and decided it was time to go. There was a navy ship anchored in the river and one of its boats was unloading a swimming party. As I was boarding the sail boat I heard this screaming and cussing and saw Cymara Britto headed for me with a twelve inch silver knife. I jumped over board and swam for the navy boat yelling "I am a navy man". They pulled me aboard and dropped me off at the ramp laughing like hell. That episode ended my trips to the Goodyear.

Christmas Leave in Rio

Christmas of nineteen forty two patrol squadron eighty three received a plane load of gifts from the USO club in Rio. When I opened mine there was a sweet letter from a girl named Billie Jean Beattie along with her address. I thought it appropriate to write and thank her. We corresponded a few times and I found out she was a part time helper at the USO. We found out later that our crew had been granted a seven days leave in Rio. When we landed they checked us into the Luxor Hotel on Copacabana beach. After settling down I caught a taxi to the USO. I walked in and asked if Billie Jean was there. They pointed her out and we introduced ourselves.

After chatting awhile, she asked me if I would like to be introduced to her father nearby. We caught a taxi and pulled up in front of a large bank. We caught an elevator and went up several floors. We walked down the hall to a door marked president with Beatties' name on it. She walked right in hugged her dads neck and said. Dad I want you to meet someone. He shook my hand and said for us to be seated. Come to find out he was the president of the City Bank of New York and they all were from Texas. Before we left he asked me if I would like to come out to their villa and have dinner the next day, of course I said yes sir. He said "Good, Billie will pick you up at the USO at four tomorrow".

I was there and this big limo pulled up and I got in and we headed for the country. We pulled into the driveway of this luxury villa and the valet opened the door. Billie Jean introduced me to her mother and she said. "Welcome, I have heard a lot about you last night from Billie and her Dad." "I have prepared a real southern meal for you". When her dad got in we washed up, sat down, and said the grace. A neatly dressed maid began bringing out the food. What a meal; cornbread, black-eyed peas, beef roast, salad, turnip greens and all kinds of desserts. What a feast. Sure beat the Spam we were used to. Before I left her dad wanted to know if there was anything he could do for me. I told him how hard Kodak film was to get, and he said before I left for Natal, to stop by the USO and Billie would have some for me. After dinner they dropped me off at the Luxor Hotel, I thanked them with all my heart and went by the USO one more time, told her how proud that it was I who received her package and could not thank her enough.

Guess it was a good thing for the both of us. All I can say is they were a beautiful and wonderful bunch of people.

I-98; Betty de Oliviera - 1943

Betty de Oliviera

There was a bar across from the Kodak shop. Both were right off the main drag. I would drop off the photos and go across the street and have a few beers. First thing I knew I was also taking film in for some of my friends. "You again", she would say. She spoke real good English and I liked to spend time in the shop talking to her. Her family would come down and she would introduce them to me. Her little niece Miriam and I enjoyed having our picture made. One of her family was in the Brazilian army and he came down and was introduced to me. One thing led to another and finally I was invited to their house for dinner. We took photos and walked the beach. We were never alone, always chaperoned.

Billie's description of his relationship with Betty de Oliviera and her family is typical of the quick rapport which developed between U.S. personnel and residents of Natal. During the 4 plus years the Americans were in Natal, many such relationships were established with some resulting in marriage.

A Wonderbar Excursion - A Memorable Night and Day in Natal

I was on temporary duty at the ramp. They had a warrant officer in charge. One day this whale boat came up the river loaded with survivors from a sunken freighter. We began to wave and they put in at the ramp. They were picked up and taken to the base. Well, we had a boat, so we cleaned it up and used it as a recreation vehicle. I got pretty good as a boatswains mate. Well, to clue you in, the ramp was next to the dock where the Pan American Clippers unloaded passengers and mail. It was the only airline from the states. Upstream from there was the Wonderbar club. A little further was another pier at the end of the main street coming down from the hotel. Anyway the warrant officer came up with a great idea.

As you know, we had a ten p.m. curfew. Here were the plans. He would spend the night at the Wonderbar and next morning we would bring the beer and food and pick him and the girls up behind the Wonderbar. Next morning we made our way behind the Wonderbar. It was rough for they had about four old rusty ships anchored there. We pulled up close and he came out on the second floor balcony in his skivvies. "Throw me a rope" he says. We did and the fool tied it to a stud holding the roof up. We waited awhile and here comes four girls down the side of the building toward the boat. We just got them aboard when we heard whistles blowing and saw a bunch of marine MP's on the city pier. Knowing they would be there soon we begin to chop the rope loose. I had the engine going and here comes the warrant officer with the marines on his tail. He made a dive as we were backing down and he caught the bow of the boat. We pulled him aboard and he added insult to injury by thumbing his nose at the marines. I put it in full throttle and headed for the far side of the river and upstream and around a bend in the river.

Little did we know that it was getting shallow. We were grounded so we ate and had a beer. The girls were getting scared so we started getting them some blankets. In doing so one of the guys pulled out some red flares that were left in the lifeboat. The girls started screaming and hollering bomba, bomba, and we had to keep them from jumping overboard. It was getting late so we took the oars and pushed out of the mud.

We got on the far side of the river and headed back to the ramp. As we looked, we could still see people on the balcony of the Wonderbar. We went nearly to the mouth of the river, came across, and pulled in at the ramp. The girls were scared to death so we hid them in the torpedo shack while we went and called a taxi. The cab picked them up and we showered and walked up to the Wonderbar. We walked in and saw two marines and a pile of rope on the balcony. We walked up and asked what had happened. Their reply was, "Some swabbies broke curfew picked up some girls, we are going to get them anyway". "Good luck", we said as we had a few beers before leaving.

I-99; Dick Hamill on Balcony of Wonderbar - 1943

The post behind Dick may have been where the escape rope was tied for the errant warrant officer noted in Billie Goodell's description of "A Wonderbar Excursion".

BILLIE GOODELL IN VB-107

In this section Billie describes experiences during the transition from the PBY's of VP-83 into the Navy's version of the B-24 and subsequent flights from Ascension Island as well as the coastal cities of Brazil. The first two episodes concern the hazards involved when pilots and air crews have short times to familiarize themselves with different planes. One facet of training entails "familiarization flights", wherein repeated take-offs and landings are practiced for several hours at a time. These were called "bounce drills" or "family hops" and were very necessary, if somewhat boring.

They would also have to sharpen accuracy of bomb drops by practicing on bombing ranges with small bombs and repetitive drops. These activities could also be hazardous as the reader will note in the subsequent anecdotes by Billie Goodell:

Unfriendly Pine Trees at Cherry Point Air Base

The PBY Catalina's that VP-83 had become too slow for the missions we were doing. Instead of the U-Boats diving, they began to stay on surface and shoot it out with us. So, we formed a new squadron, patrol bombing squadron 107. We flew the PBY's back to Norfolk and exchanged them for PB4Y-1's called the Liberator. We only had about fifteen days to get checked out on them. We flew familiarization flights and night landings.

It was pretty congested at Norfolk, so the pilot suggested we fly down to Cherry Point and use their base. I told the crew that it was no need for them, so I went along with the pilots. When you lower the landing gear there is a red latch on the gear that tells you it is locked. Only way to see it at night is with what we called Aldis lamp. Well, when we got there and started our first approach the landing gear was lowered and I went aft to check for sure. As I shined the light out the hatch, all I could see was pine trees whizzing by. I started to run forward and about that time I heard us hitting trees. We went on in and hit the landing strip. We pulled off the runway and I got out to inspect for damage. There was a tree top in the nose compartment and the hydraulic lines pulled away from the port mount. Luckily no broken lines. I got some electrical tape and patched her up and we headed for Norfolk.

A Friendly Fire Tragedy on the VB-107 Bombing Range

Look at the underside of this picture of the PB4Y Liberator and you will see nothing but the bomb bay and part of the fuselage. Here is the story. I made this from the top of a radio truck with a K20 camera. Northeast of the field we had cut the underbrush out in the shape of a U-Boat. It was about one hundred yards from the beach behind sand dunes. We used it for training purposes. The plane would get over the water and come in at fifty feet, skip over the dunes and drop a nine pound lead bomb with a shotgun shell in the nose. It would send up a wisp of white smoke and we had another crew on the ground and they would measure number of feet from the target and radio back to the plane. It was our time on the ground and the pilot in the air said for me to get atop the truck and snap his photo while he was making a dummy run. Well, I got ready and here he comes about fifty feet over my head. I snapped a photo (I-100) and you can see by the photo all I got. It blew me and camera off the truck.

I-100; PB4Y at practice bombing range - 1943

Another day we had a tragedy. We were dropping on the target and another crew was on the ground. We came in low, dropped the small bomb, and one of the crew on the ground ran prematurely toward the target to measure and our bomb hit him in the leg. We called the base and circled the ambulance to guide it to the target. I threw out our first aid kits. A blood clot formed in his leg and he died on the way back to the states.

Barrier Sweeps from Ascension Island

Patrol Squadron eighty three had been having great success with the Catalina doing convoy duty and submarine sweeps. Soon the U-Boats became desperate and instead of submerging, they would stay on the surface and throw up a lot of fire power. The commanding officer decided it was time to return the PBY's back to the states and pick up PB4Y-1's. They were faster and could carry a larger bomb load. The Germans were carrying supplies through the South Atlantic north for their war effort. They began to disguise raiders as merchant ships. When you started a run on one all of the false decking would drop and all you met was a barrage of fire power.

Admiral Ingram came up with an idea that we would patrol a barrier that would take a U-Boat or raider twenty four hours to get through before being spotted. To do this we had Ascension Island as the midway point and we kept two PB4Y-1's between Natal and Ascension, and two between Ascension and Africa. On the water we had two destroyers and a cruiser. This turned out to be a real successful operation. W e still maintained our anti submarine patrols and convoy duty.

Editorial Note:

The "Barrier Sweeps" were also based on a scientifically planned pattern of flight for the aircraft which was designed to maximize the chance of relocating a U-Boat after the original sighting occurred and the submarine had evaded hostile action by the aircraft. An organization of American scientists was recruited and some were sent to Brazil and assigned to the Fourth Fleet and Fairwing 16 to upgrade the Barrier Sweep tactics. A Dr. Steinhardt designed the so-called "Steinhardt Square" which consisted of three successive rhombic shaped patterns of flight spaced around the original scene of sighting of a submarine. Using this tactic proved to be an effective way of regaining a sighting on the U-Boats location and facilitating an attack on same. This tactic was supplemented by interception of U-Boat communications to Germany once the British captured one of the German decoding machines; the Enigma.

The Accidental Sky Diver

We had been with this convoy for a couple days and when it got out of range we went in to Belem to refuel and gas up for the trip back to Natal. After servicing the plane we all went into town on liberty. We had an ordnance man in our crew that saw a little monkey that he liked. He bought it for the return trip back to Natal. He picked it up the next morning and brought it back to the plane. He kept it tied up in the after station. We always flew with the side hatches open for we had wind reflectors to keep the wind out. Anyway he decided to untie the monkey and play with it awhile. We were flying at three thousand feet at the time. Anyway he got too close to the hatch and the monkey jerked loose and out the hatch he went. We tried to see where he hit but never saw anything. The guy was heartbroken. For days we kidded him about throwing our life rafts out of the plane for the monkey. He soon got over it. This is a true story and I am sure you have heard different versions of it.

A Near Miss on an Allied Merchant Ship

The German surface ship raiders got desperate in the South Atlantic during the last of the war. They would disguise themselves as merchant ships with false partitions. When one of our planes would go in to investigate the partitions would fall away and the plane would be met with a hail of fire. Each merchant ship had been assigned a recognition signal before they sailed, and if they did not correspond, goodbye ship. Before attacking the pilot would ask for the signal and they would run it up on a flag.

On one of my flights we spotted this merchant ship. We all manned our battle stations, mine at the time was the crown turrent located on the command deck over the radar man on the port and radioman on the starboard. The pilot circled several times trying to get the ship to respond. Still no signal. Over the ear phones we heard these words, "let's go get him." He put the plane in a steep dive, and before we had a chance to fire the pilot said, "abort, abort." The ship had run up its flag. As we pulled out of this steep dive I had my head to the side and the wind disengaged the guns, and as they flew up, the one on the port side caught me on the left side of the head and knocked me out. I went limp and fell out of the turret, landing along side of the radar man. He jumped up and told the pilot, I had regained consciousness and was bleeding from the gash over my left ear. They filled the cut with sulfa powder and bandaged my head. The pilot called Natal and told them to have an ambulance standing by, for he had a wounded crewman aboard. He also told them to send another plane out to relieve us. As we landed they unloaded me and took me to the sickbay. They shaved the cut, put six stitches in, and kept me a couple days. They kidded me and said there would be no purple heart.

Sea Urchins, Octopi, and Eels at Ascension

While spending our thirty day tour on Ascension island there was very little to do if you were not on the schedule to fly. So to entertain ourselves we would take a rolled up line with a hook and sinker and wade through a throng of noisy terns and make our way to the water's edge. There was nothing but a drop off of jagged lava rock with holes you could see the water through. We would put a piece of octopus on the hook and drop it in a hole. Immediately something would nearly jerk the line from your hand. After a struggle we would pull out a six or seven foot eel. To get them back to camp we had to tie them on a pole to keep from dragging them and two of us would sling them over our shoulder. The mess cooks would give us grease and meal for frying, then help us eat fried eel and drink warm beer.

One day I decided to go down and get some octopus for bait for the next day. There was only one place we could get to the water's edge and the lava made a flat space out into the ocean. It was full of holes and you had to watch for the ocean waves had a habit of breaking over the rocks leaving nothing but foam so if you got caught you did not know where to step. The rocks were full of sea urchins with long barbed spines which we could not pull out. The octopus clung to the rocks and we used a hook on the end of a broomstick to pull them off.

I had walked half way when I saw this large octopus, and had just hooked him, when a large wave broke over the rocks, knocked me off my feet, and I could see nothing but foam. Every time I tried to stand I would fall again. Luckily I was being washed toward the beach, and found my footing.

I was bleeding and covered with barbs from the sea urchins. I made it to the sick bay, and my white tee shirt and shorts were completely red with blood. Well, they cut on me for quite awhile to remove the barbs. Years later I could still see little black dots under my skin. I learned a big lesson. I would never go and get fish bait alone again.

Crash of the Ghost

On October the fourteenth, nineteen forty three, my crew had the day off after several anti submarine patrols. The officer of the day came up to my tent and asked if I would come down to the O.D.s office. When I came in I was asked to have a seat. He said, "Goodell, the commanding officer is going on an inspection trip to Ascension Island tomorrow, and I want you to get your plane ready."

The next day, the commanding officer, Capt. Renfro Turner and his inspection crew came out to the plane. We loaded, and for the take off we had to move most of the personnel forward. We had a couple on the catwalk in the bomb bay. My position is always standing between the pilot and copilot. Cdr. Turner was sitting behind the pilot on a piece of radio gear. He was reading a book called, "The Importance of Living". We checked the rpm and the tower gave us permission to roll.

We were up to about a hundred and fifty miles per hour and lifted off and were about two hundred feet in the air, when the plane started losing altitude. The left wing hit, and number four prop hit, and snapped off and hit the engine next to it and it hit the fuselage splitting the side where the captain was sitting. He had injuries to his back. After the prop hit, it glanced to the bow, cutting off the Plexiglas, and setting off about two hundred rounds of fifty caliber ammo. The nose wheel came up through the deck and I ended up with cuts on my leg. The men in the bomb bay had cuts and bruises. After a few bounces and skids we came to a stop. We got out fast, for we had nine bombs, and a three hundred gallon gas tank in the bomb bay. By that time all the fire and crash crew arrived. The bombs were so hot they had to spray them down before digging them out. It was a lucky day for us but the end of the Galloping Ghost. Bureau number 32052 was written off the books.

(Editorial Note: photo I-101 shows the Gallopin Ghost after it crashed.)

I-101; Crash of the Gallopin Ghost

As will be noted from this photo and Billie Goodell's description of the crash, the pilot and crew of the Ghost were fortunate to escape with minor injuries. It would appear that the plane may have been a bit overloaded.

Later, Billie took an axe and hacked out the piece of fuselage just below the word Gallopin and brought it home as a souvenir. Unfortunately his son used it as a toy and it was lost in the hurly-burly of family life.

8

Musings of an Old Naval Aviator (Lieutenant Commander Edward A. Krug (no.103998)

A life fueled by a spirit of adventure.

A Thought from the Author

This chapter is the work product of a distinguished naval aviator who clearly had (and has) a zest for life, even when confronted with dangerous circumstances.

COLLEGE, CAVALRY, NAVAL AVIATION

Ed Krug was born in Evanston, Illinois near Chicago in 1917. He went to Brown University for two years and then in 1937 enlisted in the U.S. Army, serving in the horse calvary for several years. Ed then transferred into naval aviation training ground school at Glenview, Illinois as an aviation cadet. From January, 1941 until September 1941 he was in flight school at Pensacola Naval Air Station, Florida. After graduating as an Ensign pilot in September 1941, he proceeded to Norfolk to join VP-83 as it was being formed. In photo I-102 we see Ed Krug and Mearl Taylor at tent city, Parnamirim. While in VP-83 and VB-107 he worked his way up from 3rd Pilot – Navigator to Patrol Plane Commander. At one time he was the PPC of 107-B-2. Later he served on 107-B-7 (Brown Bagger's Retreat) and subsequently became PPC of that plane.

In August 1944, while commanding B-7 out of Ascension Island, his crewmen spotted the U-843 heading south through the South Atlantic Narrows. Ed took B-7 down close to the U-Boat and planted a perfect straddle of bombs on it. The U-843 was badly damaged but did survive and slowly proceeded to Singapore for repair. After the war a Dutchman named Zimmer contacted Ed Krug to inform him that he was a friend of the family of the German skipper of the U-843 and had gone on camping trips with that family. The U-843 had been on freight duty carrying essential war material from the Far East to Germany. The U-843 was later sunk in the Baltic Sea by the RAF so I doubt if the U-Boat's skipper survived.

On September 28, 1944, 107-B-9, piloted by Lieutenant John Burton attacked and damaged U-863. Then Ed Krug, piloting B-7, bombed the U-863 and destroyed it. This was the last U-Boat sunk off Ascension.

Photo I-103, which was supplied by Ed Krug, shows 16 pilots of VB-107 in front of a PB4Y named "Heavenly Body". In the back row, left to right are: Harry Holt; Ed Krug; Sam Taylor; Joe Gentilini; H. Dixon, Jr.; Pete Gallagher; Jack Burton; and Charlie Walker. In the front row, left to right are: Tim Kiefner; Bill Boffenkamp; Butler; Len Shirley; Alan Rice; Bill Lee; Guy Brown; and Bruce Foster. There are two other signatures on the photo; P. R. Blesh and L. R. McAboy.

After the war and further naval service, Ed Krug first worked with his father on textile sales and then on his own for 30 years total. Today he is a widower, living in retirement in Arkansas. As the following recent anecdotes by Ed Krug will show, he still is keen of mind and spirit.

Ensign Ed Krug's Early Days in VP-83

Our Squadron, VP-83 was commissioned in September 1941 in Norfolk Virginia with Commander Sperry Clarke as our Commanding Officer. As a recent graduate from Pensacola Naval Air Station with my Navy Wings of Gold I was there as were two other new Ensigns who were to become my best friends, Ensign Mearl G. Taylor of Arlington, Texas and Ensign Samuel Kyle Taylor, Jr. of Whitesburg, Tennessee. Our Squadron was equipped with PBY-5B's, amphibian version of the PBY-5 Catalina manufactured by Consolidated Aircraft Corporation of California.

New Ensigns were assigned to planes as Third Pilots. This meant that they were the Navigators for their plane. If their PPC (Patrol Plane Commander) was a nice guy, they might get some time in the co-pilot's seat and some Landings and Takeoffs, popularly known as " Bounce Drill". I was assigned to Ensign Charley Daum's plane as the Third Pilot and we were scheduled to take-off on a long range anti-submarine patrol one afternoon. Two recent graduates from Flight School joined the Squadron that day we were scheduled to fly and as they badly needed flight time to keep their Flight Pay (50% on our Base Pay), I was "bumped" from the flight. Our Base Pay as Ensigns was $135.00 a month so Flight Pay, an additional 50%, was a BIG DEAL for us.

That night, Charley Daum's plane got lost and crashed into a mountain in Virginia. There was one survivor, William Preston, a 2nd Radioman on that flight, who had been sitting in the Waist Hatch with his back against the bulkhead. This had saved his life. Bill Preston later became my Radioman when we were operating out of Natal, Brazil. Bill Preston is still alive at this writing and is living in Florida with his wife. After the loss of Charley Daum's plane, I believed someone was watching over me and I felt that I would survive this war.

Editorial Note: Flight pay required at least 4 hours of flight per month to qualify – it was nicknamed "Flight Skins", the etymology remains a mystery to the author.

A Perilous Journey with Some Comic Relief

We sailed from Norfolk on the USS Nitro, a Navy ammunition ship loaded with ordnance, powder for the big Coastal guns in Panama and depth charges…in April 1942. There were about ten very new Ensigns and about twenty enlisted men with Everett Terry, a NAP (Naval Air Pilot), the senior enlisted man. Josh Tobin was a few classes ahead of me and was the senior Ensign aboard. We had our foot lockers and all our flight gear, including parachutes and winter flight gear as well. The Captain of the Nitro was what we call a "Mustang", a Reserve Officer called back from civilian life, probably in a much higher paying job to captain the lousiest job in the Navy, an ammunition ship. If you got hit, you could count on being in very little pieces He was not a happy man and having a bunch of fly-boys on board his ship, was no joy either. We took up the entire Wardroom and most available space as well.

We were escorted by two 1920's four-stack destroyers, the U.S.S. Hamilton and the U.S.S. Henderson. They had been stored upriver somewhere and the rust had been painted over. They had no Asdic Gear, no underwater detection devices and were equipped with manually-operated three-inch guns. Each had a single rack of depth charges on the stern. We got the idea that we were expendable.

We had "Boat Drill" every morning and were supposed to show up, stand in formation with our life belts on and fastened for inspection. Walt Murdock, one of our Ensigns, was a Math wizard from one of the Ivy League Schools and he calculated that with our load of high explosives, if torpedoed, we would be blown forty-three (43) miles up in the sky. We all agreed to show up for "Boat Drill" with our parachutes on…not the life jackets as required. The Captain was not pleased…he didn't think it was funny. As a result, the entire group of young Ensigns found themselves chipping paint from the decks on our hands and knees all the way down to the Canal Zone. I would swear that that chisel must have weighed twenty pounds and the hammer more. That was the very first "REALITY SHOW".

Welcome to Panama – An Old Navy Town

We passed through the Panama Canal without incident after unloading some of our cargo on the Atlantic side. The bulk of our cargo was intended for the Pacific side where the top people felt the greatest danger lay.

The Captain granted us shore leave and Josh Tobin and I went ashore, splendid in our dress whites with our gold wings proudly displayed on our chests and our shiny gold braid showing on the black shoulder boards. We were magnificent…One of the local bars took our eye…it looked pretty clean and had an English name so we went in and were ushered to a table by the Headwaiter. We had just ordered our drinks when two "Ladies of the Evening" approached our table and asked if we would like some company. They asked if we would buy them a drink and feeling in an expansive mood, Josh and I said, "Yes" and in an instant the waiter was there and the "ladies" each ordered a "BLUE MOON ESPECIAL". It wasn't another minute before the drinks were in front of the "ladies". Each drink was on a small tray…one tall glass filled with what looked like a Cola and a small shot glass filled with a light colored liquid. The "ladies" promptly poured the shot glass into the tall glass… did not even take a sip from the tall glass and promptly ordered "MAIS BLUE MOON ESPECIALS". The waiter was there in a split second and the same procedure was followed by both "ladies". Josh and I both said loudly…"Hey, we don't mind buying you drinks if you drink them, but no more of this business" The "ladies" left in a "Huff. We each were presented with a bill of ten bucks, five dollars a drink and they didn't even drink them. Our pay then as Ensigns was $135.00 a month with a 50% flight pay added and ten bucks was "A LOT OF MONEY".

On to Natal and First Attack on a U-Boat

Our group boarded the U.S.S. Patoka for our passage from Trinidad to Brazil. This time-honored oiler arrived in Natal around the end of April 1942. The Patoka was famous for having a tower on her stern where our first "Lighter Than Air" Shenandoah was tethered during tests on the capability of "Lighter Than Air" in anti-submarine warfare.

As a very junior Ensign, I was assigned as Third Pilot to a very senior PPC (Patrol Plane Commander) and as such, was actually the Navigator for the flight. The co-pilot was Thurmond Robertson, an NAP (Naval Air Pilot) who was later credited with sinking an enemy submarine by actually dive-bombing the sub from two thousand feet of altitude.

Enemy subs had been very active around Belem, one of the most important ports in Brazil. In fact, one of our supply ships loaded with aviation gasoline, ordnance, food and many essential supplies was sunk by an enemy sub just 90 miles off the mouth of the Amazon River where Belem is situated a few months earlier. It was dusk and one of our lookouts reported a surfaced submarine off our port bow. The PPC increased airspeed, put the plane nose-down and started a run. We dropped our four depth charges at about 150 knots airspeed and our PPC opened the sliding window on his side, stuck his head almost out the window and pulled up in a tight left turn, trying to spot how effective the "drop" was. The PBY started to shudder…we were going into a stall and at that altitude, we were not going to survive. I doubt to this day that our PPC knew what was happening as he was concentrating on seeing the results of the "drop". I was standing right behind the first pilot's' seat and I could feel the plane shaking…I thought…THIS IS IT. Then, slowly but surely, I saw Robertson's hands take hold of the yoke, and slowly but surely, eased up on the tight turn while putting the yoke slightly forward to pick up speed. I don't think the PPC had any idea that he was not in control of the plane at that instant. To this day, I often say to myself, "Thanks, Robbie, wherever you are". I have since learned that Thurmond Robertson was killed during the Berlin Airlift coming in to Templehof Airport at night.

I-102; E. A. Krug and M.G. Taylor
Tent City - 1942: Probably at Parnamirim

Russians at Natal and Chess Matches

VP-83 was to trade in some of their PBY-5B's for B-24 D's which would substantially increase our range and firepower (bomb load). MG Taylor, Sam Taylor and I were to fly the PBY'S back to Norfolk, train in the B-24's for thirty days and then bring back our new planes to Natal. Before that time arrived, we had a small group of Russian aviators and their Political Officers arrive on our base. We were to check them out in landings before turning some of the remaining "Catalinas" over to them. I think someone at the State Department thought that up. Their Political Officers would permit no fraternization…they had their own mess and barracks.

Some of us felt we would like to get to know something about them. They all seemed to have very well-callused hands…the hands of a workingman or farmer. There were no office workers or poets or musicians among them that we could see. Walt Murdock, our math genius played chess on his Ivy League University team and I had played with my father. We challenged them to a chess match and their Political Officers, who were their interpreters agreed. Some of our Squadron had also played chess and joined our team. All of us were University men and these Russians were laborers and farmers…what could they know about the game of chess. I knew two of the opening "gambits" and I am sure Walt knew a lot more. WELL…I lasted for three moves on my first game and I think Walt Murdock lasted about ten and it was CHECKMATE. We lost every game…didn't win one game. Then it dawned on me…CHESS is a national pastime in Russia…every kid knows the game and plays it like a champion.

So much for higher education…it doesn't win every time. We did get to know some of them and It helped to "break the ice".

(Editorial Note: Some of this Russian Pilot training was probably carried out at Lagoa Bomfim, a large lake south of Natal which had been leased by Fairwing 16 and turned into a recreational facility and training area in the 1942-44 period. The lake was in a remote, unpopulated area and was large enough for practicing water landings and take-offs of VP-83's PBY5B planes. The Navy personnel cleared an area surrounding the lake and had a shelter building and change house built for squadron personnel to use when at the lake. Naturally, in true military tradition, the facility also became a recreational spot for the air crews when they flew in from Parnamirim to carry out their familiarization flights. It was standard procedure for the crews to be told to take along their bathing suits so they could also enjoy a swim in the fresh water lake as they washed down the planes. Sometimes a trek would be made by road in trucks which were also liberally stocked with milk cans full of ice and bottles or cans of beer. The shoreline of the lake was a sandy beach. Billie Goodell recalls a large almond tree between the lakeside buildings and the beach which had a large sign warning against eating green almonds off the tree. The sign contained a large Jolly Roger skull and crossbones flag in red next to the tree. Almonds have to be roasted before they are edible, otherwise they are deadly poison (cyanide).)

Air Speed, Range, and Plane Captains' Innovation

I was assigned a brand new PB4Y-1, the Navy version of the Air force B-24. It was Number 2 Boat…still called "boats", a throwback from the day when all Patrol Bombers were seaplanes, like the PBY Catalina or the Martin PBM Mariner.

2 Boat was the slowest plane in the Squadron. I had to keep the RPM's and Manifold Pressure higher than any of the other planes just to keep our position in a five-plane sweep. This meant that I was using more gas than the other planes and would have less endurance if asked to stay out longer for some special purpose. I talked this over with our Plane Captain, Carmen D. Schaeffer originally from Iowa. Schaeffer was a great Plane Captain and I had a great crew along with him. Schaeffer asked me to come out and look at the plane…he and the crew had washed the entire plane down with water and sand and the paint was as smooth as glass. We picked up a few knots, but we were still slow. Then came the test…we had been out on patrol and on the way in were asked to divert to relieve one of our planes who was on station about 200 miles out from the Coast where one of our planes had attacked a submarine and sunk it with two or three survivors. The attacking plane had dropped a twelve man rubber raft to the survivors and they had climbed in. Being so close to land there was a good chance that they would drift to shore before dying of exposure and the Air Combat Intelligence Officers wanted to question them.

We relieved the plane and assumed our station. I put down ten degree flaps and pulled the RPM's down to 1700 and the manifold pressure down to twenty inches. We were sailing around like a big kite. Our Navigator, Chuck Hill, kept reminding me that we were getting low on fuel and were supposed to stay on station until relieved. I checked with Schaeffer and he assured me we were OK on fuel. Hill was right according to our gas load and the hours we had been in the air we were getting close. But, the Plane Captain knows his plane…he lives with it and sometimes has to die with it. I had to take his word. We stayed until relieved by Charlie Baldwin and then went back to Natal and landed with a little less than 200 gallons of fuel left in the tanks. At fifty gallons an hour per engine, we had an hour flight time left when we landed.

The next day I took Schaeffer aside and asked him, point-blank, WHERE DID THAT EXTRA FUEL COME FROM?" He told me he was filling the Outboard Wing Tanks of 120 gallons each as insurance for him and the crew. We were not supposed to use these tanks, as they tended to leak at the fittings from the flexing of the wing and could cause vapors to get into the body of the wing and ignite, causing a catastrophic explosion. Schaeffer assured me that he checked those fittings before and after each flight and found no cause for alarm. I took his word for it and we flew many missions together with no problem.

I-103; 16 pilots of VB-107 - 1943

This photo was probably taken at Ascension Island. Of the 16 officer pilots shown 3 were Pilot Plane Commanders who were credited with destruction of U-Boats. Sam Taylor finished off the U-848; Ed Krug blew the U-863 apart; John Burton had so damaged the 863 that it could not submerge contributing to Ed Krug's subsequent sinking of the U-Boat. Harry had been the navigator pilot on VP-83-10 when, under L. Ludwig as PPC, they destroyed the U-507. Sam Taylor is third from left in back row.

Then it dawned on me, we were carrying an extra 240 gallons of fuel with us on each flight and at six pounds a gallon that was an extra 1,440 pounds the other guys weren't carrying. No wonder we were slow but I decided I liked the "Insurance Factor" and I never told the Flight Officer or the Engineering Officer again about being "SLOW".

Ennui and Gin – Ascension Island

I believe it was sometime in 1943 and six planes of our Squadron were sent to Ascension Island to perform three plane sweeps of the "slot" looking for German blockade runners which were to have left the Far East with strategic war materials for the Third Reich. Somehow our intelligence had provided our A.C.I. officers with the approximate dates of departure from Singapore. We even were told names of the ships…the Burgenland, the Wesserland, and the Alstrufer.

We had a lot of time on our hands and especially in the evenings. The USO Shows never got to Ascension Island and only once to Natal, Brazil. Someone had come up with a gallon of gin and that was before straight gin became a popular drink. We had to do something with it to make it more palatable. Someone came up with a bottle of grape juice and we mixed that with the gin. We called it "PURPLE PASSION PUNCH" The grape juice improved the "looks" but didn't do much for the taste but some of us were brave, including me and Ed Hill, among others. Ed had the "duty" that night but on Ascension Island, who was going to steal anything…they couldn't get anywhere with it. It was basically a formality. I don't think Ed Hill had that much to drink but after he had left on the jeep to make his "rounds" of the field and Quonset Huts we lived in we settled down to some serious drinking. It wasn't too long before Ed Hill staggered in with his uniform all "messed up" and him looking the worst for wear. It seems that the "PURPLE PASSION PUNCH" had a bad effect on our Duty Officer and he had driven our jeep off a low embankment. The jeep could be salvaged and Ed Hill survived and I think he is still alive to this day somewhere near Colt's Neck, New Jersey.

First Encounter with the Wesserland – Blockade Runner

We were operating out of Ascension Island and had been there for some weeks. Things were dull…daily sweeps by three planes trying to intercept German Blockade Runners coming up "the Slot". The "Slot" as it was called was a channel halfway between Brazil and the coast of Africa which German Blockade Runners were supposed to be using to bring strategic supplies back to Germany from the Far East.

Then it started...M.G. Taylor encountered what looked like a British ship headed North up the "Slot". M.G. challenged the ship and the ship hauled up the required four flag hoist to answer the challenge. According to M.G. the hoist had the first two pennants correct, but the bottom two could not be read by the radioman. Every pass by the ship that M.G. made the bottom two flags looked like they were not streaming out properly and could not be read. It turned out the Germans had sewn one comer of the pennant up to one of the top comers so the flag would not "stream" out and be read. MG made the next pass much closer to the ship so the hoist could be read. The ship dropped a false bulkhead which had been hiding a rapid firing gun The "burst" hit and knocked out one of the engines and wounded the waist hatch look-out. MG sent a message and started to "home in" one of the other planes on that "sweep". M.G. was relieved quickly and started back to base and arrived safely on three engines and the wounded man was treated and hospitalized. The Blockade Runner was the German Wesserland and that story ended very soon thereafter for the Wesserland.

(Editorial Note: VB-107-B-2, piloted by Lieutenant Robert T. Johnson, relocated the Wesserland that same afternoon of 1 January, 1944. B-12 was struck by anti-aircraft fire which caused what was thought to be a minor gas leak. Unfortunately, the leak was big enough that B-12 ran out of gas and did not make it back to Ascension. It crashed 71 miles short of Ascension and all hands perished in the ocean.)

Fourth Fleet Ship and Planes Destroy the Wesserland

After the VPB-107 plane piloted by M.G. Taylor encountered the German Blockade Runner later identified as The Wesserland, the Blockade Runner turned 180 degrees and headed south at a speed we estimated at 22 knots. It was a modem motor-ship and capable of sustaining that speed for hours. Meanwhile, our Naval Squadron consisting of the vintage U.S.S. Omaha escorted by two of our most modern destroyers, the U.S.S. Jouett and the U.S.S. Somers was approximately 100 miles North of the Wesserland. At flank speed the Omaha could do 14 knots and we watched as the miles between our Naval Squadron and the enemy got greater and greater each hour of the day.

Our Skipper, Commander Renfro Turner, had the "guts" to signal Admiral Read, the commanding officer of the Squadron, a coded message which asked, "Have You Broken Down"?

My plane had been relieved on station near the Wesserland and had headed north on a set heading to determine if our Naval Squadron was "on track" for the Blockade Runner. Admiral Read had apparently read the message from our Skipper and while I was circling the group, the Somers (a destroyer) was relieved and ordered to proceed independently. The stern of that destroyer set down in the water, the bow came up and the Somers set off at what I estimated to be at least forty (40) knots. One could see the wake for miles and the seas were fluorescent (that is the only way I could describe it).

When the Somers came up on the Wesserland at night. Ed Hill and his crew were "on station" and the Captain of the Blockade Runner refused to "heave to". The Captain of the Somers asked our plane to drop flares behind the Wesserland to silhouette the ship. Ed told us that the destroyer then opened up with their rapid firing five-inch guns. Our plane on station the following morning reported that the Somers had the surviving members of the crew of the Wesserland standing on the fantail under guard of two armed men and the surface of the ocean was covered with barrels of what we guessed was tung oil, a very valuable base for marine paint.

Between our Naval Squadron and VPB- 107, almost all of the Blockade Runners were intercepted and sunk with the exception of one. The Alstrufer, a small German motorship, captained by the son of the famous Captain of the World War 1 Mystery Ship that sunk so many of the Allied merchant ships before being destroyed by Allied Naval ships, escaped by coming North and staying very close to the African Coast. History says the Alstrufer was inside the 100 mile mark.* Apparently he was never challenged as no one thought any German skipper would be that stupid to come that close to "Harm's Way".

*(Editorial Note: The Alstrufer got past Ascension and through the Atlantic Narrows but the RAF caught up to and sank it before it got all the way home. It may be that Count Felix Von Luckner was the World War I Skipper of the "Mystery Ship?")

A Disaster Avoided

We were ready to leave the line with our standard load of eight 340 lb. Torpex Depth Charges and our tanks loaded with fuel for our usual eight to ten hour anti-submarine sweep in the South Atlantic. The Tower gave us the OK to leave the line and proceed to the runway for take-off. I had previously checked the plane on the ground along with my Plane Captain and everything was OK. I checked the sheet with the gas load and everything checked out AOK. We put on the proper setting of the flaps for take-off and the cowl flaps on the engines open to the proper setting, revved up the engines to 2800 RPM and the manifold pressure to the correct range. Everything checked and I released the brakes and we started our run. We had just become airborne when the man in the waist hatch reported that the engines were streaming long trails of flames…almost reaching our tail surfaces. Something was wrong, but we were flying OK.

I called a "MAYDAY" to the tower and got permission to return to the field for an emergency landing. I called for the crew to open the bomb bay doors, asked them to check below to see if there were any native fishermen below, and then dropped my load of depth charges in the South Atlantic. We landed OK and returned to the line. A check of our fuel tanks showed that we had been loaded with thousands of gallons of 60 octane automobile fuel…not the required 100 octane our engines need to function properly. As it turned out…all the gasoline tank trucks were painted in the same green color and there was no way by sight to determine what fuel was aboard. Within a few days all trucks carrying aviation fuel were painted a bright red and the others remained in green. So much for "The Luck of the Irish" and I'm not even Irish.

Every Cloud Must Have a Silver Lining

My two closest friends, Sam Taylor and Mearl Taylor and I were assigned to return three of our old planes to Norfolk and exchange them for the newer models of the Navy version of the B-24 Liberator, the PB4Y-1. This was early in 1944 and we were to have 10 days leave.

Everything went off well…we and our crews checked out in the new aircraft and we were on our way back to Natal and coming in to Trinidad. The base we were to land at was just a few feet above sea level and we could see the island through heavy rain. A huge anvil-shaped cloud was directly in front of us and we either had to go under it or through it. We had been told that this type of cloud formation, common in this area of the world, frequently had tops about 30,000 feet and violent up-drafts could be encountered if one got into them…they were to be avoided if at all possible. Mearl and I decided to go under the cloud formation and flew through torrential rain at about 500 feet above the water. The bottoms of this cloud formation were at about 1,000 feet. Mearl and I landed safely and awaited Sam Taylor.

Sam Taylor elected to go through the clouds entering them at about 1,000 feet. According to Sam, after encountering violent up-drafts he broke out of the clouds at about 12,000 feet with half of his crew passed out from lack of oxygen. I think what saved Sam from the same fate was his large lung capacity. I know this because when we took our Schneider Tests together one time, I recall that his lung capacity was much greater than mine…by about 35 cubic centimeters. We landed safely several days later at Natal and it was determined that Sam's plane was not operational. The violent air drafts they had encountered had actually corrugated the skin of the Davis wing. The wing was bent above the fuselage and it was flyable only with minimum loads. It was going to have to be returned to the aircraft plant and have a new wing installed. The Davis Wing, unlike any other, was built in one piece, all 105 feet of it and then it was bolted down on top of the fuselage. Any other wings were built in two pieces and then fastened to either side of the fuselage.

Our Skipper, Renfro Turner, knowing that I was planning on getting married when our regular summer leave came up, asked me if I would like to fly this stripped down plane back to the States now, in February. I jumped at the chance and wired Lois Marjorie Goranson My bride-to-be, "Could we get married now in February?" That is the SILVER LINING.

Poor Lois, she already had her bridesmaids' gowns…all summer styles and now it was going to be a winter wedding. She worked her way through this problem and the wedding was splendid with Boyce McCoy, my Best Man and Harry Holt and myself in our Dress Blues. Lois' father, Walter Axel Magness Goranson had gone all-out for his youngest daughter. His older daughter had eloped and deprived him of a wedding. The huge Lutheran Church was decorated with flowers, ribbons "to the nines" and it was packed with friends of both our families. The reception was held in the Grand Ballroom of The Edgewater Beach Hotel right on Lake Michigan and known as one of the most elegant hotels in the West. The food was served in the adjacent Marine Dining Room. The wedding with pictures made The Chicago Tribune pages with the heading, and I suppose the Navy Press had something to do with it "Hero Returns to Marry Childhood Sweetheart".

9

HEDRON 16 DETACHMENT AT PARNAMIRIM

Keep them flying.

Unofficial Motto of Hedron Personnel

From December, 1941 until mid-1943 Natal (Parnamirim and the RAMPA seaplane base) was the main focal point and location for the U.S. Navy's aerial anti-submarine forces in Brrazil. During that period Natal had larger numbers of personnel than Recife or any of the advanced bases up and down the coast.

The first squadrons to arrive to Natal (VP-52 and VP-83) were nominally under the operational control of Patrol Wing II. This was before the evolution to Feet Air Wings had occurred.

Fairwing 16 was commissioned at Norfolk, Virginia on 16 February, 1943 and moved to Parnamirim in April, 1943. After a 3 month period at Natal, Captain Lyon moved his headquarters to Recife where the Fourth Fleet headquarters was located.

Earlier in the war the various patrol squadrons were complete self-sustaining units with all the required mechanics and auxiliary services necessary for their maintenance. After about six months, because of the rapid expansion of the air wings, Hedrons were formed to provide all auxiliary services to the various squadrons at each major air facility. Headquarters squadrons contained Aviation Machinists, Ordnance Men, Radiomen, Parachute Packers, Photographers, Aerographers, Storekeepers, Yeomen, and all other needed ratings.

By mid-1943, when I arrived in Brazil, central headquarters for HEDRON was at Recife where Fairwing 16's command staff under Commodore (Captain) Rossmore D. Lyons had his headquarters and where Fourth Fleet headquarters (Admiral Ingram) was located. Most of the enlisted men preferred duty at Natal, Bahia, Fortaleza or Rio so they could be away from headquarters where military regulations were more rigidly enforced. In other words, one had to put up with less C.S. (Navy slang for poultry excrement) at the advanced bases.

The small town atmosphere and fine beaches nearby also made Natal a good place to serve. The presence of a large contingent of USAAF personnel, both permanent base personnel as well as transients, made provision of more support and recreation facilities available. In addition the transient USO shows on their way overseas usually came through Natal on their way to the European, African, or Pacific theatres of war and frequently did not stop over in Recife.

Hedron 16's detachment at Natal was the second largest in number outside Recife headquarters. The next nine photos show some of the Natal personnel and describes some of their activities in support of the operating squadrons.

I-104; Photo Lab Gang

This photo shows five members of the photo lab gang of Hedron 16 at Parnamirim. From left to right sitting are: Dale E. Wright, John R. Harrison (the author); Arthur J. Sykes, R.R. England (Photographers Mate First Class in charge), and the reclining one is Robert Bronner. We didn't have either a CPO or a photographic officer at Parnamirim. It appears that Art Sykes and I are the only ones not "out of uniform". That would not have been tolerated at headquarters in Recife. An ex-officio member of the Photo Lab gang was Billie Goodell of VB-107 who spent a good bit of any free time he had on base at the Photo Lab.

I-105; Photography at Natal

This shows Billie Goodell in front of VB-107-6 (the Sea Beast). Note the Kodak Medalist 620 camera at his belt. That camera was for land use primarily, and Billie's possession of it exemplified his good standing with Photo Lab personnel.

Note the three bombers in the background waiting to be ferried via Ascension Island to Africa and on to Allied forces. The planes are PV-1 Venturas.

Eventually, VB-107 had a photo officer as a member of the squadron.

I-106; Albert J. Harrison with K-20 aerial camera - photo at Parnamirim in 1943

A.J. Harrison, Photographers Mate First Class, holds a Fairchild K-20 aerial camera in photo I-106. For photographing actions during an attack on submarines, the Fairchild K -20 aerial camera was the camera of choice.

The K-20 was an all metal camera which used a roll of 5 inch wide film in a detachable magazine and it was relatively easy to use. In the first 18 months or so of the air war with the use of PBY's , a photographer would usually be included in the crew, both to take any photographs needed and to act as a lookout sitting in the Blister on the side of the PBY. This was also the practice because during that time trained Aviation Machinists Mates, Ordnancemen, and Radiomen were scarce due to the demands of rapid build-up of air crews in the Pacific fleet.

Al was not under 21 years of age like many of my shipmates were during WWII, so he insisted on calling himself "Old Man Harrison". We were not related but he was a good friend. Al's left hand is on the handle which steadied the sturdy all metal camera. On the other side (in his right hand) would be the swiveling handle containing the shutter trigger. That handle also could be moved forward and back to advance the roll film contained in the magazine at the back of the camera. The viewfinder front piece is above and to the left of Al's hand. Over the "Bomber Jacket", Al is wearing his "Mae West" life vest. Fortunately he never had to use the "Mae West", but many of the air crew men did when they were shot down by U-Boat anti-aircraft fire.

ROLE OF PHOTOGRAPHERS MATES EVOLVES

In mid-1943, when the PB4Y's were brought into play and the problem of providing maximum firepower to suppress the antiaircraft fire from U-Boats under attack became extremely important, photographers were replaced by crew members trained in the weaponry. Earlier in the war the U-Boats normally tried to submerge and escape instead of depending more on their ability to shoot down the planes as they later discovered they could. In addition, with a modicum of instructions, the other crew members could be trained in the use of the K-20 camera.

These photographic capabilities were supplemented later by an innovative type of camera mount designed and tested by Lieutenant (jg) George Houchins, a pilot of VP-83. Some of the pilots later mounted a K-20 in the stern of the planes to ensure getting photos. One of the significant problems in aerial photography in a plane powered by reciprocating piston engines is the small vibration ever present throughout the fuselage.

If the person using a camera rests hands or arms on the surface of the plane, the vibration will make the picture fuzzy. George Houchins' camera mount avoided vibration effects and allowed remote control of the camera. Lieutenant Houchins later went to navy photography school at Pensacola and became a photo officer who participated in the subsequent aerial mapping of Greenland. Commander Prueher opined that this was a waste of a very good pilot. Lieutenant Houchins had been a co-pilot in a PBY of VP-83 which attacked and sank the Italian submarine Archimedes off the coast near Natal on 15 April, 1943.

By early 1944, the Navy had developed the concept of specific Combat Photo Units (CPU's) consisting of a trained photographic officer and three enlisted photographers mates. These units included two movie cameramen and one still photographer, though all three could handle both types of equipment. These CPU's were to go either aboard ship, on airplanes, or on invasions, according to the needs of the occasion.

I-107; Combat Photo Unit No. 6 at Natal - 1944

When Mrs. Roosevelt visited Natal in 1944, this CPU no. 6 accompanied her on what was to be a worldwide trip. The names of this group are, left to right; Webster, Burlingame, Techau, and Charette.

Edward Steichen, a prominent pre-war civilian photographer may have fostered the concept of the Combat Photo Unit. Mr. Steichen went into the Pacific Fleet early in the war and was able to make both motion pictures and still photos of battle action.

In addition to the Navy Photo School at Pensacola, Time/Life Magazine Company conducted a training school for military photographers.

The 4 x 5 Speed Graphic, the Graphic View Camera, the Kodak Medalist, and the various Fairchild aeral cameras were widely used still cameras while the Eyemo was the standard movie camera.

I-108; Gathering places for Hedron 16 Personnel

Gathering places for Hedron 16 Personnel: Other than the impromptu games of chance in the barracks, the other three off-duty hangouts for some Hedron or squadron personnel were: the Photo Lab; the ships store; and the Parachute Loft. In photo I-108 we see Eugene Webb and Art Sykes (Photographers Mates) and Charette of the Combat Photo Unit uncorking champagne for a celebration in the Photo Lab.

The three joyful lads in the photo would be joined by Billie Goodell and others from VB-107, Hedron, and the CPU for the ensuing party, all enlisted men, no officers.

I don't believe Mrs. FDR was invited because she would have been busy making the rounds to the officers club, the RAMPA and the USAAF facilities. There would also have been obligatory visits to Natal officials and Brazilian officials at Parnamirim.

I-109; Celebrating New Ships Store Natal - 1944

Celebrating the New Ship's Store: The new ships store (early 1944) at Natal was greeted with enthusiasm as we see in photo I-109. Here we see seven members of the Natal Photo Lab gang helping open the new ships store. In back is; Eugene Webb, and in front is C. Connery. Left to right in center are; J. R. Harrison, D.E. Wright, W.B. McKeehen, Art Sykes, and R. Bronner.

One interesting long lasting outcome of World War II has been the ever increasing popularity of blue jean trousers throughout the USA and the world. In the navy they were the standard work a day uniform for enlisted men but at that time they were called dungarees rather than blue jeans. Note in the latter photo of navy photographers the first evidence of "cut-off" jeans worn by Bill McKeehen in the center of the photograph. Young sailors were always trying to act "salty" as if they were well experienced in naval service and one way to do this was to wear dungarees (blue jeans) which were as bleached out as possible. This was easy to accomplish in Brazil because the sailors had their clothes washed by Brazilian Ropa women. The Ropa (clothing) women used to take them to a nearby stream and the washing procedure involved beating the wet clothes on rocks in the water. This greatly facilitated achieving a lighter bleached look on the jeans. The modern day teenager and younger people in general probably have no inkling that in wearing "distressed" blue jeans they are following the fashions of their grandfathers. Nor do they realize that many of the less than respectable terms they use (like pissed off or shacking up) are old navy barracks room language.

I-110; Hedron's Parachute Loft

As we see in photo I-110 the Loft was a roomy area so it also served as a gathering place for off-duty personnel. To the left of the improvised hot plate grill is a sewing machine used in repairing parachutes. It was also used to fabricate "Parachute Bag" type luggage from heavy gray canvas cloth. These loft made bags were equipped with heavy fabric handles for carrying purpose as a replacement for navy issue sea bags. Charles Sirignano is the one making toast. On the right is Art Sykes with a sandwich in one hand and a coffee mug in the other. The long table on which Art is sitting was utilized in packing chutes.

I-111; Chief Petty Officers of Hedron 16 at Natal

This photo, I-111, which I took in late 1943, shows the six CPO's of Hedron 16 right after some formal ceremony. Most of the CPO's at that time were "Regular Navy" (not reservists) who had been in service several years before the war. They really ran things and were the first and most competent line of management. Note the two hash marks denoting eight years of prior naval service on several of the CPO's sleeves.

I-112; Officers of Hedron 16 at Natal

The odds are that these gentlemen in photo no. I-112 were all “90 Day Wonders” who had either college educations or had some sort of jobs requiring leadership skills in civilian life or had academic grades in school which got them into Officers Candidate School (OCS). The 90 day comment refers to the length of training most would have received before being commissioned as officers in the Naval Reserve. Their best hope for success was to have a good crop of experienced CPO’s to lean on.

I-113; Doctors and Medics at Parnamirim: 1943

This photo (courtesy of Billie Goodell) appears to be the Naval medical staff of Hedron 16 at Parnamirim; doctors and pharmacists mates (chancre mechanics).

For the first 12 to 18 months of the war these gentlemen were very busy dealing with cases of venereal disease. Noting the toll that their local brothels were having on the health of the U.S. military personnel, the military officials and the local government cooperated in efforts to minimize this problem.

Cooperative supervision of the health of the local "Ladies of the Night" was initiated to supplement earlier warnings by indoctrination films and lectures.

Both at Natal and Recife the authorities had done fine on mosquito control so we did not to use mosquito netting and malaria was not a threat. That may not have been true at other bases.

I-114; Pets at Parnamirim - 1944

In addition to the occasional monkey, sailors sometimes adopted puppies like this one being held in this photo by a Chief Petty Officer. One sailor bought a horse which turned out to be too old and decrepit for riding very much.

10

Distinguished Visitors to Natal

A clean sweep down, fore and aft

Standard Order Before Inspections

Whenever a military base is about to receive distinguished visitors, either from high ranking officers or notable civilian officials, feverish sprucing up of the base and personnel occurs. Because it had become the "Crossroads of the World", visits to Natal by dignitaries of high rank were frequent.

PRESIDENT ROOSEVELT AT NATAL

One of the most notable visits occurred on January 28, 1943 when FDR arrived in Natal on his way back from the Casablanca conference with Winston Churchill. FDR had notified President Vargas about his itinerary via Natal so the two leaders seized the opportunity to meet again. At this meeting President Vargas agreed to send 3 divisions of Brazilian Infantry and a fighter plane squadron to the European theater of war.

Field Marshall Kesselrings' skillful use of the mountainous terrain in Italy enabled the Germans to make the advance of the Allied armies very costly in casualties, materials, and time. Brazil's contribution of infantry and a fighter squadron particularly adept at supporting infantry efforts was to prove very helpful in the Italian campaign.

The contribution of the Brazilians to the Italian campaign as well as their excellent cooperation in the anti-submarine and Ferry Command work would not have happened without the diplomatic efforts by FDR and by Admiral Ingram over the years preceding Brazil's entry into the war.

The U.S. Navy and Brazilian Navy officers had become friendly during World War I and that ongoing relationship had been greatly strengthened between the wars, particularly by the efforts of Admiral Ingram. At this time the Allies were more confident since the Battle of Stalingrad had just finished and the German Wehrmacht had thereby been shown to be vincible in the struggle with the Red Army. All of the fatally flawed battlefield meddling by Hitler had finally taken a fearsome toll on the German led forces.

The battlefield weakness of the Romanian and Italian divisions on the Russian front had become apparent during the Battle of Stalingrad. The willingness of the Red Army to sacrifice many lives for the defense of Stalingrad on a house by house basis signalled a dramatic change in the results of the German efforts in the Soviet Union. Nonetheless several substantial military conflicts were still to be fought.

One of the more difficult European theatre campaigns to come later was the struggle by the Allies up the Italian peninsula to oust some of the best German divisions from Italy. Both the Brazilian fighter squadron and Brazilian infantry division took active roles in the Italian campaign.

The three following photographs commemorate the meetings of heads of state at Natal.

I-115; Jovial in a Jeep

Clear evidence of the good personal relationship between President Vargas and FDR and Admiral Ingram is obvious in the relaxed demeanor of all present in this photo of the group in a jeep next to the Pan Air do Brasil Archway building at the RAMPA.

I-116; Meeting on the Humboldt

In January, 1943, the RAMPA base still had limited and rudimentary facilities for entertaining dignitaries so most of the discussions were held on the U.S.S. Humboldt, a seaplane tender anchored in the Potengi River. In photo I-116 we see, from left to right, Harry Hopkins (special assistant to FDR), President Getulio Vargas, FDR, and Jefferson Caffrey (U.S. ambassador to Brazil), all seated. Standing are Rear Admiral Ross McIntire, Brigadier General Robert L. Walsh (USAAF), Rear Admiral Jonas H. Ingram, and Rear Admiral A.I. Beauregard.

I-117; Birthday Cake on a Boeing 314 Clipper

FDR's sixtieth birthday came as he was on his Casablanca trip. By January of 1943 a Pan Am Boeing Clipper was available to the President. In photo I-117 we see him about to serve his birthday cake to his entourage. These photos show that in early 1943 FDR seemed to be in good health. Unfortunately, the stress of two more years of war and atrociously poor medical care would find his life ended a short 2 plus years later.

MRS. FRANKLIN DELANO ROOSEVELT AT NATAL

Eleanor Roosevelt, in the early phase of the worldwide tour, came to Natal in March of 1944, she was on her way to Africa, the Middle East, and the Pacific theatre of war. She would make overnight stops along the way to visit with Allied forces.

From Natal, Mrs. FDR and her entourage went on to Recife and points beyond. Since the ground transportation system between Natal and Recife was not adequate at that time one of the VB-107's PB4Y's was fitted out especially with bathroom facilities for tranport of Mrs.. FDR.

Captain Rossmore D. Lyon, Commander of Fleet Air Wing 16 reads comments introducing the first lady. Note the news reel cameraman on the right in to the photo.

The following 3 photos also were made during Mrs. FDR's visit to Natal.

I-118; Commodore Lyon Introducing Mrs. FDR

I-119; Pinning the DFC on Lieutenant Sam Taylor

Note the intense expression on Eleanor Roosevelt's face in photo I-119. At that time Mrs. FDR was filing daily stories to the U.S. press describing her activities.

After this medal pinning adventure she noted how difficult it was to get the medal pin through those navy whites.

When I managed to get a copy of this photo carried back to my mother a few weeks later she was able to deduce that I was at Natal because she had read Eleanor Roosevelt's column in which she had described being at Natal and the difficulty she had in pinning on medals.

In the background on the right are the musicians of Admiral Ingram's Fourth Fleet Band from Recife.

On the left in the background by the nose hanger, a portion of the hundreds of officers and men of Fleet Air Wing 16 are lined up.

I-120; Mrs. FDR with Officers

As expected, the top brass from Recife headquarters was on hand to greet Mrs. FDR. In this photo we see an Admiral (Read?), a navy Lieutenant and Brigadier General Walsh of the USAAF. Note the Southern Cross emblem on General Walsh's shoulder.

I-121; Mrs. FDR and Female Entourage

The female officer on the right in this photo is either of the USAAF or the U.S. Army. The younger lady may well be with the Red Cross. Presumably, the lady to Eleanor Roosevelt's left is a traveling companion. Note Mrs. FDR's "pilgrim" shoes.

HISTORICAL NOTES ABOUT ELEANOR ROOSEVELT AND FDR

Eleanor Roosevelt was a "Woman of Substance" who played a significant role in her husbands' life, in World War II; and in national affairs in subsequent years. Many of her contributions were positive and she was generally revered.

However, all serious students of history need to note that her comprehension of geopolitics and the relative merits of various governments and leaders around the world was seriously naïve and constituted a great threat to the national interests of the people of the USA and the free world (and to the general populace of the Soviet Union). The most graphic evidence of her naiveté was her total misunderstanding of the character and purposes of Joseph Stalin and the Russian Communist Party, the leaders of the Soviet Union. Like most Americans she equated Russia with the Soviet Union instead of realizing that the Soviet Union was an imperialistic continental empire which was started by Catherine the Great and greatly expanded by the Russian Communists after World War I. The Soviet Union was created by the force of arms. The two million members of the Communist Party ruled over the total population of one hundred ninety million citizens of the Soviet Union. The communists had become the "New Aristocracy".

To understand these comments the reader is referred to passages in the excellent biography of Harry Truman by David McCullough (Reference 13). In that work the story is related of how Eleanor Roosevelt tried mightily to have Henry Wallace (a "fellow traveler" of the Communists) placed on the Democratic ticket as Vice President in 1944. Had Mrs. FDR succeeded we would have had Henry Wallace succeeding FDR in April 1945. Mr. Wallace was campaigning for the USA to provide Marshall Plan type aid to the Soviet Union after the conclusion of World War II which would have hampered our ability to provide such aid to our Western European allies. Eleanor Roosevelt falsely envisioned the most savage mass murderer of all recorded history, Joseph Stalin, as Uncle Joe. FDR also referred to him as Uncle Joe. The following quote from Reference 13 shows how oblivious Henry Wallace was to the real nature of Stalin and the Soviet Union.

> "Nothing better symbolized the blind eye that the Western Powers now turned to Stalin's crimes than the American Vice President Henry Wallace's visit to the Kolyma Gulag (in Russia) in May 1944. "No other two countries are more alike than the Soviet Union and the United States", he told his hosts. He added, "Both the Russians and the Americans, in their different ways, are groping for a way of life that will enable the common man everywhere in the world to get the most good out of modern technology. There is nothing irreconcilable in our aims and purposes."

How's that for the Fellow Traveler philosophy? Fortunately, by dint of back stage political maneuvering, other Democrat party leaders (mostly heads of labor unions) successfully opposed Mrs. FDR's efforts and a truly bona fide American hero, Harry Truman, was nominated as Vice President in 1944. As a result, President Truman courageously led our nation through the critical last 4 months of the war and the first 7 years of the Cold War. He had to overcome the gross errors made by FDR who in his last year of life also seriously misunderstood the character and motives of Joseph Stalin and the Communists. FDR was, unfortunately, a dying man with diminished capacities from mid-1944 until his death. He worked himself to a premature death in service to his country.

The tragic final year of FDR's life does not seriously degrade his place in history as a great president. Even though FDR's New Deal had flaws and did not get us out of the depression (the 1937 Depression occurred 5 years after he was in office), he did correct some of the defects of what Edward Heath - Prime Minister of Britain - rightly labelled "The unacceptable face of unbridled capitalism". It is difficult, if not impossible; to envision the great will and strength of character he exhibited in overcoming the crushing physical disease which he endured while still in the prime of life and until his passing. Literally, he became a casualty of war just as much as any serviceman killed in battle. He had his faults but they were miniscule compared to his valiant service to his country and to the world.

THE COMMODORE OF FAIRWING 16

Captain Rossmore Denham Lyon (the Commodore) came to Natal frequently and he was always greeted with enthusiasm. He was a popular commander because he followed policies favorable to all under his command. The Commodore was a pioneer in Naval Aviation who had worked his way up through the ranks which probably explains his compassionate approach to enlisted men as well as officers.

The following thumbnail sketch of the Commodore's distinguished career is an excerpt from "The Command History of FAW 16".

Captain Rossmore D. Lyon, USN 38766

Captain Rossmore D. Lyon, former Commanding Officer of the Naval Air Station at Corpus Christi, Texas was ordered to duty as skipper of Fleet Air Wing Sixteen at the Wing's inception February 16, 1943 and he has held that position up to the present time (December 31, 1944). Captain Lyon's previous Navy career has amply qualified him for this assignment.

A native of Poughkeepsie, New York, where he was born in 1895, he has been in the Navy and naval aviation since 1917. In that year he joined the National Volunteers of New York State, the first aero-division in the United States Navy. This volunteer group, who were checked out in seaplanes known as F-boats, were trained in Riverview Academy in Poughkeepsie, later in Tarrytown, New York and Bay Shore, Long Island, where the Navy took over from a Yale Unit training there.

Two years later Captain Lyon was an instructor in aerial gunnery, after tours of duty in Key West, Florida, and the Massachusetts Institute of Technology (where he attended a Ground School for Flight Training) he returned to Pensacola. After another brief tour of duty in Key West, he became an Inspector of Recruiting operating out of Chicago, covering the territory contained in the triangular area of which Omaha, Detroit, and Memphis are the apexes. In 1920, he reported for duty at San Diego where he took an active part in the development of aviation in connection with Fleet operations. During his tour of duty at San Diego he participated in a mass flight to Panama. Then, after being commissioned as Ensign, was transferred in 1921 to Pensacola where he was Assistant Superintendent of Flight Training. He remained at Pensacola until 1923.

When the Navy-planned expedition to the North Pole via Spitzbergen failed to materialize, Captain Lyon, then a senior grade Lieutenant, was then ordered to the U.S.S. Langley, which was engaged in cold weather maneuvers at Anacostia. Here he set a world record by remaining aloft in an airplane for 21 hours and 10 minutes. He did this in 1924 in a single engine seaplane just before being assigned to the Langley which was commissioned as the first aircraft carrier in 1924. The first carrier to participate in Fleet Operations, it cruised in 1925 to Hawaii, operating then out of Pearl Harbor. Here Captain Lyon learned the newly devised technique of carrier deck take-off, night landings, catapult shots and other procedures then in an experimental status. He left the USS Langley in 1927 to report for duty at Camden, New Jersey where the USS Saratoga was being fitted out and commissioned. While assigned to this ship he witnessed the abortive attempt of the dirigible Los Angles to land on the carrier.

In 1928, he returned to Pensacola as a squadron commander and officer in charge of Cory field where his men were checked out in such land based planes as N3Ns. Three years later he reported to VS1 at Norfolk as Squadron Commander. From 1931 to 1933 he was again assigned to the Langley. Meanwhile, in 1931 he was married in Richmond, Virginia.

In 1933, he went to Pearl Harbor as Commanding Officer of VP-6. Two years after this he was transferred to a VOS squadron, the observation unit of the Third Division of the Fleet, consisting of the battleships Idaho, Mississippi, and New Mexico. At this time seaplanes were landed near ships for the first time in maneuvers.

In 1936, Captain Lyon was Assistant Air Officer on the U.S.S. Yorktown, and then two years later squadron commander of VP-11, stationed at San Diego. He cruised to Alaska and made a non-stop flight to Panama. In 1938 he once more became Officer-in-Charge of Cory Field at Pensacola at the time when several new landing fields were being developed. In 1940 he left to report to the new Air Station at Corpus Christi as Executive Officer and was instrumental in getting the station established and in operation as a training base. After serving as the acting Commandant, he became the Commanding Officer of NAS Corpus Christi, retaining the position until February 1943, when he was ordered to set up Fleet Air Wing Sixteen and take command of that unit as it was being formed to go to Brazil.

(Editorial Note: The Commodore proved to be an inspirational leader as the record of Fairwing 16 demonstrates.)

ADMIRAL INGRAM AT NATAL

Admiral Ingram came to Natal in October, 1943 (Navy Day) to formally present medals to Thurman Robertson and Gerald Bradford and their air crews for the destruction of the Italian submarine, the Archimedes on April 15th of 1943. In photo I-122 we see the Admiral addressing the assemblage. The group on the platform includes Eduardo Gomes of the Brazilian Air Force; he is directly behind Admiral Ingram. General Gomes was instrumental in having John Buyers appointed as liaison officer to help form and train the Brazilian Air Force Squadron which would later serve with great distinction In the Italian campaign.

Reflections about Admiral Ingram

While we give credit to the Commodore it should be noted that Admiral Ingram was also the well liked commander of the Fourth Fleet and its air arm who gave the Commodore the latitude to promulgate the morale boosting personnel policies previously noted.

One of Billie Goodell's anecdotes on the immediate aftermath of VP-83's destruction of the U-164 (The First Kill) is illustrative of the enthusiasm and verve of the Admiral. Admiral Ingram had also carried out a very successful cooperative effort with our Brazilian counterparts and much of the success of the Fourth Fleet and its air arm (FAW 16) can be traced to the Admiral's executive ability. His performance was acknowledged when he was promoted to Commander in Chief Atlantic Fleet (CINCLANT) in the latter days of the war. In photo I-123 we see him meeting with the Secretary of the Navy (James Forrestal) and Fleet Admiral Ernest J. King, Chief of Naval Operations.

A Life of Distinguished Service

Even before World War II, Jonas H. Ingram had performed exceptionally well in his lengthy career as a leader of men in the U.S. Navy. From his entry into the Naval Academy at Annapolis in 1903 until he retired in 1947, his record of service was most impressive.

After graduation in 1907, Ingram went to sea on several battleships, cruisers, and destroyers over a seven year period. On April 22, 1914 he was the Gun Turret Officer on the Battleship USS Arkansas as it engaged in an attack on Vera Cruz, Mexico during the Mexican Revolution. During that action he established a record for firing rate by the 12 inch guns of a battleship. As a result he was awarded a Congressional Medal of Honor, our nation's highest military decoration.

After serving as head football coach at the Naval Academy from 1915 to 1917, he was posted to the staff of Rear Admiral Hugh Rodman who commanded Division Nine, Battle Force, Atlantic Fleet. This work gave Ingram some valuable experience in the anti-submarine warfare of World War I.

By 1924, he had achieved the rank of Commander and became the commanding officer of a destroyer, the Stoddert. From 1926 to 1930 he was Athletic Director and Head Football Coach at the Naval Academy where he had previously starred as an outstanding player during his academic career. It was in 1926 that he is reputed to have made the following observation, "The Navy had no place for good losers! The Navy needs tough sons of bitches who can go out there and win." Later, in World War II, he repeated this philosophical insight to the men of the Fourth Fleet and Fairwing 16.

Ingram then became commanding officer of the Battleship Pennsylvania for a period of time followed by service as Officer-in-Charge of the public relations branch. This latter assignment was an indication of his communication skills which were to serve him so well in developing his subsequent rapport with Getulio Vargas and the Brazilian Armed Forces in World War II.

By 1935, after being an aide to the Secretary of the Navy, Ingram was promoted to Captain and returned to sea as Commander of Destroyer Squadron Six and then the Battleship Tennessee.
On January 10, 1941 Ingram was promoted to Rear Admiral in charge of Task Force Three prior to his designation as Commander South Atlantic Force, U.S. Atlantic Fleet, with the rank of Vice-Admiral. This force was based in Brazil.

In addition to developing these forces to successfully counteract and destroy Axis Power U-Boats, surface raiders and blockade runners, Ingram led the effort to equip and train Brazilian Navy Units.

On November 15, 1944, he was designated as Commander-in-Chief, U.S. Atlantic Fleet and directed the containment and destruction of Axis Power naval units throughout both the North and South Atlantic.

I-122; Admiral Ingram at Natal October, 1943

Admirial Ingram at Natal - October, 1943: The U.S. Naval officers on the left side of the platform are both wearing fourragere braid on their left sides denoting membership on Admiral Ingrams Fourth Fleet Staff. To the right of them is a Brazilian Aviator. At this ceremony six awards were made on a typical sunny day at Parnamirim. Brazilian Air Force General Eduardo Gomes sits in back of Admiral Ingram.

I-123; Admirals King and Ingram with James Forrestal

This photo was probably taken in Washington, DC at the time when Admiral Ingram was being promoted to Commander - in - Chief of the Atlantic Fleet. Admiral Ernest J. King was Chief of Naval Operations throughout World War II. He very clearly was successful in selecting his Admirals. Picking C.W. Nimitz for Commander - in Chief of the Pacific Fleet also proved an excellent choice.

Ascension Island - An Important Allied Air Base

Build an airstrip on a volcano? Impracticable if not impossible!

British Authorities

THE STRATEGIC ROCK

Prior to 1942, Ascension, a British possession, was best known as a small rocky place favored by sea turtles and large birds which nested there and deposited large amounts of guano (excrement with a high nitrate content). The few people (200 or so), who inhabited this 35 square mile island recovered and processed the guano which was sold as a fertilizer.

The Allied forces had three significant reasons to build air base facilities on Ascension Island. As a perusal of a map of the South Atlantic ocean reveals, Ascension is roughly half way between the northeast coast of Brazil and Africa. It was clearly in a strategic location.

The U.S. Army Air Force (USAAF) had the difficult task of ferrying thousands of airplanes carrying personnel and military supplies to the European, Mediterranean, and Far Eastern theatres of war. It was a daunting task because of the limited range of many of the planes involved as well as the relative inexperience of many of the Ferry Command pilots. An airport at Ascension was very much needed by the USAAF. The lament of Ferry Command pilots was to become, “If we don’t hit Ascension, my wife gets a pension.”

Fairwing 16 and its Brazilian allies also needed an advanced base at Ascension to close the mid-ocean convoy coverage gap which existed because even the new PB4Y’s arriving in 1943 still did not have enough range to close that gap while flying solely out of Brazil or out of African bases. This problem was sadly illustrated by the loss of 107-B-1 and Commander Prueher and his crew. The third reason for making Ascension Island a real military base with available air power there was the fear during the 1940-42 period that the Axis Powers would seize the island and convert it to a military base for their purposes. The island, a British possession, remained essentially undefended until late in 1941. Minimal efforts to provide a military garrison presence and defensive artillery commenced in mid and late 1941. As a result there was a real scare in December, 1941 when a force of 500 armed survivors of a sunken German surface raider (an armed and disguised merchant ship) accompanied by four U-Boats were in the general area and were in position to possibly invade and occupy Ascension Island. Indeed, in early December, 1941, the U-124 surfaced off Ascension and was preparing to shell the island but it was driven off by fire from on-shore defensive cannon.

Finally acting firmly against the threat, the British Royal Navy sent some cruisers with escorts and moved three infantry companies to Ascension. This served to protect the small HF/DF (Huff Duff) direction finding installations the British had installed in 1940. Once the German Enigma code was broken, these and other facilities enabled the station at Ascension to monitor the radio traffic between the U-Boats and Axis surface vessels so they knew where those forces were during the course of the war.

IMPRACTICALITY IS OVERCOME

The attitude of the British engineers on the possibility of building an air base on Ascension is aptly depicted in the sentence below the title of this chapter. However after much discussion, they permitted the U.S. Army Corps of Engineers (USACE) to construct an air strip on Ascension in the May-July period of 1942. Photo I-124, shows how the air strip was squeezed in between the volcanic hills on Ascension Island.

I-124; Aerial View - Ascension Island

Aerial view of Ascension Island - 1944: this photo was taken when the island was at its peak use. It shows how the runway appears to have a "crowned" contour with the lengthwise center being higher than the edges. This must have been done to insure drainage.

In August of 1942, three PBY5B's of VP-83 operated successfully out of Ascension for several weeks. Their presence on Ascension was important due to the concern about a vital convoy then going across the South Atlantic carrying many Sherman tanks and artillery pieces urgently needed by General Montgomery who was trying to keep the Afrika Korps from advancing toward the Suez Canal. The convoy got through, the Afrika Korps was later defeated at El Alamein, and Churchill finally got a much needed victory after many defeats. For some unknown reason the PBY's left Ascension in September, 1942 and did not return. A full year would again elapse before some of VB-107's planes would be sent to Ascension.

WATER AND SUPPLY PROBLEMS

In addition to the inhospitable and difficult topography and geologic structure of Ascension Island there was a distinct lack of water resources and vegetation. The only original source of water was from the condensation of clouds on the top of the 2,800 foot peak of Green Mountain which had only a thin layer of soil and meager vegetation. Later on, the Americans brought in distillation type desalination units to provide a barely acceptable level of water availability. Even in mid 1943 the weekly water ration was only 5 gallons per week per man for all purposes.

Photo I-125, (from Reference 3) shows a U.S. soldier au naturel attempting to bath from a basin. Photo I-126 (from Ed Krug) shows Danny Diebler (a VB-107 pilot) shaving while M.G. Taylor observes his water usage technique. By the time VB-107 got to Ascension in the fall of 1943, a bit more water distillation capacity had been provided.

Another difficulty at Ascension was that it did not have a natural harbor and getting seaborne supplies required anchoring offshore and "lightering" in materials via small vessels. Eventually an 1,100 foot pipeline was put in position on the sea bottom to allow facile delivery of petroleum products from tankers anchored offshore. It might have been that the USAAF needed all the water, fuel, and other supplies then available at Ascension and this precluded further anti-submarine flights from the island by Fairwing 16 until October, 1943?

The fortification and usage of Ascension Island was not publicized until late 1943 for strategic reasons. An article was published in December, 1943 and it spelled out the importance of Ascension to the Allied forces. As the reader will note not all the information in the news article was correct since the air strip was in operation in July, 1942, not 1943.

Wartime Publicity About Ascension

On December 29, 1943 the Associated Press (AP) distributed a news article about Ascension Island. The title of this press release noted that this tiny island was playing a significant role in the strategy of "Air War".

The AP story emphasized that the USAAF Ferry Command was using Ascension Island as a vital link in the chain of air bases from the USA via South America and the west coast of Africa to the various theatres of war. It claimed that 5,000 planes had taken the route which passed through Ascension.

During the previous April, the USAAF had stated that Lockheed Lightning P-38 fighter planes were able to cross from South America to Africa under their own power once the Ascension Air Base became operational. Previously only larger planes could make the non-stop flight from South America directly to Africa.

According to AP's report, construction of Wide Awake field on Ascension was started March 30, 1943 by the USACE. It was a difficult job because of the huge amounts of volcanic rock which had to be broken up and moved.

Like many stories in the press during wartime, erroneous items were included, either by design or by accident.

Wideawake Field was built in 1942, not 1943 as reported in the war department's press lease to AP on December 29, 1943. During August, 1942 three PBY's of VP-83 operated out of Wideawake field on Ascension. The PBY's provided protection for several convoys. One of the convoys was carrying a cargo of tanks and artillery shells to the British Eighth Army in North Africa that was preparing for the Battle of El Alamein.

The AP report went on the note that the large flocks of Sooty Terns (Wideawakes) on Ascension were a problem for air traffic. A large number of cats were brought to Ascension to help eliminate some of the birds. The AP story claimed that this tactic did not work as the birds ate the cats. Actually, according to current information, the cats were not eradicated and succeeding feline progeny (Feral cats) have and continue to be a problem in maintaining bird populations on Ascension. Importation of cats to Ascension has been forbidden for decades so that the bird population will no longer be threatened.

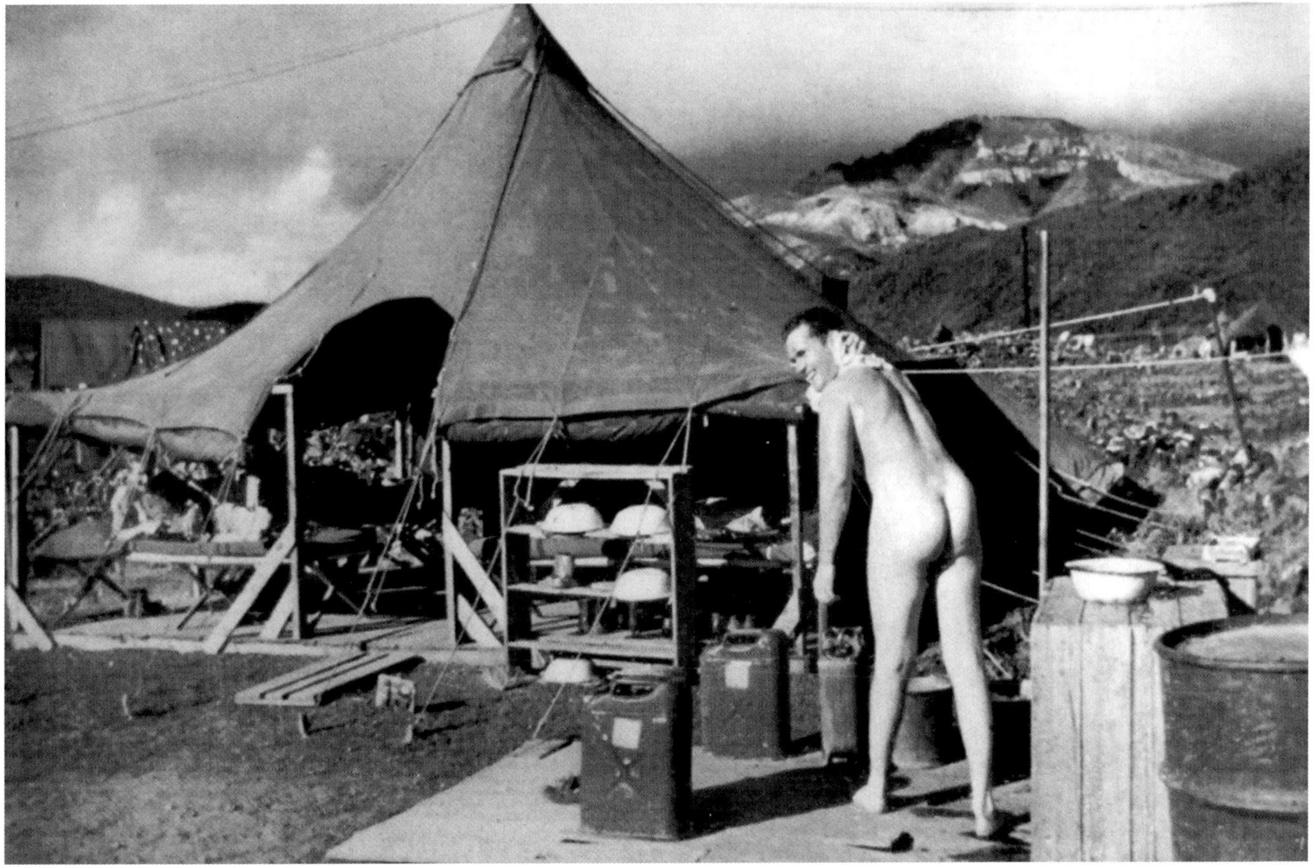

I-125; Soldier Au Naturel - Bathing (Reference 5)

I-126; Dan Diebler and Mearl Taylor

The degree of hardship felt by the USAAF soldiers was undoubtedly significant. However, 5 gallons of water per week per individual for all purposes mandated the practice of a spartan sponge bath, probably once per week.

For former city dwellers accustomed to copious supplies of hot water and more frequent baths or showers this would have been irksome.

For a country boy whose hot water for his once per week bath (whether he needed it or not) was carried in pots from the black iron kitchen stove up to the bath tub in a bed room, this would not seem to be such a great hardship. At least at Ascension he did not have to light a small portable kerosene heater in a normally unheated bedroom in order to keep warm as he stepped out of the bath at home.

Fairwing 16 pilots shaving: even though most of VB-107's men were in their 20's, shaving practically every day was a necessity. Beards were not permitted and practically no one used an electric razor. As a result, water use for shaving consumed a chunk of the 5 gallon per week supply. Perhaps Dan Diebler had a low water use technique as observed by Mearl Taylor?

The Laconia Incident

USAAF planes from Ascension were involved in this famous (or infamous) occurrence near the island in September, 1942.

A U-Boat (U-156) had sunk an ocean liner (The Laconia) which was carrying 1800 Italian prisoners of war as well as Polish soldiers acting as guards and some British women and children. As a result most of the passengers were soon in lifeboats about 250 miles from Ascension.

The U-507 surfaced and took some of the lifeboats in tow. Two other U-Boats (506 and 507) were summoned by U-507's captain to help in the rescue effort. Allied forces on Ascension were aware of the U-Boats efforts to rescue the survivors but typically in the "Fog of War" they did not restrain USAAF B-24s from attacking the three U-Boats involved in the rescue effort. The U-Boats broke off their rescue attempts and escaped.

In view of this incident Admiral Doenitz issued an order that from then on the U-Boats should not attempt to rescue survivors of U-Boat attacks or aid survivors in any way. After the war this Laconia order by Admiral Doenitz was used as primary evidence against him at the Nuremburg trials. This evidence was used despite the fact that Admiral Nimitz orders to the Pacific Fleet were the same about not aiding survivors.

In any event, as noted herein, the FAW 16 Squadrons and many other US Naval forces usually did rescue survivors.

RENTAL ARRANGEMENTS

For the privilege of using Ascension Island the British Government charged the U.S. Forces a landing fee and a takeoff fee for every plane passing through, even for those planes which we were giving, gratis, to the British Armed Forces. Since 25,000 planes were to transit Ascension this was lucrative for the British

FAIRWING 16 AT ASCENSION ISLAND

Due to successes of the anti-submarine sweeps by both Fairwing 16 and the Brazilian air forces off the coast of Brazil, Admiral Doenitz moved most of his U-Boats away from the close-by coast more toward Africa in the latter part of the summer of 1943. This prompted Fairwing 16 to consider further basing of anti-submarine aircraft on Ascension Island. There was also a need to intercept Axis blockade runners which transited nearer Ascension.

Air strip capability and support facilities at Ascension Island had been expanded to the point that by September 1943, the decision was made to move a detachment of Fairwing 16 patrol bombers to that rocky island. This extended the coverage range for the planes. This move was greeted with mixed emotions by the PB4Y Liberator air crews. They realized the military advantages but also missed the friendly confines of Natal and Recife. There were no Wonderbars or Estrela de Pratas (Silver Stars) on the desolate island know as "The Rock" by U.S. personnel. However, there were many worse places to be based. In keeping with the enlightened policies of the Fourth fleet, the various air crews and planes of VB-107 rotated periodically in and out of Ascension. Photo I-127 shows Ascension Island personnel of VB-107 on one occasion.

I first became really aware of Ascension Island in late August, 1943. A group of five photographers (including me) who had been shipped from Fleet Air Wing 9 at Quonset Point in June, 1943 were serving at Recife and living in tents because Ibura field had not yet been updated with barracks. Four of us were just getting ready to leave our tent from lunch break to go back to the Photo Lab when Jim Tracy, Photographers Mate First Class, came in with a message. He said the four of us were to draw straws to see which one of us was going to draw the short draw and thereby be selected to go to Ascension Island to set up a Photo Lab and become the solo resident photographer there. None of us trusted Jim Tracy and we insisted that we all go back to Ibura Photo Lab to do the drawing of straws in front of the resident Chief Photographers Mate. Sure enough, when we got to the lab we found that Jim Tracy was supposed to be included in the drawing of the straws and thus a potential transferee to Ascension. Unfortunately, Billy Rodman, instead of Tracy, drew the short straw. Apparently it wasn't such a bad assignment for Bill Rodman for two reasons. Firstly he liked the personal freedom to run his own lab and secondarily it helped him keep up his almost daily correspondence with his lady friend, Johanna, who became his wife after the war. His letters from Ascension were always cheery.

Ascension Island Today

Since World War II, Ascension has been used for various purposes by the British government, the U.S. Air Force, NASA and communication companies. The Falklands war prompted the British into expanding facilities on the island. Today it has a population of 1100, and is important to British and U.S. military forces.

I-127; VB-107 Personnel on Ascension

VB-107 personnel on Ascension Island: This photo of VB-107 pilots and air crewmen was taken in late 1943. In the second row (standing) are 19 pilots and 2 air crewmen. Third from left is Stan Shedakar-AMM1/c. Fourth from left is Zoom Pinnell, Ninth from right is Sam Taylor - one pilot is missing.

12

Fernando de Noronha
Advanced Base of Fairwing 16

It extends operating range by 200 miles out and 200 miles back.

Headquarter's rationale for this base

A THIRTY-DAY EXILE

In January, 1944 the author was sent from Natal to Fernando de Noronha, an island archipelago some 200 miles out in the Atlantic from Natal for a 30 day tour of duty. The air strip was on the Ilha Fernando de Noronha, the main island. Prior to the construction of a U.S. Navy/ Brazilian air field, the main island had served as a prison colony. The Brazilian Army had a significant detachment on Fernando. In photo I-128 we see a large number of Brazilian troops, as well as civilians and U.S. Navy sailors. The U.S. Navy used Fernando as an advanced base and as a potential emergency air field for crippled planes, either for navy planes shot up by submarines or Ferry Command planes experiencing problems. The island base also enabled extending the range of planes like the Lockheed PV-1 Ventura so they might make lengthier sweeps eastward toward Africa in the Atlantic Narrows.

Photo I-129 is one which I took with a K-20 aerial camera during a patrol flight out of Fernando de Noronha. The main island, though small, had sufficient space for an airstrip and base. It also had a few hills as we see in photo I-130 of a morning muster of Fairwing 16. (Photo courtesy of Dr. Clyde Smith, Jr.)

Every few days a PV-1 would fly out of Natal to Fernando carrying freight, mail and or transferees. The end of the runway was at an escarpment with a steep cliff-like fall off down to the ocean. One pilot liked to approach the island at high speed just above the ocean and well below the sight line of the control tower or sailors at the field. He would then zoom up steeply and appear suddenly over the end of the runway, scaring the daylights out of onlookers.The air strip and water treatment facilities appear in photo I-131.

(Photo from Dr. Clyde Smith, Jr., Reference 16) Understandably, most personnel of Fairwing 16 preferred duty at Natal, Fortaleza, Recife, Bahia, or Rio rather than Fernando.

During my stay on Fernando I was puzzled by the fact that even though it had served as a prison there did not seem to be any large prison buildings. We learned later that prison cells were not required since the prisoners couldn't go anywhere. This may well have changed in the 1964-85 period when the military dictatorships then ruling Brazil once again used Fernando as a prison for political prisoners.

Fernando de Noronha Today

Since World War II, the main island of the archipelago (Ilha de Fernando de Noronha) has become a well known tourist location for those with an ecological interest. It's relative isolation from the mainland and its protection as a Marine National Park has preserved the extensive avian wildlife and made it a paradise for birdwatchers. The crystal clear seas surrounding Fernando abound with fish, whales, sponges, dolphins, and coral. There are plenty of beautiful beaches and a reasonably constant 78°F water temperature means that wet suits are unnecessary. There is regular air service from Natal or Recife. Fernando has a permanent population of about 3000 people and interestingly, only 540 tourists are permitted on the island at any one time. This means beaches and nature trails are not overcrowded and helps preserve the natural habitats on the island.

The Fernando de Noronha Archipelago is now owned and administered by the State of Pernambuco even though it is closer to Natal.

I-128; Allied personnel on Fernando - 1944

The title of the photo may not be totally accurate. While there are Brazilian Army troops and US Sailors in the photo, there also are Brazilian civilians of different ages. Perhaps some of them were political prisoners.

I-129; Lockheed Ventura PV-1 in flight - 1944

The two planes were proceeding back to Fernado from an Anti-submarine patrol flight when I took this photo.There were 5 different PV-1 squadrons in Fairwing 16 at various times so I don't know which squadron this No. 6 belonged to: probably VB-126 or VB-145.

I-130; Morning muster on Fernando - 1944

I-131; Air strip and water treatment plant - Fernando - 1944

The “Ships Company” of Fairwing 16’s Fernando detachment salutes both the USA and Brazilian flags at morning muster and flag raising ceremony.

It is notable that there is significant vegetation at ground level and on hillsides. It looks as if there was a surface water treatment pant at the base.

13

Natal, Brazil
People, Places, Buildings, 1943-44

Friendly people, a fine seaside town, good duty.

Universal opinion of U.S. Military personnel

Most of the following photographs were taken in Natal by the author in the period between October 1943 and April 1944 while he was stationed in Fairwing 16 at Parnamirim Field. Where the photograph was taken by others, the notation identifies and credits the source. The authors' photographs were made using either a Kodak Medalist 620 camera or a 2x3 Miniature Speed Graphic. Many of the negatives were not printed until the 1999-2002 period and most of them can be enlarged to a 16x20 size print.

The first 6 pictures which follow (I-132through I-137) were all taken on one December day in 1943. This is substantiated by the fact that in photo I-133 we see a Consolidated Coronado. This new very large seaplane, appears in the mid-left portion of the photo as it floats on the Potengi River at the RAMPA area. The Coronado had made its first overseas flight from Patuxent River, Maryland, Naval Air Station non-stop to Natal.

The Mercado Publico

This public market shown in photo I-132 was primarily a local farmer's market. It was an important place in Natal during the war. In December 1941, when Marshall Jamison, the first Army Air Force officer to come to Natal (he was the original commander at Parnamirim) the essential elements of a supply function from the USA were not in place. He notes that in order to provide food for the U.S. personnel coming to or passing through Natal, he would go to the Mercado Publico to obtain food supplies. Marshall, through his service stint at Natal, developed a bond with the people and the city. As a result he has revisited Natal many times and frequently spends several months at a time in the city. He maintains an apartment there. Note the burros in the front yard of the Mercado Publico. I have been told that the Mercado Publico is no longer there. I have also been told that the Banco do Brasil building now occupies the site of the old Mercado Publico.

In order to get a good location from which to take a landscape photo of the Ribeira/RAMPA area and the Potengi River I had gone up the hill to the edge of Cidade Alta and thence climbed up into a church steeple. From that vantage point, I just happened to notice the Mercado Publico on the right and the people flowing in and out of it.

At that time I was not aware of Marshall Jamison's 1941-42 use of the Mercado Publico's facilities to obtain food supplies for the transient air crews who were transiting through Natal to Africa. I was intrigued by the size of the public market and was curious to see how it compared with the ""Farmers' Markets" present in my home state.

The rest of the photographs in this chapter were taken during other days when I or my shipmates were fortunate enough to go "on liberty" from Parnamirim into Natal. The friendliness of the many Brasileros toward Americans is amply demonstrated in their facial expressions as they well tolerated having me take their pictures. It helped that I had learned a bit of Portuguese and knew the words for "take a picture" (tirar retrato).

I-132; The Mercado Publico- Natal-1943

The presence of 7 burros loaded up shows how some locals got their produce from the outlying areas into market. This was a busy place during the war years. It was a large Farmer's Market building.

I-133; Ribeira from Cidade Alta church steeple

In the right center of photo I-133 is the open area in front of the Mercado Publico. In the center left is the Potengi River and the Ribeira section with the ocean beyond. The Coronado flying boat can be seen moored in the Potengi River at the Pan Am dock.

I-134; Skyline of Cidade Alta from Potengi River

On the left in photo I-134 the Mercado Publico in visible. The church in the center may be the Igreja de Santo Antonio (also known as Igreja do Galo – the church of the rooster). It was built in the 1600's. Just right of center the church known as Igreja Matriz de N.S. da Apresentacao Cathedral, the first in Natal, was originally built as a wattle and daub chapel in 1599. One can see a total of four church steeples in this 1943 photo.

I-135; Irma, Irmao

Just inside one of the doorways of the Mercado Publico at the counter of a booth I saw this brother and sister sitting contemplating the young sailor with the Kodak Medalist camera in his hand. As usual with the young Brasileros who saw an American, they were smiling. This is an available light indoor photo, hence the good flesh tones.

I-136; Mae, Menina

The little girl's mother graciously agreed to let me photograph her and her daughter. One can see the contented mother-daughter relationship in the caring smiles. As my British friends might say, they may not have had "many brass farthings to their name" but that did not dim their happy demeanor nor their obvious affection for one another. This photo was also taken at a small booth just inside a doorway of the Mercado Publico.

I-137; Bananas and Coconuts

In photo I-137 we see a gentleman about to purchase a bunch of bananas from a produce stand inside the Mercado Publico. In addition to the unusual type of melon in the lower right corner, pineapples (abacaxi) were abundant around Natal. The Mercado Publico was a very useful facility. Presumably there must be another such farmer's market in Natal today?

Aldagisa

This young lady shown in photo I-138 was a popular waitress at one of the several small café-bars in the Ribeira which is the older riverside section of Natal. The two such places which I remember served cerveja (beer), fruit juices, and some food. I cannot recall the names of the two café-bars which my friends and I frequented in Natal but I am certain they were not the Wonderbar or the Maria Boa or the Goodyear which were primarily brothels. Since I had been nurtured in a household with a Victorian set of values, alcoholic beverages were taboo. My drink was either guarana (a local soft drink) or suco de uva (grape juice). Also, we were well aware of the dangers of venereal diseases which had been rampant during the early 1941-1942 years among the American servicemen in Natal (as a consequence of the contacts at the brothels). These facts, plus the influence of training films were sufficient for me to keep out of trouble in Natal.

Aldagesa was not a prostitute; it took many entreaties from a certain red-headed electricians mate before she would consent to go out with him. The results of their liaison were not totally satisfactory.

Sailors Casa in Natal

There were occasions when a group of likeminded sailors from Parnamirim needed a place in Natal to stay when they had an overnight pass and did not wish to be confined to a room at the Hotel Grande which was really the only good hotel in town at that time. Accordingly, several of them rented a house in the Cidade Alta section of Natal. Photo I-139 is of the house which was used also to host parties with young ladies from Natal. The young ladies were not from the Wonderbar or Maria Boa or Goodyear, which were, by that time, supervised brothel facilities.

There was an attractive well dressed young lady who just showed up at the Casa without invitation on several occasions. She must have been the Brazilian equivalent of a "desperate housewife" who had noted the presence of three or four American sailors at the Casa. My more mature shipmates were glad to do her the honors by helping her "celebrate" life.

There were 3 distinct types of young girls in Natal. Prostitutes mostly inhabited the Goodyear, Wonderbar and Maria Boa. A second group, mostly waitresses or store workers, sometimes could be cajoled into romantic interludes. The third group were from serious families and they were always well-chaperoned and not apt to indulge in any dalliances.

Orvacio Olivera Feitosa

Orvacio was one of two Brasilero custodians of the building housing the photographic department's office and photo lab of Hedron 16's detachment at Parnamirim, Natal. Altogether by 1945, about 2,800 native Brazilians were employed at the air base which contained over 400 buildings on its 3,301 acres of land. Parnamirim and Natal were accurately dubbed the "Crossroads of the Worlds". There were facilities for 6,600 people at Parnamirim.

I regret that the photo I-140 caught Orvacio in an unusually pensive, reflective mood as he normally was perpetually smiling and laughing when we conversed with him in our halting quality Portuguese. Orvacio was fascinated by American coinage and usually got around to asking if he could be given what he called "a shiny dime" an American ten cent piece. He seemed to be a good person well adjusted to life despite what must have been a frugal life style by American standards. At the time I did not realize that 10 cents was two thirds of a day's pay for Orvacio. The Brazilian workers pay of 15 cents per day was considered to be very good wages by the local populace.

Lady with a Pipe

The facial features, skin color, and hair of this lady outside the Mercado Publico in photo I-141 might enable an anthropologist to assess her ethnic background but I am certain I could not accurately do so. It is clear that her pipe adds to her contentment but I do not know what she is smoking. I did not see a lot of Brasileros using tobacco but in a subsequent photo we do see a small store selling tobacco products. Note the quizzical look in her eyes and one wonders what her thoughts were?

I-138; Adalgisa

The pleasant and trusting smile on her face is typical of the way the folks of Natal welcomed Americanos. Aldalgisa worked at Dolly's Bar Nacional at 199 Rua Barata. She was a reluctant Amorato of "Red", an Electrician mate.

I-139; Sailors Casa in Natal

I think this casa was in Cidade Alta not very far from Plaza Pius XII. As can be seen the window - like openings did not contain windows. There were shutters attached and they could be easily closed to provide privacy. Louvers provided ventilation.

The house directly across the street, which was one in a row of conjoined houses, had a number above it's front door which I think is 53. In my photo of the house across the street, the shutters and shuttered door were closed.

It was convenient for several reasons, to have a place in town.

I-140; Orvacio Oliviera Feitosa

The always cheerful Orvacio Oliveira Feitosa, would that everyone would be as well adjusted to life as this Brasileiro.

I-141; Lady with a pipe

How much native indian and how much Africano in her ethnic make-up?

THE RIBEIRA

Both the local citizens and the visiting Americans tended to gravitate to the Ribeira during the war years because that riverside area was "downtown" during that era.

There was a "Liberty Bus" which ran on a regular schedule between Parnamirim and Natal. In addition we could occasionally hitch a ride with Jim Tortorice and his supply truck or some other base vehicle while making the journey.

I don't recall anything about taxi service between Parnamirim and Natal like there was in Recife. Parnamirim was such a large base and there was frequent traffic to the RAMPA area which was in the Ribeira so it was usually not difficult to get back and forth from town.

Our designated times for being allowed to take off work or "go ashore" in navy terms varied but generally were on the weekend.

The main drop-off and pick-up point for the Liberty Bus was at a small park like plaza area at the edge of the Ribeira. Photo I-142; Park, Nova Aurora, and USO shows the location of that bus stop at the edge of the Ribeira.

Photos I-142 through I-162 following show what the Ribeira looked like in the 1943-44 period when I had the opportunity to visit there many times.

The downtown USO club and the various stores and shops in the Ribeira drew the attention and patronage of residents of Natal and its outlying areas as well as that of the thousands of visiting Americans and other Allied personnel. The folks from the outlying areas tended to come into the Ribeira on the weekends, particularly on Saturdays.

People from across the river in the Redinha and other areas came by small boats since the road system was not extensive at that time. There was Bonde trolley service between Cidade Alta and Petropolis areas to the Ribeira which was frequent, dependable, affordable, and widely used.

I-142; Park, Nova Aurora and Downtown USO

This was the "Bus Stop" for U.S. vehicles to drop off or pick up riders to or from Parnamirim. The downtown USO is on the left. The Ribeira section with stores, cafe-bars, and other commercial establishments are straight ahead.

I-143; Downtown USO and Bonde

The street car to Petropolis is loaded as usual. The gentleman pushing the cart may be a street cleaner? While the downtown USO was popular, the USO at the oceanside beach area was even more so. I don't remember many military police or shore patrol in Natal.

I-144; Street of shops - Ribeira

These stores are across from the Park Plaza bus stop area at the edge of the Ribeira. The Confeitaria Delicia was a "sweets" shop. The only other store which is familiar is the Drogeria Limeira which was a drug store. The street to the left of Nova Aurora may be Rua Barata.

I-145; Lojas Paulista store in the Ribeira

Presumably this dry goods (fabric) store was in competition with Casa Rio. The automobile looks like a 1936 Ford. The two ladies and young girl on the right are interested in the black and white puppy in the box belonging to the two kneeling men.

I-146; Saturday afternoon in the Ribeira area

This photo shows groups of young Brasileiros who are out on the town on Saturday afternoon. According to notation on the envelope of this negative they are on Rua Barata in the Ribeira section. On the right is Pharmacia Montiero and one hanging sign says Casa Gloria. I think that one of the café-bars we frequented was in this area on this street. Ribeira means riverside and all the coastal towns seem to have a section called the Ribeira. During the 1940's, the Ribeira was the "Downtown" area of Natal.

I-147; Cane-ada stand

I-148; A Cane-ada Customer

Sugar cane and cotton were predominant crops in the colonial era of the Brazilian Northeast, particularly in Salvador-Bahia and Recife areas, less so at Natal. In photo I-147 we see that sugar cane was still significant in Natal in the war years. A stalk of sugar cane is passed through a press with the liquid sugar solution resulting being sold on the spot.

An elderly gentleman gets a sugary pick-me-up at the Cane-ada stand in Natal photo. Poetic license was used to employ the word; Cane-ada, since I cannot find it in my Portuguese-English dictionary. I just used the phonetic version of what my Brazilian friends called the drink.

I-149; Grande Hotel - Natal - 1943

This was the only large hotel in Natal during the war years so it was very busy. The owner, Theodorico Bezzerra made a fortune on the hotel and casino within the hotel. There were questions about financial maneuvering during that period.

I-150; Casino - Grande Hotel - Natal, 1943

I-151; The 5 and 10 cent store - Natal, 1943

It took considerable political acumen for the owner of the Grande hotel to obtain a license permitting a casino in this establishment.

The presence of the thousands of American troops and Airmen in the Natal area provided a large and steady stream of gamblers to patronize the casino.

The sailor leaning over the roulette table at the position of 7th from the front on the left side is Albert J. Harrison, Photographers Mate-First Class. The older sailor, third from the front on the left bears an uncanny resemblance to Robbie Robinson who went AWOL in Trinidad.

I am not sure where this store was located but it may have been in the Mercado Publico.

The garland on the ceiling was probably a Christmas decoration.

The signs on the counters show prices of 7 cruzeiros and 3.5 cruzeiros (milreis) which seems a bit expensive since 20 cruzeiros equals on U.S. dollar, this may be due to the fact that much of the merchandise was imported.

It would seem that Brazilian workers from Parnamirim who were paid 3 cruzeiros per day would likely not be able to afford to buy goods at the 5 and 10 cent store. Perhaps the Brazilian soldiers and sailors shown in this photo were better paid.

I-152; The leather goods store

Alligator belts and ladies handbags were popular souvenirs. On the counter in this photo is a medium size satchel, one of which I brought home. Natal was famous for boots which were not as tall as American cowboy boots and were made of flexible soft leather. They were popular with the American aviators. I do not believe that this is the leather shop that made those famous boots.

I-153; Confeitaria Avenida-Ribeira

This small shop clearly sold things other than confections since there are advertisements for toothpaste and lifebouy soap and candy jars on the counter.

I-154; J. Tortorice and Friends - Ribeira

This photo shows the ever-popular storekeeper and a group of friends in a cafe-bar which could have been at 199 Rua Barata (Bar Nacional - Dollys) or one of those on a Venida Taures de Lyra, near the RAMPA.

In any event, the photo shows both food and drink on the tables which confirms my memory of eating in the Ribeira at various cafe-bars.

There was one of these establishments my gang favored and I remember the names of two of the more popular waitresses. One was called Irasuda and the other was Louisenette. They had sunny dispositions and were good young ladies who resisted all the amorous entreaties by my more adventurous colleagues.

I will have to ask Jim Tortorice if he recalls the name of this particular cafe-bar.

I-155; Jangada Ashore

This photo shows Eugene Webb, photographers mate second class, pretending to use the large oar used to steer a jangada. Ahead of him was the large creel for holding fish and other appurtenances.

I-156; Jangada Afloat

An oblong wooden raft with a sail and a chair for the helmsman constitutes the primary makeup of small fishing craft along the coast of Brazilian towns. Here in this photo we see such a jangada with one man working the sail and another one the helm. The Jangadas are still used in the coastal cities, particularly for recreation.

This church is in the Ribeira area. It is visible from the balcony of the Hotel Grande.

In one photo in Reference 3 of soldiers sitting on a balcony of the Hotel Grande drinking beer this church is visible in the background.

Unlike many Brazilian churches this one has both steeples complete. I was told that those with a steeple on only one side were maintained that way by the clergy in order to show why the supplicants needed to provide more funds to the church, possibly this is an apocryphal story.

On the sunny day in which I took this photo the church was not open. I would have liked to have seen the inside of this church.

The steeples would also have provided a good view of the nearby areas.

I-157; Igreja Bom Jesus - Natal

I-158; Teatro Carlos Gomes

This theatre in Natal photo I-158 and its impressive architectural front has had a name change since 1943. It is now named the Theatro Alberto Maranho, evidently a spillover of political changes? There was a General Gomes at Natal who eventually ran in a presidential election against Getulio Vargas.

I-159; Grupo Escolar Augusto Severo

Augusto Severo was a notable person from Natal. Not only was this school named for him but also the name of the airport at Natal is now "The Augusto Severo Airport". Mr. Severo was an early proponent of aviation activities and was noted for flying in hot-air balloons locally and reportedly in Europe.

I-160; Christmas in Natal - 1943

In the park we find Santa Claus giving out gifts to children. Clyde Smith makes reference to the fact that in 1944 American servicemen at Parnamirim made voluntary contributions toward a celebration by the Christmas Committee of Natal that the Committee gave for Natal's underprivileged children. This photograph shows part of that type of celebration event which took place in December, 1943.

I-161; Fortune Teller at Christmas Festival

The wigwam houses a young lady from Natal acting as a fortune teller. I do not remember what she said about my future prospects at that time.

I-162; Young Lady of Photo Shop

This young lady worked at Joao Alves Kodak photo shop. He was a good friend. I enlarged some of his pictures for him.

I-163; Bonde Making a Turn

The Bonde (trolley) system in Natal was an excellent facility and really indispensable for the citizens at that time. This Bonde is making a turn from a side street onto Rua Tavares de Lira which connects the dockside at the river to the location of the Hotel Grande. Photo I-163 shows a typical well-filled Bonde.

THE PINHEIRO - ARAUJO - FONTES FAMILIES

The presence of Americans in Natal effected the evolution of those referenced families in a very positive way. In his book about Parnamirim concerning the postitive financial impact on Natal by Americans (Reference 6), Clyde Smith wrote the following: "Others who made money were, Vincete Mesquita, Joao Pinhero, nicknamed Joao da Casa Rio, the owner of the shoestore, Leao do Norte, and...." The following text and four photographs delineate my knowledge of how the Casa Rio's success enhanced the well-being of the extended Pinheiro-Araujo-Fontes family.

Casa Rio and Guinora

If my memory is accurate, the Casa Rio, a dry goods store, founded by Joao Pinheiro and then operated by Alcides Araujo, was up the hill between the Ribeira and Cidade Alta proper. The Casa Rio was notable because Guinora Pinheiro, Alcides young sister-in-law spoke English. Perhaps her sister Giomar, (who is the wife of Alcides), and also Alciides himself spoke English (I do not recall). In any event here in photo I-164 we see the attractive (about 17) Guinora outside Casa Rio with a U.S. officer by a Jeep.

Jim Tortorice, a navy storekeeper from Hedron 16 at Natal and a friend of mine, had a definite yen for Giunora (as did a lot of other servicemen). Jim got me to take photos of Guinora and of her mother, sisters, and niece. Within the past few years a Brazilian friend (Fred Nicolau) of Sao Paulo traced Guinora and Jim Tortorice both via the Internet.

Guinora Pinheiro married an Argentinean airline employee named Machado and lived for a number of years in Argentina. After the passing of her husband she returned to live in Rio de Janeiro. Her son became an airline pilot. She also had a daughter (and now has a granddaughter) at home with her in Rio.

Alcides Araujo became a very successful business man in Natal and is today the proprietor of a large department store complex in Natal. In photo I-165 we see Alcides showing two Army men some fabric at Casa Rio. Guinora is in center of the photo and Giomar (Alcides' wife) peers over his shoulder (Photo from Clyde Smith, Jr.) Jim Tortorice came back to Pennsylvania after the war. I have talked to him recently and exchanged correspondence.

Guinora Pinheiro on Steps of Casa Rio

Photo I-166 of Guinora I took for Jim Tortorice. Apparently, after many years of living in Argentina speaking Spanish, her capabilities in English have diminished to some degree. However, it may be that a future conversation with her may elicit additional information about Natal which will clear some of the cobwebs from my memory of people and places there.

Jim Tortorice – Storekeeper

Jim had done a bit of barbering before joining the Navy. When he first came to Parnamirim, his superiors insisted that he take over the barber shop work, displacing the native Brazilian, who had been cutting hair for navy personnel. After a while Jim convinced them that this was not good for Navy-Brazilian relations so they let him return to work as a storekeeper. His duties required frequent trips to Natal, both the city and the RAMPA. This is how he became acquainted with Guinora Pinheiro. Photo I-167 shows Jim by his truck in Natal.

Guinora Pinheiros Extended Family

Guinora had four sisters: Giomar, Grenauta, Vilma, and Teresa. Vilma and Teresa appear next to their mother (Rosa) in photo I-168. Rosa is holding her granddaughter (Magaly) who is Giomar and Alcides Araujo's daughter and therefore Guinora's niece. Guinora also had 2 brothers, Joao and Tatio.

Alberto Fontes, a Brazilian Air Force Officer, and Grenauta Pinheiro Fontes had four daughters; Regina, Denise, Diana, and Katia. Regina married an American (Leroy Foster) and they live in the Dallas, Texas area. Alberto Fontes had two sisters in Recife who married American servicemen. Dolores Fontes married Dell Livingston of the U.S. Army and they live in Texas near Regina and Leroy Foster. Carmen Fontes married Tony Perrone (a sailor) and they live in Connecticut.

I-164; Giunora and Officer at Casa Rio - 1944

Here we see an American Naval Officer on what must have been an unofficial stop at Casa Rio. Who can fault him for pausing to visit with such a beautiful and gracious "Moca" like Guinora Pinheiro?

I-165; Alcides Araujo, Giomar Pinheiro Araujo, Gunora Pinheiro and solders on the steps of Casa Rio

Alcides has two American soldiers interested in buying silk stockings to send or take home. His wife, Giomar, smiles approvingly over Alcides shoulder, and Guinora is typically cheerful. Guinora and Giomars' father Joao Pinheiro had founded Casa Rio in 1937 and he also had businesses in the interior of the state. By 1944 Joao Pinheiro was incapacitated and Alcides seemed to be in charge of Casa Rio. Guinora's fluency in English and her persona materially aided economic results at Casa Rio.

I-166 Close-up of Guinora Pinheiro
A Brazilian Beauty in front of the Casa Rio Store in 1944.

Perhaps when Giomar Pinheiro Araujo, Guinora's older sister, completes her memoir of the Pinheiro - Araujo family we will learn how and why Guinora was able to learn to speak English. We will also know whether or not Giomar herself or Alcides developed that capability.

Certainly whoever encouraged Guinora to learn English before the war broke out had great foresight since there had previously been no great indication that an English language skill would be such a boon to a store in Natal like Casa Rio.

The Germans, Italians, and French had been much more active in all of Brazil prior to World War II while the American and even English presence and influence in Brazil during that period was very minor in comparison. Those three non English speaking countries were operating airlines to Natal and other cities in Brazil. The Germans and Italians had and were emigrating into Brazil in large numbers.

As the war progressed a USAAF officer developed a relationship with Guinora which resulted in her considering marriage. However, apparently a member of Guinora's family discouraged the union because they did not want her to leave. Subsequently a potential union with a Brazilian Air Force Officer met the same fate. Finally an Argentine Airman came along and the "die was cast". Guinora married him and off they went to Argentina.

I-167; Jim Tortorice - Storekeeper

This photo shows Jim with his truck parked under the trees in the Plaza where the Liberty bus stopped. This was on the day on which I had ridden into Natal with Jim with one purpose being to take some photos of Guinora Pinheiro and her family.

I-168; Rosa Pinheiro, Daughters and Grand Daughter

Rosa Pinheiro's smile is a reflection of her joy at holding her grand daughter with two of her daughters beside her. Rosa looks to be in goodhealth and to be coping well with the task of raising her four daughters and two sons.

CIDADE ALTA AND THE SUBURBS

We did not normally spend a lot of time in the upper city of Natal except when we stayed in the "Sailors' Casa". We were much more likely to be in the Ribeira at the Cafe-Bars or various stores or at the USO Beach Club on the ocean front or Ponte Negra beach.

The "Kodak" photo store was also in the Ribeira and I was there frequently to cajole the owner of the store into selling me roll film for the Medalist or film packs for my Speed Graphic since Navy film was off limits for use in what was called Cumshaw or personal activities. Apparently that word was a garbled version of the older word Scrimshaw which was the term from sailing ship days for carvings made by the sailors in their off-duty time.

One place in the Cidade Alta which was at time frequented by Allied service men from Parnamirim and the RAMPA bases was the Plaza Pius XII which is depicted in photo I-169. That plaza was a favorite spot for sailors and soldiers to rendezvous with young ladies from Cidade Alta who liked to stroll through the Plaza in the early evening or on the weekends.

My friendship with Jim Tortorice enabled me to visit some of the outlying areas adjacent to Natal proper without having to walk for miles. That was how I was able to photograph a typical settlement of small homes outside Natal as show in photo I-170 which I call "suburbs of Natal" as well as I-171 which is a close-up of a typical small home.

We also stopped at Alecrim which at that time was outside Natal proper and a small encave all its own. Photos I-172, I-173 and I-174 all depict scenes in Alecrim in 1944.

The man and boy at the pineapple stand remind me that one of the photos I enlarged for Joao Alves, the proprietor of the Kodak photo store was a picture of a field of pineapples outside Natal. The Natal area had an abundant supply of fruits and of seafood.

As will be noted in photos I-173 and I-174, Alecrim with its Casa Leite, Mercearia Delicia, Casa Primos and Armazem Potyguar, had a business district of its own.

I-169; Plaza - Pius XII

This picture was taken across the park-like plaza of Pius XII, which is in Cidade Alta, it shows the well appointed homes in that section of Natal in 1943. One of my shipmates noted that this Plaza was a favorite rendezvous spot for American sailors and the nubile young ladies of Natal. There were a few weddings of Natalanese girls and Americans during and at the end of the war.

I-170; Suburbs of Natal

Outside of town one could see the typical small one or two room thatched roof houses where many people lived amongst the palm trees. These were the homes of the less well off folks around Natal. They still look better than the Favelas which have sprung up around other and larger Brazilian cities since the war.

I-171; Small Suburban Home - Natal

Photo I-171 shows an attempt to beautify this small home by decorating the front of it. "Be it ever so humble." They sure didn't have to go far for coconuts.

I-172; The Abacaxi Stand

The lad enjoys his fresh pinapple while the farmer wonders if I plan to buy one. I cannot remember the price but do believe it would have been reasonable.

I-173; Alecrim-Rio Grande do Norte

In 1943-44, Alecrim was a small village. It was a stop on the local bus line as can be seen in this photo. Casa Leite (House of Milk) provided refreshments of various types. Clearly the bus was carrying a full (or overfull) contingent of passengers.

I-174; Armazem Potyguar - Alecrim - 1943

Note the advertisemet for the movie Sergeant York in this photo of an establishment in Alecrim. The advertisement may have been for the movie theatre called the Rex. There were too many other diversions in Natal so we generally depended on movies at Parnamirim for that activity.

I-175; USAAF Ceremony at Alecrim Cemetery

Alecrim was the site of an American Military Cemetery. At the end of the war all but one of the servicemen who had lost their lived in the Battle of the South Atlantic were returned to the United States for final burial. The one who was left was the fiance of a local Brazilian girl who convinced the servicemen 's parents that he should remain at Alecrim. His name was Thomas Browning.

I-176; U.S. Navy Ceremony - Alecrim Cemetary

This photo shows U.S. Navy and Marine Corps Honor Guard in a funeral ceremony. In April of 1947, a U.S. Navy ship came to Natal on a mission called "Operation Glory" to remove the bodies of the 146 American servicemen and return them to the USA.

14

Recife
An Important Allied Base in World War II

This port is strategically well located for operations off Cape San Roque which is the most vital strategic point in the South Atlantic area.

Admiral Ingram on September 4, 1941

LOCATION OF RECIFE

Recife, which is about 200 miles south of Natal and about 400 miles north of Bahia (Salvador), became important to the U.S. Naval forces in 1941 due to its central location on the Northeast Coast of Brazil. Though Natal was the best place to concentrate aerial anti-submarine activities it did not have adequate seaport facilities to accommodate the cruisers, destroyers, and various auxiliary vessels in Admiral Ingram's surface fleet. Salvador (Bahia) was too far south to be chosen as headquarters.

The Map no. 3 (see previous page 17) shows the northeast hump of Brazil's coast line and the central location of Recife which is the capital of the state of Pernambuco.

HISTORY OF RECIFE

The Portuguese had come to the general area of what became Recife in the 1500's and established sugar plantations around Olinda, a small city they built just north of what is now Recife.

In the 1620's, the Dutch, in their eagerness to take over the lucrative sugar production operation of the Portuguese plantations in northeast Brazil began a military campaign against the Portuguese. They started by destroying a Portuguese fleet at Bahia (Salvador) resulting in their capture of that city in 1624. In 1630 they attacked and burned the small city of Olinda which had been the "sugar capital". The Dutch followed up by capturing Natal in 1633. While they continued to occupy Natal and Salvador they also turned much of their efforts toward what became the city of Recife. They did this by using their European land reclamation skills to drain the marshy area where three rivers flowed through what is now the city of Recife. Essentially, Recife is on land reclaimed from wetlands by the Dutch.

It took about 20 years of guerilla warfare by the Portuguese settlers to later recapture Recife and Olinda. The Portuguese also recaptured Natal and Salvador during that same period. The Spanish aided the Portuguese in their battles against the Dutch. This was a corollary to European continental wars between the Spanish and the Dutch. Those wars were based both on religious differences and commercial empire rivalries. Treaties defining the boundaries between Spain and Portugal's colonies were developed with the help of the Vatican. These boundaries were not always strictly adhered to.

RECIFE IN WORLD WAR II

By 1941, Recife had become one of the larger cities in Brazil with a population of about 250,000. It was and is a beautiful city with rivers flowing around and about its several components on their way into the South Atlantic. Map No. 11, I-176 (reproduced with permission from Brazil Travel Survival Kit 3 at 1996 Lonely Planet Publications) is an overhead view showing the principal components of Recife. The suburbs of Recife have grown and sprawled on the mainland adjacent to the three islands of the main city.

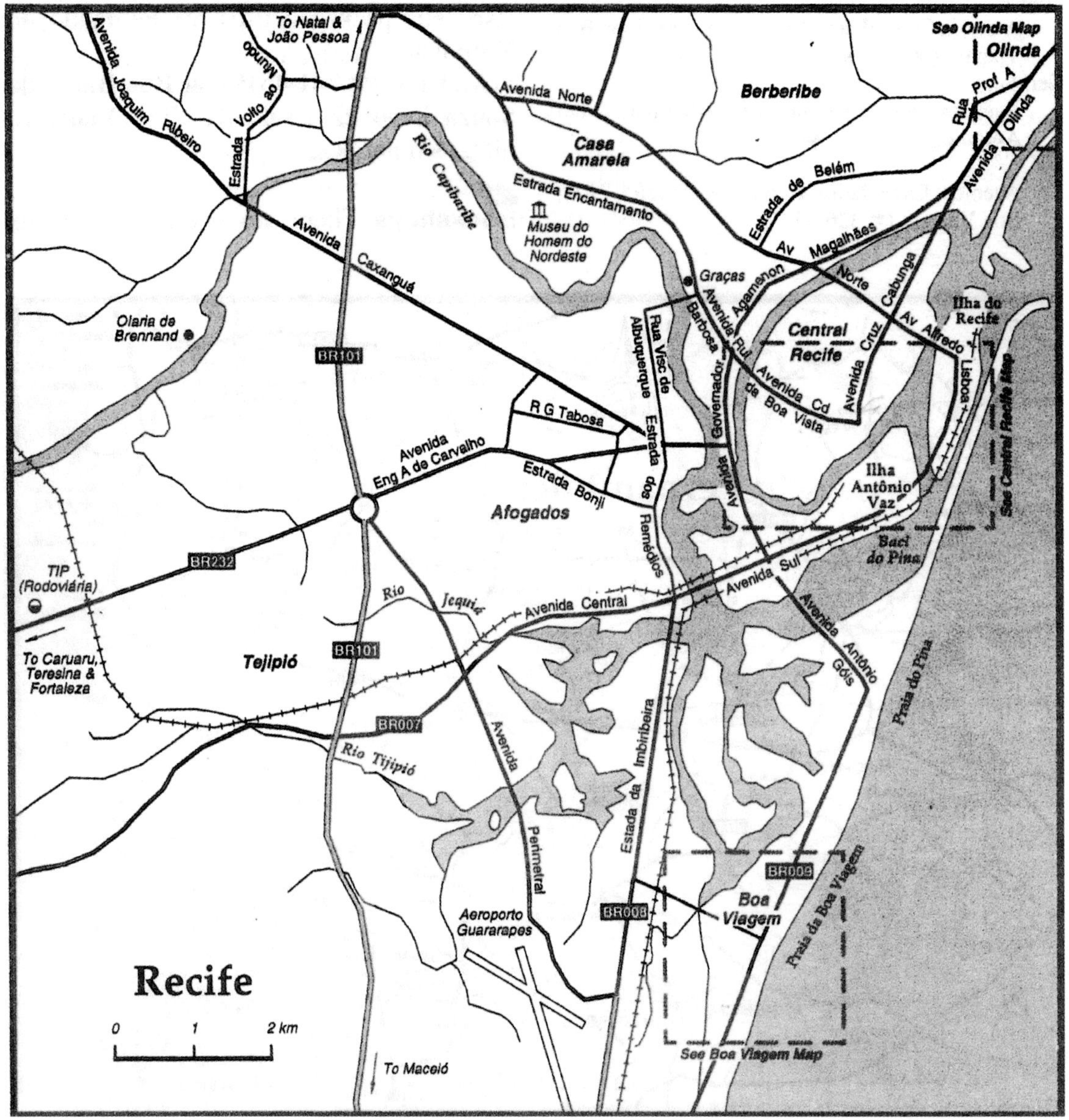

I-177; Map No. 11; Modern Recife

Recife is Portugese for Reef which is what this city used to be. The city is a monument to the Dutch engineers who constructed this beautiful dwelling place with its many waterways around its islands. Map from Reference number eight.

The main parts of Recife Proper are its 3 islands and 2 peninsulas. Recife Island contains the port facilities and some of the business district. Santa Antonio Island, considered to be central Recife since it contains most of the businesses, lies between Recife Island and the Boa Vista Peninsular area. Ilha Antonio Vaz is south of the central area. Boa Viagem, where the main beaches are, is a peninsula south of the central sectors.

South of central portions of Recife and west of Boa Viagem, the U.S. Navy, in a cooperative project with the Brazilian Air Force enlarged the existing IBURA air base to accommodate the planes of Fairwing 16 and those of the growing Brazilian forces. The expansion of Ibura field occurred in 1943 (later than the work at Parnamirim) and when our group of transferees arrived in Recife in mid-1943, we had to live in tents (at least they had floors) until the barracks were built at IBURA field.

Because of its larger size and population, Recife was not as greatly impacted by the presence of many American sailors, soldiers, and airmen as Natal had been. Being a much larger city it did offer more restaurants, upscale bars, and other amenities. However, it became headquarters which meant much more adherence to regulations. Nevertheless, American military personnel considered Recife to be a "Good Duty City".

TASK FORCE 3 – PRECURSOR OF THE FOURTH FLEET

As of June, 1941, Admiral Ingram had the heavy cruiser, Memphis, three light cruisers, a squadron of destroyers, and a number of auxiliary vessels to utilize in the South Atlantic. Recife and Bahia port facilities were made available to the Admiral by September 1941. That group of ships, designated as Task Force 3, was to patrol most of the South Atlantic ocean from below Trinidad to the river Plate in Uruguay. This was to prove to be a daunting assignment for many months before additional forces became available to Admiral Ingram. The presence of Task Force 3 was an indication of the Brazilian government's early association with the Allied cause even though they still had not dropped the figurative "second shoe" in early 1941.

Prior to December 1941, Admiral Ingram did not have an aviation force in Brazil because of Brazilian sensitivity about having land based U.S. forces on Brazilian soil. In the 8 March, 1941 to 6 December, 1941 period the U-Boats destroyed 62 merchant ships in the South Atlantic Narrows, most of them in mid-ocean or near the African coast. The losses of Allied merchant ships in the North Atlantic sector and off the North African coast were even greater. The main allied effort on convoy protection focused on the North Atlantic where forces also had to be committed to secure both Iceland and Greenland from German occupation and to prevent further domination of the North Atlantic by German forces. These were perilous times.

It was clear that Admiral Ingram had neither the forces nor the authority to fully protect shipping in the South Atlantic during this period of Axis Power ascendancy. All of that would begin to change with Pearl Harbor and the German's failure to completely succeed in the Soviet Union in December of 1941. The Admiral would finally get authorization from the Brazilians to bring the planes of VP-52 (December 11, 1941) to Natal harbor to operate from a seaplane tender thus allowing the Brazilians to maintain a semblance of neutrality. They also would only allow six American planes in transit on Brazilian soil at any one time for quite a few months thereafter.

It would be another 12 months before Admiral Ingram had enough planes and ships to begin effectively countering Axis naval units in the South Atlantic.

After Pearl Harbor the degree of cooperation from and with the Brazilians kept increasing and when the U-Boats sank a few Brazilian ships in August, 1942, their government declared war on the Axis Powers and they became staunch allies to the Allied Powers. Both the land based and surface ships naval forces of the U.S. and their Brazilian counterparts thereafter operated jointly up and down the coast of Brazil and at Fernando de Noronha and Ascension Island. Recife became the focal point for these joint activities.

THE U.S. ARMY IN RECIFE

The U.S. Army Corp of Engineers (USACE) also would place its Brazilian headquarters at Recife. All the work on the air bases and port facilities in the Brazilian coastal cities was a task of such magnitude that the USACE had a significant number of personnel, both of the army and civilian staff at Recife. These capable people worked closely with their Brazilian counterparts in this effort, both at Recife and the other coastal bases.

The U.S. Army Air force also had personnel in Recife even though their principal efforts were from Belem southward to Natal and on to Ascension Island and the southern route of the Air Transport Command across the ocean.

FOURTH FLEET AND FAIRWING 16 IN RECIFE

When the U.S. Fourth Fleet officially became into being on March 1, 1943, Admiral Ingram had his headquarters on a naval vessel in Recife Harbor. As time progressed he established a headquarters on Recife Island. Fleet Air Wing 16 was set up in the spring of 1943 with headquarters initially at Parnamirim at Natal. As soon as reasonable facilities existed at Ibura, Captain Rossmore D. Lyon, the "Commodore" of Fairwing 16 moved his headquarters to Recife in July 1943.

Camp Ingram

As the total complement of personnel in the Fourth Fleet and Fairwing 16 grew in 1943-44, a Navy Rest and Rehabilitation (R + R) installation known as Camp Ingram was established in the Recife area. A Captain Roper was in charge at Camp Ingram.

Headquarters Building – Fairwing 16

Fairwing 16's headquarters were in a multi-story building which had been rented on Rua Madre de Deus on either Recife Island or Santo Antonio Island. This building had at least seven floors and featured various occupants of some passing interest. The building had formerly housed the Brazilian Bank Employees Pension Institute.

I remember that Fairwing 16 had its Operations Office on the second deck and it's Administration Office on the 6th deck. Also located in the building were: Shore Patrol headquarters; a photo lab for Fourth Fleet; a brothel, a prophylactic station; and a dance hall/night club on the top floor. The building had an interior rectangular staircase of significant size that went from the street level floor and wound within the interior all the way to the top deck (floor) which housed the large dance floor in the night club.

With a group of my friends we walked up the stairway one Saturday night to get to the dance hall. On the way we had to keep walking while avoiding the entreaties of the young ladies hanging out the doors of the brothel. To curb the venereal disease problem I believe the brothel may have been regulated by the military. Nonetheless our only visit to any of the areas of this unusual collection of facilities was to the Dance Hall on the top floor. The long walk resulted in the very entertaining spectacle of Brazilian sailors and soldiers dancing the Samba with their girl friends. I have not seen any couples since who could dance the Samba with the same fervor and skill as did the Brazilian couples that evening. It had to be seen to be believed.

Fourth Fleet Expansion

In the December, 1941 through 1942 period, auxiliary vessels like the USS Albemarle (Able Mable - photo I-178) were very important vessels in the US Navy's efforts in Brazil.

The Fourth Fleet surface vessel capabilities grew in the 1943-44 period with an increase in the number of surface ships including Jeep aircraft carriers and auxiliary vessels including the sea-going tugboat (the USS Seneca). One of my school friends (Charles Ogorek) served on the Seneca which was used to pick up survivors from torpedoed merchant ships or downed navy aircraft or to tow damaged merchant ships to port for repairs. I was unable to make contact with Charley as our tours of duty in Brazil only overlapped for a month or so and he was at sea a lot.

I-178; USS Albemarle - Atlantic Fleet seaplane tender

Seaplane tenders were always essential to the maintenance and repair of the PBY's, PBM's and other seaplanes of Fairwing 16 and Task Force 3 and the Fourth Fleet,. They were also supply ships for ordinance, fuel, etc. In the early days of the war before Parnamirim, Ibura, Ipitanga, etc. were completed facilities to service amphibian aircraft, ships like the Albemarle and Humboldt were indispensable. The Albemarle at times also served in the North Atlantic so its crew experienced the arctic climate as well as the balmy weather of Brazil.

FOURTH FLEET AIRCRAFT

Early on the PBY5A was the most important airplane for anti-submarine work in Brazil. Though it continued to be important, a large share of the flight coverage was soon (after July 1943) to be shared with the PB4Y Consolidated Liberators, the PV-1 Lockheed Venturas, and the PBM-3 Martin Mariners.

In September, 1943 Fleet Airship Wing 4 (squadrons 41 and 42) with their K-class blimps arrived to carry out ASW patrols, escort duties, air/sea and jungle search and rescue missions. They were primarily based at Fortaleza, Sao Luiz and Maceio

When, in 1944, the jeep escort carriers joined the Fourth Fleet, they utilized Grumman TBF Avengers as bombers and Grumman F4F Wildcats as fighter –bombers. I recall seeing three F4F's fly into Ibura field at Recife and they landed together almost wing tip to wing tip, like a flock of geese. Some of the Cruisers were probably equipped with OS2U observation seaplanes.

The next seven photos show various planes used by Fairwing 16.

The Martin Mariner: PBM-3

The PBM was strictly a seaplane and three squadrons of them, VP-74, VP-203 and VP-211 were assigned to Fairwing 16. Though some were based at various times at the RAMPA in Natal or at Aratu in Bahia, they also operated at times out of Rio de Janeiro. In photo I-179 we see a PBM-3 of VP-204 at Quonset Point, Rhode Island in 1942. This PBM seaplane has wheels and undercarriage attached by the "Beach Crew" to trundle it up onto the tarmac to be serviced.

Beaching a PBM at Quonset Point and getting it up onto the land was an arduous task requiring a number of sailors in arm pit high waters to get into Narragansett Bay in the winter. Service in the Beach Crew was a favorite disciplinary tactic imposed upon miscreant enlisted men. The photo lab at Quonset was a 24/7 operation due to work volume. One time a striker named Thibodeaux was drying the graveyard shifts output of 8x10 prints while also eating a peanut butter sandwich. The inevitable happened and when Chief Sanders noted the prints spotted with peanut butter, the unfortunate striker was sentenced to a few weeks on the Beach Crew.

Both Quonset Point Naval Air Station on Naragansett Bay in Rhode Island and Norfolk Naval Air Station in Virginia served as marshalling points for receipt and inspection of recently manufactured and newly delivered airplanes. Thes aircraft had to be checked out for quality control purposes before being accepted and turned over to the various squadrons in the Air Force - Atlantic Fleet. In additioin to flight tests, a close examination of individual pieces of equipment was carried out When, inevitably, defective or damaged parts were detected, pohotographic evidence was required for government reporting purposes, hence the heavy work load on the photo lab.

I-179; PBM 204-P-1 (Martin Mariner)

The PBM was not the favorite airplane of most of the pilots of Fairwing 16. Both the dependable PBY and the PB4Y were more highly regarded. The early models of the PBM which came into service seemed to be underpowered. If the airplane had to be taxied in the water for any significant distance a great strain was put on the engines which caused more than normal downtime for the maintenance and repair of the engines.

The huge fuselage hull of the airplane made it a bit ungainly. Eventually more powerful engines were put on the PBM's which alleviated the problem to some degree.

Pilots still preferred choppy water to aid in take-off, particularly when the PBM was loaded.

I-180; Grumman Goose (J2F6)

For auxiliary flight purposes including photographic missions, planes like the Grumman J2F6 were employed. In photo I-180 we see Billie Goodell of VP-83, (later VB-107) with R. R. England, Photographers Mate 1/c (who was in charge of the photo lab at Natal), alongside a Goose on the tarmac at Natal.

On the fuselage under the wing in back of the engine nacelle is a port or small hatch which can be opened in flight for photo purposes. However, we quickly learned not to tarry long hanging out that opening to take photos because the exhaust from the engine was noxious. Later, in late 1944, I was back at Norfolk Naval Air Station in VD-2 (Photographic Squadron 2) and took a photo flight from Norfolk to Anacostia, D.C. in a Goose. A WAVE officer was given a ride to Anacostia and she sat in the bilge with me. She insisted, despite my warnings, to continually hang her head out the hatch watching the scenery during the flight. Predictably, about 5 minutes from Anacostia she got violently sick and puked all over herself and me. The last time I saw her she was running toward the Anacostia terminal in tears.

I-181; Grumman Avenger (TBF)

The aviation branches of the U.S. Army and the U.S. Navy were generally not well prepared in 1941 in terms of well designed fighter planes, torpedo planes, dive bombers, or long range heavy bombers. There were some exceptions wherein Glenn L. Martin and his coterie of young disciples like Bill Boeing, Donald Douglas, etc., had been able to design, build, and start producing some planes which were of sound and adequate capability.

The U.S. Navy had particularly good fortune with the results of work by Leroy Grumman and his team of aeronautical engineers with the development of the TBF torpedo bomber. In photo I-181 we see a Grumman TBF Avenger which saw yeoman service in the Pacific on fleet carriers and in the South Atlantic on jeep convoy escort carriers. This photo was supplied by Keith G. Watland, photographers mate first class. It shows an Avenger in flight over Narragansett Bay. The TBF's were used as bombers flying off jeep escort carriers during the last 18 months of the Battle of the Atlantic.

To illustrate how prewar planning on aircraft design and procurement could have been much improved we need to reflect on the status of the navy's prewar program for fighter planes. Before Grumman developed the F4F Wildcat fighter the Navy had selected the Brewster Buffalo, definitely not a propitious choice because the plane was slow and unwieldy, particularly in comparison to the fine Japanese Zero. Little did I know when I built a detailed model of the Brewster Buffalo in 1940 that I was admiring an airplane that was essentially outmoded before it first was put into service. A photo I-182 of the author (age 15) holding the model of the Brewster Buffalo is shown. At the time I had no premonition at all that I would, within just over 2 years, be sitting on a jump seat in a blister of a PBY circling a convoy in the North Atlantic.

Design and procurement of the Brewster Buffalo did not fit the normal pattern of U.S. Navy aircraft development programs. The more familiar names are: Grumman; Consolidated; Martin, Douglas; and, North American. A review of how Brewster won this early fighter plane contest might prove of some interest.

I-182; The Brewster Buffalo Fighter Plane

I-183; The Grumman F4F – Wildcat

This photo shows an F4F fighter plane in flight. It was definitely better than the Buffalo, but it was still inferior to the Zero in several respects, as our pilots soon found out. When our pilots successfully battled Zeros it was because of the skills of the pilots. Fortunately our F4F pilots in the South Atlantic did not have to encounter the Zero. The Japanese had been at war for quite a few years before 1941 so they had developed some superior weapons.

I-184; The Lockheed Hudson

This plane was a reasonably successful medium patrol bomber but we had not produced many by 1941 when the war started. This photo I-184 shows a Hudson of VP-82-10, flying out of Quonset Point in 1942. Clearly this plane was a Lockheed transport version which had been hastily converted to military use because we can see the many windows along the fuselage typical of airline planes. England was not the only country asleep in the 1935-39 period. The range of these planes limited their effectiveness in anti-submarine convoy coverage patrol.

I-185; The OS2U (Kingfisher)

This observation scouting plane was made both in land plane form or on a float to enable it to function as a seaplane. At Natal we had OS2U seaplanes and at Recife we had the land plane version of the OS2U.

In photo I-185 we see a land plane based OS2U flying out of Quonset Point Naval Air Station on a photographic mission. One can see an F-56 type aerial camera held by Keith Watland of Patrol Wing Nine in the rear cockpit. The goal of this photo flight was to track the run of torpedoes being fired by PT boats based on Narragansett Bay to determine accuracy of the torpedo firing. The U.S. Navy Bureau of Ordnance had great difficulty matching the performance of the Japanese "Long Lance" torpedo. Our submarine sailors of the Silent Service paid a heavy price at times, not only because our torpedo designs lacked matching effectiveness but also because there were many defective torpedoes supplied to them. Not only would they take erratic paths but also sometimes curled back and hit the submarine which fired it. Probably the most tragic example of defective torpedoes was the story of how Richard O'Kane, the most highly decorated naval office of World War II (the Medal of Honor) had his submarine, the Tang, sunk by an errant torpedo which came back after being fired. Commander O'Kane's submarine was responsible for sinking more enemy ships than any other U.S. submarine skipper. For the full story of Commander O'Kane and the crew of the Tang the reader is referred to the excellent book, "The Bravest Man," by William Tuohy (Reference no.15).

I-186; PT Boat

This photo shows a PT boat maneuvering off the training base in Narragansett Bay. Note the "ash can" depth charges amidship and the torpedo tubes near the bow. We did not have any PT boats in the Fourth Fleet.

15

Ibura Air Base
Recife

Please try to get me reassigned to Fairwing 16 in Recife.

A.E. West, Photographer's Mate to the Photo Officer at Ibura a few months after having been rotated back to the USA from Recife.

A GOOD DUTY POSTING

Red West was a regular Navy sailor (see photo on p. 248) who already had one "hash mark" signifying completion of a four year portion of his first six year hitch in the Navy. One might ask, why would a sailor who was stateside request a transfer back to Recife, Brazil where he had already served for 18 months. I believe it was because Recife was really good duty for both enlisted men and officers. Well before the time Red West had rotated back to the U.S.A., Ibura field amenities such as barracks, ship's store, etc., had been upgraded and the food supply was excellent.

Admiral Ingram early on leased a 250 acre farm near Recife which was used to raise vegetables, meat animals, and dairy products to supplement the Commissary supply from elsewhere in Brazil and the USA. Even more importantly, Recife was a "good liberty town". One could safely get a very good meal in Recife, there was ample female companionship readily available (of all varieties), and the climate was benign. Ibura field had been easier to upgrade because more facilities were there to start with. Recife had been a gateway aviation city to airplanes and zeppelins in the 1930's.

Some of the staff officers of both Fairwing 16 and the Fourth Fleet early on recognized the good duty to be had at Recife and lobbied as hard as they could to stay as long as possible at Recife. Who can blame them? Later on, as those who rotated back to the USA spread the word, it became a bit more difficult for the ones who had been at Recife for a protracted period to avoid being rotated back to the USA or to the Pacific.

ACTIVITIES AT IBURA FIELD

While VP-83 planes did stop at Ibura field much during 1942 and early 1943 during their forays up and down the coast, no squadron was based at Ibura till 1943 when part of VB-129 (PV-1's) were based there. The Brazilian Air Force usually had 3 squadrons based at Ibura field. By December, 1943 VB-143 with PV-1's was based at Ibura and when the jeep aircraft carriers arrived in 1944, the carrier based planes frequently landed at Ibura. The Naval Air Transport Service (NATS) operated its local fleet of the Navy's version of the Douglas DC-3 out of Recife.

The Fairwing 16 photographic officer, one Lieutenant Ralston L. Rundquist, originally from Rockford, Illinois, had his office in the photo lab at Ibura. He lived in a rented home in Boa Viagem.

Photographing the Commodore's Plane

The Commodore (Captain Lyon) also had a PV-1 at his disposal at Ibura field. One day the Fairwing 16, Hedron, Photo Officer, one Lieutenant Ralston L. Rundquist picked three photographers to each take a different camera to go photograph the Commodore's plane on the tarmac at Ibura. I was one of the three chosen and took the photo I-187 shown. Luckily, the Photo Officer chose mine as the best shot. He said my reward was to be to go up in an OS2U and take aerial photos of Recife and its harbor which contained ships of the Fourth Fleet. Lieutenant Rundquist was preparing a large collection of photographs of all the U.S. bases (and the cities) for the Commodore. He personally was going to (and did) fly up and down the coast taking the balance of the photos for the Commodore's collection himself.

Naturally I made a series of 18x22 prints of the beautiful photos I was able to take of Recife and its harbor for myself. However, when I returned to the USA and in February, 1945 was sent to the Richmond Florida Naval Air Station (a blimp base) I put the photos of Recife in my locker at the Photo Lab. When, in September, 1945 a hurricane passed through the greater Miami area and the Blimp Hangers, one of which contained the Photo Lab, were all burnt to the ground. My Recife photos and other contraband from my three plus years in the Navy were all burned up.

I had had the good fortune of marrying my childhood friend in April, 1945 and was ashore (at home in Miami) the night when the hurricane came through and destroyed the blimp hangers. Fortunately, most of my other negatives and prints from Brazil were at home with my parents. This good fortune has enabled me to prepare the photos in this compilation. Despite repeated attempts I have not yet been able to locate the other photos made for the Commodore's album but hope to do so in the future. I believe that another FAW 16 photographer does have a set of those photos.

In this photo I-187 of the Commodore's plane we note that there still were tents being used as they appear in the background under the nose of the plane.

Secretary of the Navy Comes to Recife

During World War II, President Roosevelt encouraged a bi-partisan approach to the war. At that time, "Politics stopped at the water's edge". One of the ways he did this was by naming Republicans to cabinet posts. One such appointment was that of Frank Knox as the Secretary of the Navy. In 1944, Mr. Knox visited Recife and Ibura field. In photo I-188 we see Secretary Knox riding in a jeep at Ibura field with Admiral Ingram, a flag officer and Captain Lyon in the back seat.

Photo Lab Gang – Ibura Field

Photo I-189 was taken during April, 1944 because at about that time I had been transferred back to Recife from Natal after serving at Natal for about 6 months starting in October, 1943. The pictures show some of the new barracks at Ibura in background. Back row, left to right, are: Ugo Anthony Marinelli; Shannon: Robert Bronner; and front row are: Dale Ernst Wright; Arthur J. Sykes; and Moyer.

Shannon, when he first came to Brazil, lobbied hard and successfully to be sent to Fortaleza to set up a one man photo lab near that beautiful city north of Natal. Bronner, Wright, Sykes and myself had all come from Natal to Recife in late March, 1944. Moyer had been at Recife all the time and was a close friend of the Photo Officer who was located there. Since Moyer was in Recife for probably 2 years or more he must have had a substantial collection of photographs. Hopefully his descendants may read this book and then get in touch with me.

I had wondered why Shannon was so determined to go to Fortaleza. At that time I did not know what a beautiful city Fortaleza was (and is).

Admiral Ingram's Plane

Early on the Admiral's plane was also a PV-1 as we see in Photo I-190. He upgraded to a PB4Y (B-24) in 1944.

I-187; The Commodore's Plane

Captain Lyon was a veteran pioneering pilot but I believe he depended on some of his younger pilots to do the flying when he went on his inspection trips from Amapa in the north to Florianapolis in southern most Brazil.

I-188; Secretary of Navy in jeep

I-189; Ibura field photographers - 1944

Frank Knox was a life long Republican but also was highly respected by both political parties. He was to visit the bases in Brazil several times during the course of the war.

The 2 U.S. Navy captains in the back of the jeep with Admiral Ingram were unknown to me. It may have been that they were both skippers of the light cruisers in Fourth Fleet's surface vessel force. Admiral Ingram, by this time, had 5 light cruisers in Fourth Fleet and each cruiser had a captain as skipper.

The lieutenant doing the driving is on the Admiral's staff at Recife. Behind the officers is a NAT's DC-3 transport.

The photo officer (Lieutenant Rundquist) had a policy of rotating photographers periodically to different bases. Thus I went from Recife to Natal and back to Recife in a 12 month period. Only the two chief photographers mates and Moyer stayed always at Recife.

Back row - left to right are Ugo Anthony Marinelli, Shannon and R. Bronner. Kneeling are D.E. Wright, A.J. Sykes and Moyer. Shannon would leave soon thereafter to go to Fortaleza.

Moyer would be promoted rapidly to Photographer's Mate First Class and then to Chief Photographer's Mate. Lieutenant Rundquist would stay at Recife till near the end of the war.

I-190; The Admiral's Plane - 1943

In this photo we see the pilot and co-pilot of the Admiral's plane in 1943 with his three star Comsolant emblem. Subsequently the Admiral became CinClant, Commander in Chief Atlantic Fleet. Later on, Admiral Ingram was allotted a PB4Y (The Southern Cross). Lieutenant Vance Dawkins of VB-107 became the Admiral's pilot and Aviation Chief Radioman Dick Carper became the plane's Crew Chief.

Most important to we enlisted men, Recife was both Fairwing 16 and Fourth-Fleet headquarters so regulations were strictly enforced. Ibura was only a cab ride from town and Boa Viagem was only about 3 miles away so going into town on liberty was convenient. Given the opportunity most of the photographers would choose duty at Fortaleza, Natal, Bahia or Rio even though Recife was still considered to be "Good Duty".

A Wartime Romance – How Did it Culminate?

In a park in Recife, one fine Sunday we see in photo 191, Art Sykes and Dale Wright and Dale's immorata whose name I unfortunately do not remember. A month or two after Dale was rotated back to the states the young lady gave birth (mid 1944) to twin girls fathered by Dale. All of what happened subsequently I do not know except that at least for the several more months that Art Sykes was still at Recife, Dale was sending him money for transmittal to Dale's lady friend. Did Dale eventually marry her or bring her to the States later? In any event, those twins would be 61 years old now and their mother about 83 or so. Maybe we can solve this mystery later? So far my inquiries to current contacts who live in Recife have not developed any information about Dale's twin daughters.

A.E. West and Moyer (Photographers from Ibura) in Recife

On February 18th, a group of four of us from Natal were flying to Rio to go on a 7 day leave. The leave period encompassed three nights of carnival time. We had expected to be in Rio de Janeiro for all of the Carnival. As luck would have it we got bumped off the flight in midday of the 18th and spent the first night of the Carnival in Recife. That afternoon we went in to Recife and I took some photographs. This one photo 192 shows A.E. (Red) West in the front of the jeep with Moyer in the back with a Leica camera. That afternoon and night, I took some photos of the carnival celebrants both in the streets and in their homes.

These 2 Navy photographers would each spend over 2 years at Recife so no doubt they had many interesting photos taken during that period. Moyer porobably made kodachrome color photos.

The Dead-Beat Taxi-Cab Passenger Incident at Ibura

Ibura field was only about 1.7 miles from Boa Viagem. Boa Viagem was served by Bondes from central Recife. This proximity of Ibura to areas of Recife was convenient both for the many navy officers who rented homes on Boa Viagem but also to sailors going to and from Recife and Boa Viagem. One could take a taxi from either place to Ibura and vice versa since the taxicabs were allowed to come right into the air base by the barracks.

The system of transportation worked well until one miscreant sailor pulled a maneuver which forced a change in procedure for the taxicabs. One late Saturday night (or early Sunday A:M) a sailor took a cab back to Ibura knowing full well he did not have any money to pay the cabbie. When the cab pulled up to the barracks, the miscreant sailor jumped out, ran into the darkened barracks and hopped into a bunk and pulled up his covers. The poor cabbie knew he couldn't go into the barracks and search for his passenger but he could and did report the incident to the authorities. Thereafter procedures were put into effect to prevent such misdeeds. That particular sailor was not popular thereafter.

The Ropa Woman Incident – Ibura Field

There was one young sailor with an abnormally great libido who cut a large swath among the willing young ladies of Recife. However, in his amorous adventures he managed to get into a fight in town and for disciplinary purposes he was confined to base for a 30 day period. He survived the first 3 weeks alright, but during his fourth week of no liberty privilege he managed to seduce one of the Ropa women who were allowed on base to pick up laundry and to return it to the sailors when they had finished washing and drying it. Most of the Ropa women were "long in the tooth" but he managed to ensnare one of the younger ones. Frequently mother and daughter combinations were in the group of Ropa Women. One wonders why he chose a Ropa girl instead of the many attractive young females working at the ship's store, etc?

Unfortunately for the errant sailor, the mother of the young lady who was seduced was also among the Ropa women and when her daughter became pregnant, she brought the matter to the attention of the base commander and the sailor was punished, but I do not remember the extent or the type of disciplinary action imposed.

I-191; Art Sykes, Lady L., Dale E. Wright

This happy trio in a park in Recife must have been aware that Lady L. was several months pregnant because the photo was taken about April, 1944.

Dale's twin daughters were born in July-August, 1944. One must assume that appropriate plans had been made.

I-192; A.E. West and Moyer in Recife

These 2 sailor photographers each spent over 2 years at Ibura Field near Recife. No doubt they both would have many interesting photos of Recife. Moyer was probably shooting Kodachrome color film. West was from Illinois but I don't know what state Moyer was from.

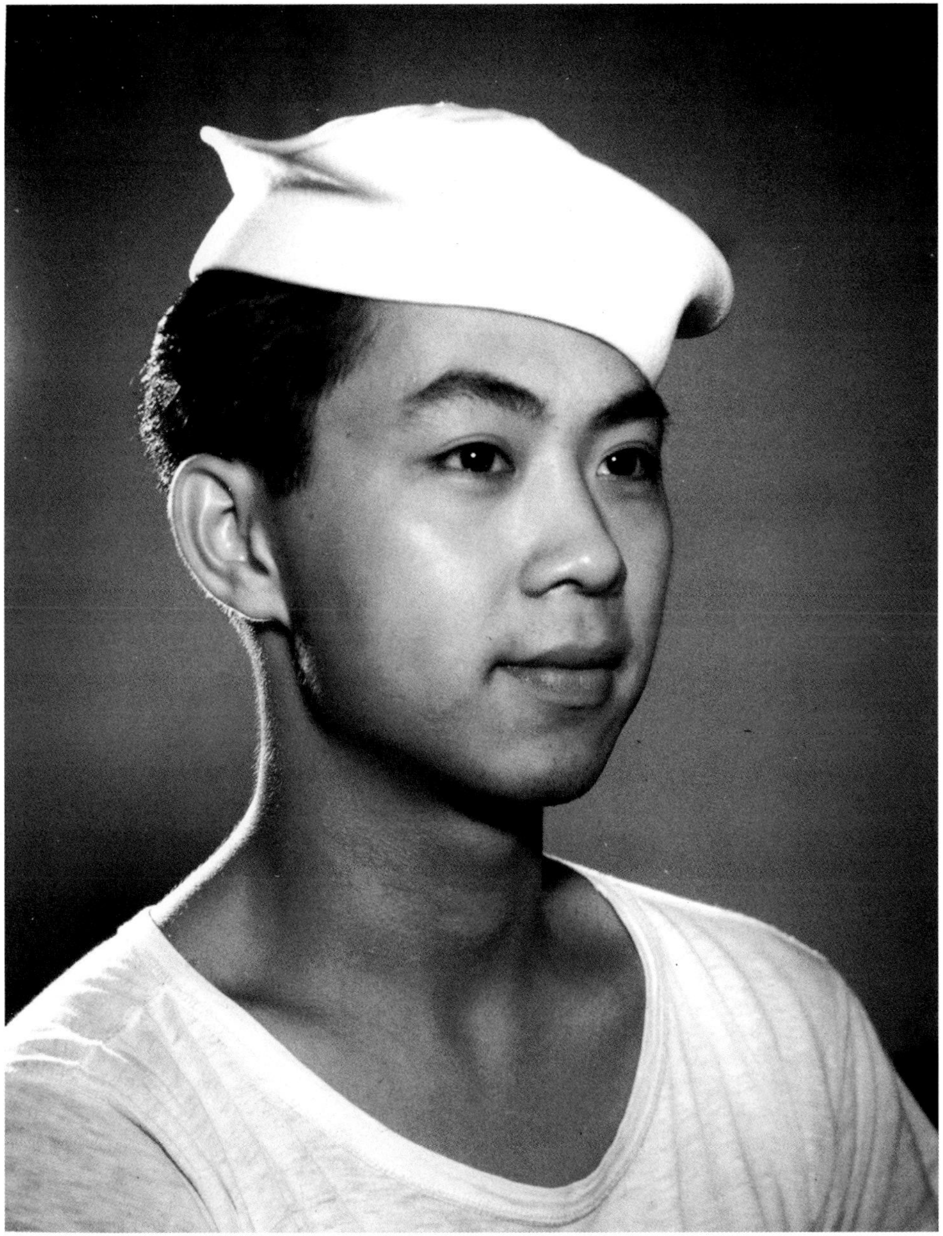

I-193; Moo Thick Soo Hoo, PhoM2/c
Ibura Field - 1944

AN AMERICAN SUCCESS STORY

This young gentleman, by 1944 when this portrait was made, had matured considerably since that day in 1935 or 1936 when he (age 13) had arrived in Boston from his birthplace in Canton, China.

His face reflects composure and confidence. No doubt developed by the need to learn English while attending grade school in Boston where only English was spoken and by working long hard hours in his family's laundry.

Having to cope with overt racial prejudice all his life and being able to overcome it also had a character building aspect. At this point in his life I suspect that he did not realize that he had found a new, almost lifetime home in the U.S. Navy. His unique skill as a camera repairman set him apart a bit and would also have bolstered his self confidence. He was robustly healthy, handsome and self assured, as attested to by the faint hint of a smile in this portrait. He also knew how to square his hat properly.

The following six pages describe some of the life experiences of this very successful emigre to the USA.

Then I was transferred from Natal back to Recife in March 1944 there had been several changes in photo lab personnel. One of the new sailors in the photo lab was a photographer's mate third class named Soo Hoo who was also a camera repairman. Moo was happy to be in the navy and had a buoyant personality. We became friends. He was a virile young man who enjoyed the company of some of the ready, willing, and able young "mocas" of Recife. He exhibited a joie de vivre that made him a boon shipmate. The preceding photo I-193 is a portrait of Moo shortly after he arrived in Recife.

After I returned to the USA in 1944 to Photographic Squadron 2 (VD-2) at Norfolk, Virginia, we corresponded with one another. This kept Moo and his shipmates up to date on happenings at Atlantic Fleet photo headquarters (VD-2) and myself aware of how Moo and my Fairwing 16 friends were coping with activities in Brazil.

I had last heard from Moo in a letter of October 10, 1945 when he wrote from his new duty billet at the Naval Air Station in Atlanta, Georgia where he was, as a Photographer's Mate First Class, in charge of the photo lab. In February, 2007, as I was beginning to write a paragraph about the portrait of Moo to explain its significance I thought it would be of interest to see if he were still around and if I could find him. One of my relatives who is expert in searches for people found a phone number and address that seemed to be of my friend Moo who I had not been in touch with for 62 years. Amazingly, as soon as he answered the phone I knew I had reached my old friend. Voices do not seem to change a lot.

Over the past few months we have talked several times over the phone and Moo has related to me the interesting story of his family background and his career of 30 years in the US Navy and subsequent activities. Moo's grandfather was "shanghaied" from Southern China in the mid 1800's to work as a coolie on the railroad building gangs in the western half of the USA. While here in the USA he fathered a child who in turn became Moo's father, which made Moo a US citizen even though he was born near Canton, China in December 1922.

Moo's father, because he was a US citizen, could freely travel between the USA and China. He would work a few years in the USA to accumulate money and then return to China for a couple of years and then he repeated the cycle of residing alternately in the USA and China for several decades. In the process he had three successive Chinese wives and produced children with all three of them. According to Moo, who was the last child born of the third wife, he wore the first two wives out. He was 60 years of age when Moo was born.

Moo's father was obviously an industrious "man among men" and he eventually became a prosperous landowner near Canton. Unfortunately he was in China when war broke out so he had to remain there for the remainder of his life. When the Communists took over his area they tied him to a pole in the Village Center and put a placard on him labeling him a "Capitalist Pig" because he was a landowner. He and his third wife lived until the late 1940's and he was 84 when he passed away. What an adventurous life he lived and what tumultuous times and dramatic events he witnessed and participated in. As we will note, "the apple does not fall far from the tree." Sangfroid can be passed from father to son.

Moo Thick Soo Hoo was 13 when he was put aboard a Canadian ship in Hong Kong by himself to sail to the USA to join his father and his uncle (his mother's brother) in Boston. His uncle owned a laundry in Needham, Massachusetts and two of Moo's brothers were also there. Aboard ship an adult fellow passenger befriended Moo and counseled him on what to do to catch a cross-country train and how to deal with immigration authorities. Moo's mother remained in China because at that time Chinese immigrants who were American citizens could not automatically bring in alien wives.

When Moo arrived in Boston the immigration authorities did not believe that he was a US citizen because they did not believe that he was his father's son. He was incarcerated for 30 days but finally his father was able to show some family records that convinced them Moo indeed was the son of a US citizen. At that time Moo did not speak or understand English.

Moo then went to work in his Uncle's laundry. He gradually learned to speak English by sitting through many double feature Cowboy and Indian movies, which, at that time, only cost 10 cents or so to get in. Even though he had gone to the sixth grade in the Chinese school at the Canton area he had to start in the first grade in Massachusetts public school at the town of Franklin. The language barrier must have been significant until Moo could sit through many movies to learn English. He went through 7th grade prior to enlisting in the Navy in 1942. Quite obviously he was to do a good bit of home self schooling in subsequent years in order to complete his education to allow him to achieve the many things he was to accomplish in life.

Like many of us, Moo's life changed dramatically after Pearl Harbor. In early 1942 two of Moo's brothers were drafted into the US Army. Their letters back to Boston about army life convinced Moo that he would rather serve in the US Navy. He almost failed the physical due to a heart murmur but he convinced the recruiter that it had come from working 16 hours a day for 7 days per week in his Uncle's laundry. By taking the physical the second time he was able to enlist on August 16, 1942.

After boot camp at Newport, Rhode Island, he was assigned to the receiving station at Boston. Earlier he had been told that he should become a mess boy or cook, probably a bit of racial prejudice. He demurred and talked them into letting him serve as a coxswain and in a few months he took the test for Boatswain's Mate third class and passed it. In a second instance of racism he was not promoted because BM3/C is a right arm rate and regular navy personnel then considered those ratings should only go to regular navy men of the right color.

He got his first break when he was transferred to Argentia, Newfoundland to serve as a striker (apprentice) in the photo lab. He had wanted to be a navy photographer. He spent 6 months at Argentia Naval Air Station in the photo lab and while there he passed the test for Pho M 3/C and did obtain that rating.

Moo then went to VD-2 in Norfolk, Virginia in mid 1943 and was chosen to go both to Fairchild Camera Company and then Folmer Graflex, both in New York, to be trained as a camera repairman. After a brief period back at VD-2 he was sent on a cargo ship to Recife, Brazil to become the camera repairman for Fairwing 16. The journey to Brazil took 30 days and Moo arrived in Recife in the first quarter of 1944.

At Recife it only took a few months for him to make Pho M 2/C. In photo I-194 we see him standing at an inspection being conducted by Commodore Lyon.

Moo spent 14 months in Fairwing 16 in Brazil and by September of 1945 when he was sent to the Atlanta Naval Air Station he became a Pho M 1/C in charge of the photo lab.

Shortly after the war ended, the navy began a rapid demobilization and by early 1946 there were only 103 photographers left in the entire navy. Then came the decision in very early 1946 to use our two remaining atomic bombs in experimental detonations at Bikini Atoll in the Pacific to determine the effect of these powerful new weapons on various types of naval vessels. Moo and Ken Ainsworth (with whom I had served at Quonset Point) and John Richter (Paul Richter's brother) were among the many navy photographers who were put on a specially equipped navy ship and sent to Bikini to photograph the tests and the damage done to the vessels subjected to the bombing. The group was to spend 6 months at Bikini and Kwajalein on this assignment.

Among the many ships assembled to be subjected to the blasts of the atomic bombs were: the German heavy cruiser (the Prinz Eugen): the Nagato (the giant Japanese battleship) and the old aircraft carrier (the USS Saratoga). The first two ships named had obviously been recovered and sufficiently refurbished that they could be brought to Bikini Atoll. One of the atom bombs was placed under the keel of the Saratoga and detonated. The other bomb was dropped from the air. In addition to photographing the detonations per se, all the ships had to be photographed before and after the bombings, inside and out, in great detail. A very large task.

Prior to one test a decision was made to have a Life magazine photographer go up in a plane and photograph one of the detonations but at the last minute he backed out of the assignment. Moo volunteered to take his place and was able to make some excellent photographs. A short time later some of the photos appeared in Life magazine and they were mistakenly credited as having been taken by the Life photographer who had refused the assignment.

After Bikini the navy photographers remaining were given leeway to participate on determination of their next assignment. Moo chose to attend the navy photo school at Pensacola to learn motion picture techniques. In addition to completing that training he became an instructor at Pensacola for a number of months in early 1947.

Like many of us he still maintained an urge to go to sea so he secured a transfer to a seaplane tender (the USS Salisbury Sound) which was on its way to the Pacific in mid 1947. From Hawaii the ship sailed on to China. When it put into port Moo had his hair cut in Chinese fashion, donned peasant clothes, and thus disguised made his way to his parents home near Canton for what would be his last visit with his father, mother and other relatives. This was a risky business, not only because it was not authorized but also there was a war going on between the Chinese nationalist's forces and those of the Communists. Good fortune smiled on Moo and he made his last visit, returned to his ship, and did not get caught in the process.

The Salisbury Sound returned to the West Coast and was alternately in the Bay area or at Long Beach. In 1947 he met an attractive Japanese-American lady, Nancy Kumasaki, and after a few months in 1948 they were married.

Nancy Kumasaki was born in Fresno, California where her father worked as a farm laborer. Unfortunately, when Nancy was 6 years old her mother died while giving birth. Nancy was taken in by a Mexican family on a nearby farm and was raised by that caring family. During World War II, having been reunited with her Japanese – American family members, she and the family were interned and sent to a poorly equipped internment camp in Arizona. She was released after a period of time and went to live in New York City. However when matters were resolved she returned to California where happily she met Moo. Since Moo had earlier and would later manage to survive episodes of racial prejudice, no doubt he could empathize with Nancy concerning her internment.

There were some complicating matters for both Nancy and Moo in relationships with their families which they were able to deal with. Some of Moo's relatives had family members at' Nanking at the time of the notorious "Rape of Nanking" where the Japanese army murdered hundreds of thousands of Chinese men, women, and children in a most barbarous act. In turn, Nancy had family relatives at Hiroshima when the atom bomb was dropped but most fortunately they all survived. Despite these stresses they had a successful 55 year marriage and produced two talented and successful daughters before Nancy passed away in 2003.

In 1951, while stationed at Alameda, California, Moo was promoted to Chief Photographer's Mate and became personal photographer to Fleet Admiral Chester Nimitz, the chief architect of victory in the naval warfare in the Pacific. After this assignment he went to sea again on the aircraft carrier, USS Yorktown II for a 20 month tour of duty. While on the Yorktown, and after surviving another racial prejudice episode, he passed the test for and became a warrant officer. For the next 10 years or so he would serve at various naval bases and work his way up to Lieutenant. In 1964 he was transferred to Atsugi Naval Air Station in Japan and was put in charge of all photographic activity in the Western Pacific. He was able to bring Nancy and his two young daughters to Japan and they went to Hiroshima to visit Nancy's relatives during their 5 year stay at Atsugi. By this time, Moo Soo Hoo had served in World War II, the Korean War, and the Vietnam War and his meritorious record enabled him to be cleared for promotion to Lieutenant Commander. In photo I-195, we see Moo donning his jacket with the new epaulets. It had been a long and eventful journey for the 13 year old from Canton, China. In photo I-196 we see Nancy and Moo at a social event.

During the latter 16 years of Moo's 30 years of naval service, Moo had been doing two things to prepare for that day in 1972 (at the age of 49) when he would resume civilian life. Over the years, he bought properties at several places in the USA and Hawaii wherever he was stationed. He also took college level courses so that when he came back from Atsugi to Point Mugu in California for his final days of service he was able to obtain his Bachelor of Arts in Economics.

After leaving the navy Moo served as a financial officer for the city and county of San Francisco for a decade and then concentrated on management of real estate interests. Today he lives in the San Francisco bay area, travels frequently and also helps his medical doctor daughter Sonia and her husband Michael Black by babysitting his three granddaughters. His other daughter, Mona, is an attorney in Los Angeles.

When Moo's life journey ends, he will join that pantheon of patriots in Arlington National cemetery where his wife Nancy is interred.

I-194; Commodores inspection - Ibura Field

It appears that Captain Lyon is pausing a bit as he passes by Moo Thick Soo Hoo standing at attention. Hopefully and probably the Captain's gaze was strictly one of curiosity and not a querulous or disapproving one.

I-195; Moo Thick Soo Hoo - Lieutenant Commander - USN

The twists and turns of events; from an immigrant lad of 13 learning to speak English by watching double feature cowboy movies in a Boston theatre; serves his adopted country through three wars and becomes a distinguished naval officer; amazing.

I-196; Moo Soo Hoo and Nancy Kumasaki Soo Hoo

Nancy Kumasaki and her parents and siblings also had their trials and tribulations before, during, and after World War II as noted previously. Nancy's father was very strongly disillusioned by the governments treatment of Japanese Americans during the war. Nancy's father had originally come to the USA to work as a blacksmith on the railroad early in the 20th century. He had obtained a Japanese bride by mail order through a catalog with pictures. After her passing he struggled to raise the family but obviously succeeded.

Once World War II was over Mr. Kumasaki renounced his U.S. citizenship and returned to Japan hoping to resume operation of his small family farm. However, other relatives had taken it over so he needed and wanted to return to his family in the USA. It took an act of Congress to permit him to recover American citizenship which he then did and he was able to rejoin Nancy and Moo.

Nancy and Moo's daughter (Sonia) married an Irishman so Moo now has several beautiful Chinese-Japanese-Irish-American granddaughters with black hair and green eyes. Their other daughter (Mona) is an attorney. The success story continues.

16

Views of City of Recife, 1943 – 44

Recife was the high water mark for Dutch colonizers (empire builders) in the western hemisphere.

Observation by the author

THE CREATED ISLAND CITY

The Portuguese word Recife means reef. The Dutch built Recife's islands behind reefs on land reclaimed from the sea to provide an excellent harbor. In so doing, they created what is sometimes referred to as the "Venice of Brazil". Chapter 24 contains views of modern Recife.

Central Recife

I-197: Map No. 12 is a map of modern Central Recife (from Reference 8) showing the six bridges connecting the main business district of Santa Antonio Island with Boa Vista on the mainland and Ilha de Recife, the dockside island. Two of the three rivers which flow into Recife are shown on this map.

The next seventeen photos are scenes from Recife Proper and depict what that city looked like in 1943-44. There follows six photos of the less affluent sections around Recife which I call the "suburbs".

Recife – August 1943 – A Parade and a Surprise Welcome

Folks everywhere seem to like a parade and citizens of Recife seemed to particularly like them. While Carnival time was the pinnacle, there seemed to be many other occasions for parades in Recife. The crowded scene in photo I-198 was a religious festival of some kind which happened during my first liberty to Recife. Note the two U.S. Sailors on the far side of the street to the left of the umbrella. My first contact with a Brazilian was a bit startling. I was standing with other sailors watching the parade when suddenly I felt a pain in my groin which quickly dissipated. Then I noticed three young ladies who had just passed looking back and laughing and smiling at us. One of them had grabbed my crotch as they passed by. The one who had done so was a bit dusky and had on rather striking purple lipstick. Naturally, my companions thought the incident was hilarious but I was just startled.

At the time I was eighteen years old and most of my companion sailors were a few years older and much wiser in the ways of the world whereas I could best be described as still a "bit wet behind the ears". Being born at home and subsequently raised in a small bucolic rural village surrounded by family farms and wooded hillsides had been a wonderful childhood but my sheltered early life did not provide any significant degree of worldliness or sophistication. This may have been a blessing.

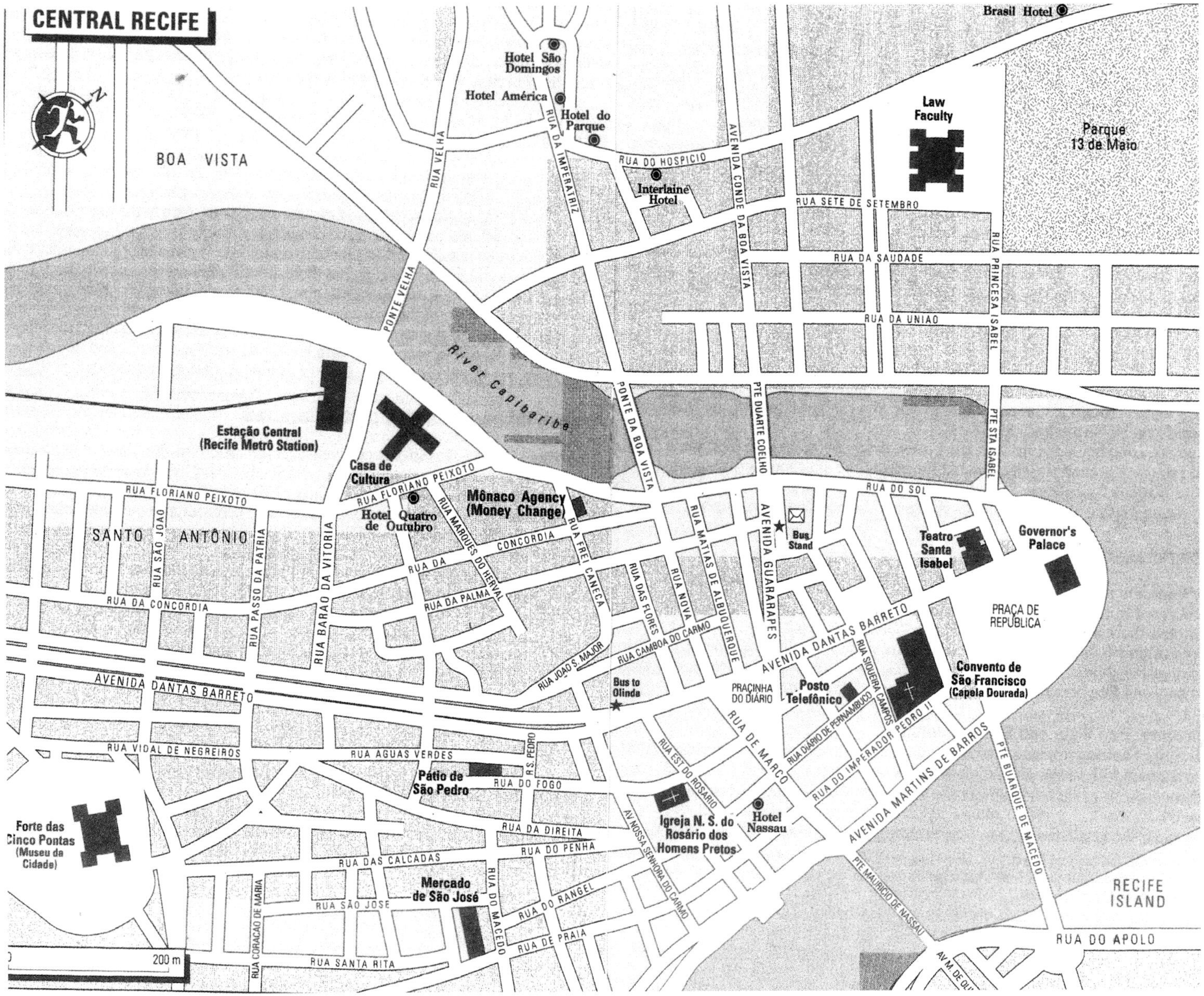

I-197; Map No. 12 - Central Recife

Map is reproduced with permission from Brazil Travel Survival Kit 3 at 1996, Lonely Planet Publications. It shows how the most central island (Santa Antonio) which is the main business district is connected to Boa Vista and Recife Islands by the bridges depicted in several of the following photos. The church depicted in later photos is most likely the Igreja N.S. do Rosario dos Homens Preto (Rosario of Black Men).

I-198; Religious parade in Recife

On the left side of this photo the front of a Bonde with a destination sigh labelled Pinheiro is visible. When these parades occurred both the streets and sidewalks would become crowded and Bonde or other vehicle traffic was difficult.

I-199; Ponta Duarte Coelho - Recife

While standing on the Santa Antonio end of Ponta Isabel I took this photo I-199 which shows this bridge as it crosses over Capibaribe River to Boa Vista section of Recife. This is one of the 39 bridges connecting the three main islands to each other and to the mainland. There are three church steeples in the center portion of this photo.

I-200; Closer view of Ponta Duarte Coelho

This is a second photo of Ponta Duarte Coelho. It may be that the Estrela de Prata (Silver Star), a favorite café-bar for American servicemen, was located at the far end of this bridge on the right hand side of the road facing the River Capibaribe.

I-201; Foot and truck traffic on Ponta Duarte Coelho

As can be seen in this photo this particular bridge was one of the busiest roadways in Recife. The Bonde tracks also show that Avenida Guararapes was a main thoroughfare at that time.

I-202; Ponta Sta Isabel - bondes and buses

The domed building is a significant structure. It is the Legislative Assembly Headquarters. The bridge shown in this photo is Ponta Sta Isabel. There are two traditional Bondes as well as two buses on this bridge.

I-203; View of Rua Aurora across River Capibaribe

The small boat in this photo is typical of many used for a variety of purposes in and around Recife. The street on the far side of the river is Rua Aurora in Boa Vista. A color photo of Rua Aurora as it appears today is in the later chapter on modern Recife.

I-204; Ponta da Boa Vista

This bridge with its criss-cross girders shown in this photo connects Rua Nova, a main business street of central Recife with Rua de Imperatiz in Boa Vista. Note the closed Bonde behind the more familiar open sided bonde.

I-205; Pastoral Boa Viagem

Boa Viagem is a beach section of Recife on a peninsula south of the three main islands making up Recife proper. During World War II Boa Viagem, which was connected to Recife by the Bonde line on an avenue running southward, was a pastoral area featuring many modest homes facing the ocean over the avenue. Note the absence of high-rise buildings.

I-206; Front porch Boa Viagem beachfront home - 1943

This photo shows how close the tiled roof homes along the avenue on Boa Viagem were to the ocean. Many officers from Fairwing 16 in groups of 3 or 4 rented homes along Boa Viagem beach. The officers would get their provisions and ice from the commissary at Ibura field. They had housekeepers and other local helpers to cook and clean, etc., in these houses. I do not recall too many of them griping about service in Brazil or requesting transfers to other places. It must be remembered however that a fair number lost their lives when their planes were shot down in the war against the U-Boats.

Once in a while a victory party would be held in one of the larger homes to celebrate the sinking of a submarine or blockade runner. The Commodore (Captain Lyon) was a respected hard worker but he also liked to lead the group singing by getting up on the top of a flat top piano at one of the houses once the party got into full swing. Normally these parties would be well stocked with nurses, USED girls, Red Cross ladies, USO females, if not also some ladies from Recife. One night I was chosen to take some photographs at one of these parties. During the course of the evening one particular young lady, who was there with a member of the Commodores staff decided she liked the "cut of my jib" and began making amorous overtures. My protestations (I knew she was there with an important person and I knew on which side my bread was buttered) were of no avail for a while. I finally was able to convince the photo officer (my boss) that I had used up all my film and he kindly let me leave and return to Ibura, a narrow escape from exile to Ascension Island.

I-207; Church in Recife - 1944

From a steeple of one of the many churches in Recife I took this photo of an adjacent church. The steeple in which I stood was higher indicating that the church to which it was attached was much larger than the adjacent church in the photo.

This leads me to believe that I was standing in a steeple of the Igreja N.S. do Rosario dos Homens Preto (Rosario of Black Men) when I took this photo. However, since there are dozens of colonial era churches in Recife it may have been a different one.

Note the cylindrical gas holder next to and closer than the smoke stacks, on of which must have been "blowing soot" at the time I took the photo. There must have been a coal gasification plant in Recife or else they were bringing in natural gas in 1944.

I-208; Interior of church - Recife - 1944

This photo shows a detailed and elaborate display on the wall of one of Recife's many churches. While this nave is impressive it is much smaller and less ornate than decorative areas in other early Brazilian churches, gold was clearly plentiful in church coffers when this church was planned and built.

The lavish interior architecture of the churches built in the 1500 and 1600's is a reflection of the position of the church in the culture and political hierarchy during the colonial ascendancy of the Portugese.

The relative simplicity of form and structure of the houses of worship of the more austere branches of the protestant religious groups is striking by contrast. The Pentecostal protestant churches have, in contemporary times, experienced much growth in Brazil.

I-209; Thatched roof homes - suburbs of Recife

In this photo the author is using a 35 millimeter Retina to take some color photos of the decidedly less affluent areas outside of Recife. One of the houses shown has the prevalent thatched roof and there are unused bundles of thatch in front of it. Note the utility poles and wires in the upper right area.

The two boys observing are thin but they at least do not appear to be malnourished. They all seemed happy and friendly despite their relatively low standard of living.

Whoever went along with me on this visit took this photo. Unfortunately I only got the Retina and one roll of color film just a week or two before I left Brazil to return to Norfolk; Virginia, Naval Air Station. Thus practically all my photos of Brazil are black and white.

I-210; Menina in front of mud hut

The house in this photo was not the usual masonry thatched roof home. One must remember our own pioneers who went west and lived on the prairies in “Soddys” which were made from Sod. But that was in the 1800’s and a temporary arrangement.

The block-like bits on the front wall of the house look like “wattle and daub” of English usage?

The Menina looks well-fed but pensive and not quite sure what the young Americanos were up to. She was also pleased when we were able to speak to her with a few words of Portugese. Then off she ran to join a group of other youngsters.

I-211; Hillside homes - Recife

As can be seen in this photo, not only were there no paved roads in this area but also the roadway that did exist was deeply rutted. The man in photo I-211 does have a shirt even though it is holely. Note the third house down has a mud block exterior.

I-212; Painted house with a fence

There were gradations in quality of the modest dwellings in the hilly suburb areas on the mainland opposite the mostly island city of Recife. This particular house was one of the very few that had a fence, albeit not a particularly sturdy one.

The steep hill at the rear of the house was in sharp contrast to the low level flatness of Recife's island nearby.

There did not seem to be any vegetable gardens in the area. Perhaps the folks living there did not have enough ground area to facilitate gardens. Presumably the residents worked either in Recife or on outlying farms in the area.

I-213; Our gang in the suburbs

This group of youngsters appears to be as happy and carefree as such a group most anywhere in the world. Just from their facial expressions one might assume that the one who is the second from the right just might be the unofficial "leader of the pack"?

I can well remember similar photos my mother took of a group of youngsters in our neighborhood with similar poses and varying facial expressions.

They are standing on a small bridge of some sort. The area around Recife had many tributary streams which discharge into the rivers surrounding Recife's island. There is a building with a smoke stack in the background.

I-214; Broad Street in Recife suburbs

A group of young mothers and some of their children are curious about the two Americano sailors with their cameras walking around their neighborhood. A smile and a few words spoken in Portugese clears the air.

17

People in Recife, 1943 - 44

The mixed Portuguese, Dutch, Indian and African heritage of Recife's people is displayed in daily life and at Carnival.

A blinding glimpse of the obvious for the author

AN ETHNIC MELTING POT

The following fifteen photos include images of the spectrum of citizens of Recife.

Silver Star (Estrela de Prata) – From the Entrance

A favorite spot for American sailors and soldiers was a bar-café called the Silver Star. I believe it was located in Boa Vista at where the Ponte Boa Vista reached the far bank of the Rio Capibaribe. In photo I-215 we note the lady co-proprietress of the Silver Star at the back end of the bar. She got me to take this and the next photo so she could get souvenir post cards made to sell to her customers. The young lady at the extreme right behind the bar was named Sevola Maria Olivera. She was a friend but that didn't stop her from teasing me about my usual beverage of Suco de Uva (grape juice) instead of beer, which was their principal drink. Sometimes I would drink Guarana which was treated like coca-cola by the Brasileros. As a matter of fact it was not at all like coca-cola in taste and was a refreshing drink.

Silver Star – From the Rear

In photo I-217, taken from the back of the Silver Star shows the gentleman who was co-proprietor. He is wearing the typical lightweight white suit favored by Brasilero business men. The Silver Star was a well run place and generally was free of any incidents. However, one evening a group of navy personnel from a jeep carrier were present and an officer in the group tried to pry one of my sailor friend's young Brazilian girl friend away and an altercation ensued. What the officer didn't know was that the sailor's lady fair was just pregnant and they were a serious couple. There were fisticuffs involved with our Chief Photographers Mate decking the transgressing officer. No charges were pressed. A Brazilian secret service agent named Mario Amorim Campos (photo I-216) frequented the Silver Star and had befriended many of us. He was a fine fellow and his presence may have affected the outcome of the incident just described. I was not present in the Silver Star when this incident of fisticuffs allegedly occurred so I cannot vouch for the accuracy of all the sequential events.

We also had a favorite restaurant in Recife called the Green Front which, I think, was on a street at the edge of a small park. We had "bife assado" (roast beef) on occasion at the Green Front. I still have an image in my mind of the diminutive mustachioed Brazilian waiter at the Green Front who was kind enough to puzzle out our meal order conveyed to him in broken Portugese.

I-215; Silver Star (Estrela de Prata) from the entrance

I took this photo at the request of the lady with the feather in her hat at the back end of the bar. She was coproprietor of this most popular cafe-bar in Recife.

I-216; Mario Amorim Campos

This gentleman was a member of the Brazilian Police in Recife.

He was a congenial man and I think he could speak and understand some English.

We saw him on occasion at the Silver Star.

His presence was particularly fortuitous on one occasion mentioned in the text.

Recife was full of soldiers and sailors. On very infrequent occasions, the police were needed.

I-217; Silver Star from the rear

Here we see the coproprietor in the white suit in the center of the photo. Out beyond the swinging front doors one can see the characteristic railing of the Ponte da Boa Vista. This helped me discern the location of the Silver Star in Boa Vista. Apparently it is no longer there.

I-218; Da Cunha - street photographer

In this photo we see my friend, da Cunha, in action. I cannot remember his first name. He would take photos of passerbys and give them a card with his name and number so they could contact him for copies.

I-219; Da Cunha and lady friend

My friend was a real bon vivant. This was not the only pretty lady who stopped to talk to him. I don't know whether or not he was a family man. His photo beat was on the main street of the Santa Antonio business and shopping district. His business was successful.

I-220; Vende coconuts

At a public open air market in Recife we see a gentleman selling coconuts. One could speculate he must have some reasonable source of income since he sports a watch, a ring, and an umbrella.

I-221; Brazilian with marmoset

There are stories about sailors purchasing or somehow ending up having small creatures including monkeys in which the subsequent behavior of the critters was a real problem. I don't know about the Marmoset which appears in this photo. My Portuguese-English dictionary doesn't list a Marmoset.

I-222; Al's girl plus her friend

I-223; Vende doce

My negative cover for this photo contains the notation, Al's girl friend. Al was a sailor who had maintained his abstinence from conjugal relations with Brazilian ladies for his first year in Brazil. Finally he succumbed and I believe it was to the charms of the young lady on the right.

This lad is carrying coconut based squares of candy on the plate on his head in this photo. He must have had a good sense of balance even when confronted by my camera. The look on his face is pensive and quizzical.

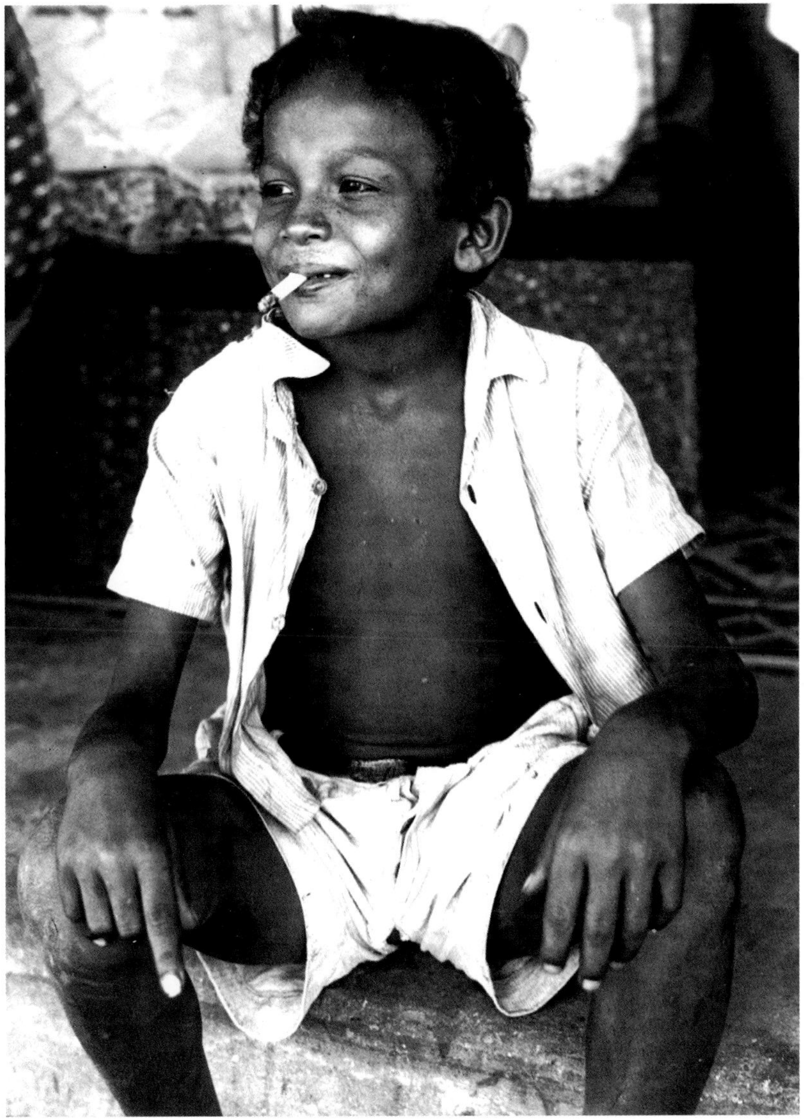

I-224; Menino Freshkoo

The lad in this photo taken in Recife conveys the impression of someone with "street smarts". My negative envelope contained the title Menino Freshkoo. The second word is probably a phonetic spelling of a Portuguese word which I had heard but not seen in print at that time. There is a Brazilian word Frescura, meaning freshness. I don't remember seeing a lot of cigarette smoking by Brazilians, even though Bahia-Salvador was a tobacco growing area.

I-225; Raggedy Man

The necktie is an interesting touch on this otherwise tramp – like costume. Certainly the many Brasileros of modest means all seemed to use carnival as a time for celebration and perhaps unconsciously as a safety valve in preparation for the strictures of the Lenten season to follow.

I-226; Dock workers in Recife

In this photo we note the unloading of a small vessel carrying flour to the Recife Docks from either up river or from another coastal town. This was a typical way of moving goods in Brazil since the rail and road transportation system at that time (43/44) was not extensive or widely used.

I-227; Carnival - Recife - boys - girls

In Recife in 1944 there was as much or more impromptu dancing and prancing in the streets during carnival as there was an organized parade. In this photo we see a group of revelers in costumes and with obviously varied ethnic backgrounds. We note, in the right hand of the second person in the front left side of the picture a small metallic cylinder containing a very volatile liquid. They used these containers to spray the back legs of unsuspecting females. Physicians used to use this technique to freeze areas of skin, an unusual but prevalent prank at carnival time. The use of these "Lanca Perfume" spray cylinders was later prohibited by law.

I-228; Sailors with costumed girls

On the main street in Recife this photo shows a pair of young bonneted ladies and a Yeoman 2nd class who seem to be on familiar terms. I do not know the significance of these carnival costumes; they seem almost colonial in nature. They may be due to the remnant of Dutch influence in Recife.

I-129; Brass and string bands

In this photo the street crowd mills about the 12 man band marching up the street on February 18, 1944 in Recife. This appears to be a Maracatus (an African procession accompanied by percussion musicians at Carnaval). We can see 9 umbrellas scattered throughout the crowd. These were to shield their holders from the sun, even though the temperature was not oppressive at all.

I-230; Familia

An extended family kindly allowed me to enter their home to take photos of the street scene below their front windows. In turn I made this photo of them. They were in the midst of enjoying some food and Cerveja when I intruded on them. I relied on the aura of a general feeling of friendliness prevalent during carnival.

18

Olinda - 1944
Early Capital of Brazil

O Linda situacao para uma vila.

Comment by first Portuguese Governor
on arrival at site of the new town

The old colonial city of Olinda is supposed to have derived its name from the first two words of this utterance by the emissary from Portugal who had been designated to govern the first capital of Portuguese Brazil in the early 1500's. The site of Olinda certainly was and is a beautiful location for a town.

TOPOGRAPHY

The Portuguese chose the hilly area overlooking the beaches bordering the Atlantic rather than the more southerly swampy marshland of the site which would later become Recife for their first settlement in what would later become the state of Pernambuco. They did use the Recife area as a port but Olinda, 4 miles north of the marshland had both climatic and military advantages as well as being a much more attractive place to live at that time.

HISTORY

Olinda came into being because of the Europeans need for sugar. The settlement grew into a small city in the 1500's because of the concentration of cane sugar plantations which grew up in that area. As part of the Dutch effort to take over as much of the northeast Portuguese Brazilian sugar industry as possible, the Dutch, after first conquering Salvador da Bahia, conquered Olinda in 1630 and burnt the city to the ground. Fourteen years later an uprising by the many sugar planter barons and their minions drove out the Dutch and recaptured Olinda and the port city of Recife.

The Dutch had converted much of the marshland surrounding the small port of Recife into habitable land by draining the swamps, building canals and forming a larger Recife. The effort by the Dutch at Olinda and Recife and Natal was their last attempt to wrest control of Northeast Brazil from the Portuguese. The Dutch had previously been driven out of Salvador da Bahia so when they lost Recife, Olinda and Natal they ended their attempts to take over Northeast Brazil.

Salvador da Bahia had quickly grown and by 1549 that city had become the capital of Portuguese Brazil so Olinda's reign as the capital was very short. In turn, the seat of Portuguese Brazilian government was transferred from Salvador da Bahia in 1763 to Rio de Janeiro when the "Gold Rush" occurred in Minas Gerais, the state near where Rio is located. Once they had routed the Dutch the sugar barons and their supporters rebuilt Olinda into a beautiful colonial city, very similar to the pre-Dutch invasion condition. As time progressed, Recife grew much more rapidly than Olinda and accordingly people generally consider Olinda as part of the Recife metropolitan area. However, the sheer beauty, historical and cultural aspects of Olinda have enabled it to maintain a sense of individual identity.

I-231; Olinda from hill - 1944

This photo shows a religious enclave in 1944 on one of Olinda's typical hills overlooking the South Atlantic Ocean. The large rectangular structure in the center is the Seminaria de Olinda and next to it is the Igreja NS da Graca (church) both date to 1549. Further down the hill is the Convento Sao Francisco (1585) and the Capela de Sao Roque and the Igreja de NS das Neves. Recife appears in the distance in the upper right quadrant.

I-232; Olinda - a closer view - 1944

The second photo of Olinda is further down the hill toward the ocean and gives a closer view of the Igreja de NS das Neves and its surroundings. Olinda, in combination with Recife and its Boa Viagem beaches has developed into a popular center for Brazilian and foreign tourists at carnival time which lasts now for 11 days in this area. One reason for this is overcrowding in Rio de Janeiro plus the fact that Recife, the fourth largest city in Brazil is increasingly the first port of call for many of the foreign tourists flying to Brazil.

19

Salvador da Bahia
Brazil - 1944

Bahia is far superior to Recife as a
naval base in every respect, except position.

Admiral Ingram on September 1944

LOCATION AND TOPOGRAPHY – SALVADOR

As Admiral Ingram noted, Bahia and its capital city, Salvador, was about 400 miles too far south to be the central home port for Allied naval forces in the South Atlantic. Salvador, the fourth largest city of Brazil (and capital of the state of Bahia) with a population of about 300,000 in the early 1940's, had excellent harbor facilities so it did become an auxiliary base for surface ships. Since the Bahia area was about midway between Belem and southernmost Brazil it also became an important base for Allied air power for use in combating Axis naval forces.

Map no. 7 (preceding page 55) shows the location of Salvador in the Northeast section of Brazil. Salvador da Bahia is located on the tip of a peninsula at the entrance to the Bahia de Todos Santos within an area known as the Reconcavo as seen in Map No.12 - I-233 (reproduced with permission of Rough Guides LTD, publishers of the 5th edition of the Rough Guide to Brazil, in 2003).

During the war most American sailors referred to Salvador as Bahia. Most Brazilians also refer to Salvador as Bahia. Indeed I do not even remember hearing the name Salvador during my stay in that country and city. This was probably because the two Navy air bases were outside Salvador City.

Just as with Recife and Rio de Janeiro, the topography of Salvador da Bahia was most significant in its founding and subsequent history. The large embayment and the steep cliff above a natural harbor at the bottom of the peninsula bordering the ocean made for a great defensive position for a settlement to be built on the top of the hill overlooking the bay.

A most poetic description of Salvador da Bahia was by one William Scully who wrote in his 1866 guidebook to Brazil as follows:

> "Here, sheltered from every wind and surrounded by a country exuberantly rich, fleets may ride at anchor in a gulf which seems as if formed by nature to be the emporium of the world and receive its shipping while the town itself, seen picturesquely crowning the high bluff that circles round the eastern side of the bay, appears a fitting mistress of the lovely scene."

At the time of early colonization by competing European countries it was inevitable that small wars would be fought over advantageous areas by the European competitors whose objective was to acquire territory, natural resources, and riches. The initial settlement by the Portuguese was on top of the cliff at Salvador, in a position to defend the whole area surrounding the Bay of All Saints and its fertile area known as the Reconcavo (bay area).

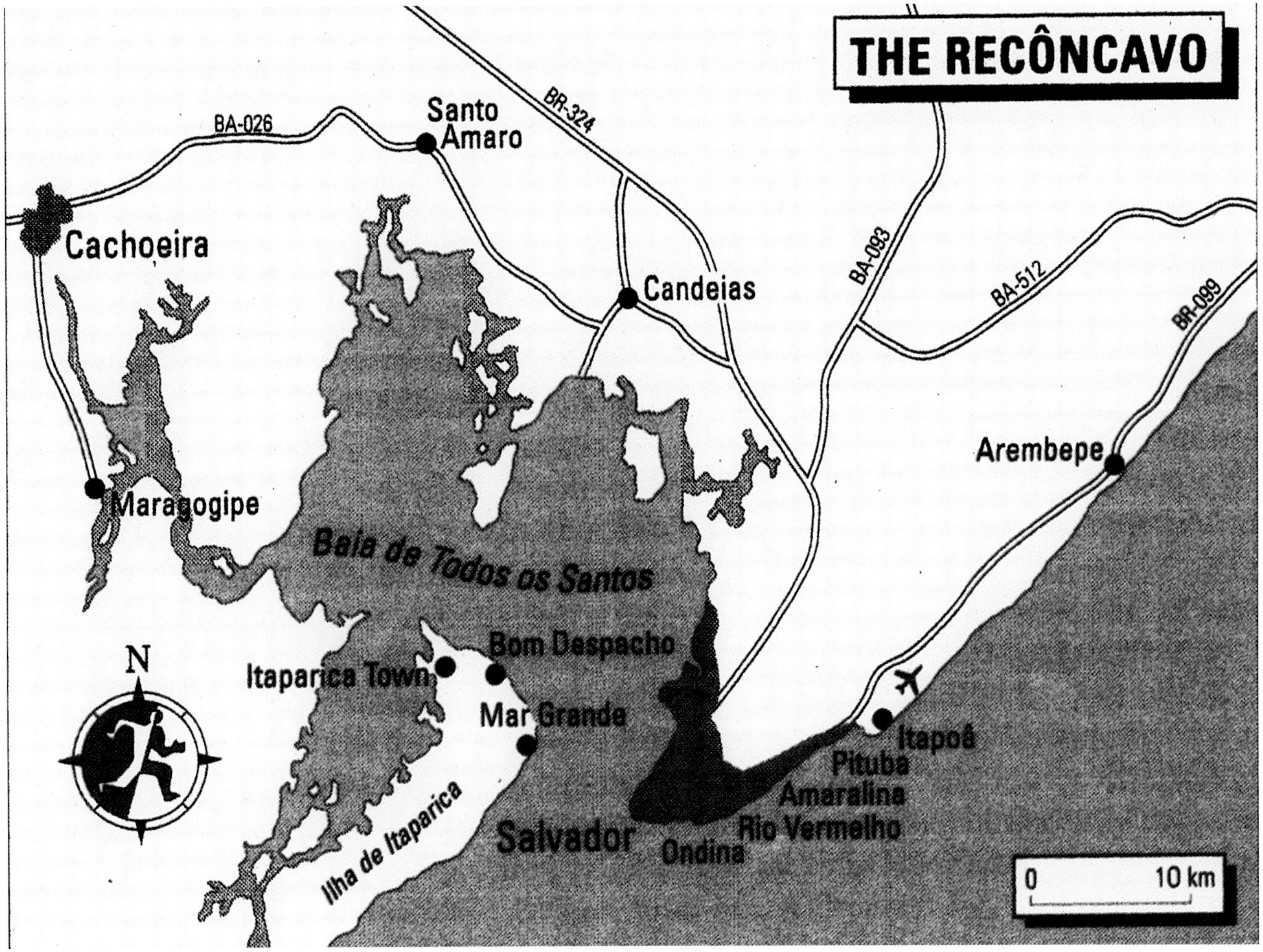

I-233; Map No. 12 - the Reconcavo

Once again, the early colonizers of Brazil chose a spectacular bay area (Reconcavo in Portugese) for an early strategic colony. In this case there were three great advantages for the Reconcavo and Salvador on the southern tip of a peninsula. The Bay of All Saints was and is a great natural harbor where ships could hide.

The topography of Salvador made it a fine place to erect defenses against intruders and the area around the bay was very fertile.

It is not difficult to envision why the Portugese made it an early capital of the Brazilian colony. It is also easy to realize why they quickly recaptured Salvador in 1625 after allowing the Dutch invaders to keep the colony for only about one year.

The region around the bay has always been widely used for agricultural crops of various types.

This map is reproduced with permission from Brazil Survival kit 3 at 1996, Lonely Planet Publications.

THE U.S. NAVY IN BAHIA

Early difficulties

The Trinidad – Bahia (Salvador) convoy route was a busy sea lane which had to be protected. During the first 18 months after Pearl Harbor that task was not well fulfilled because the skimpy combined Allied Forces present were only beginning to assemble and become able to perform adequately. The subsequent story of Convoy BT-6 will illustrate the difficulties.

One of the problems with both merchant seamen and navy sailors being on liberty in port cities during wartime when submarine warfare is occurring is the likelihood of leaks of information about convoy sailings and routes. The following quotation from reference no.3 about a leak at Salvador da Bahia in March 1943 is an example:

> "That northbound convoy (BT-6) consisted of 29 vessels, some of which had come from the Indies via Capetown, and many of which had no convoy experience. It included five Liberty ships, whose 11-knot speed was cramped in an 8 knot convoy. Security, survivors asserted, was very slightly observed at Bahia, where Torpedo Annie, a handsome redhead who consorted with nobody under the rank of Master, was suspected of passing along to the Nazi spies such confidences as she was able to extort during hours of amorous dalliance. This belle dame sans merci owed her romantic sobriquet to the observed fact that her lovers, shortly after parting, were apt to go down with their ships."

Six ships of Convoy BT-6 were torpedoed. Cherchez la femme. Fortunately, after mid 1943 improved security provisions and better regulation of convoy maneuvers were put into place.
In early 1943 an Atlantic Fleet analyst made the following comment about the fate of Convoy BT-6, "It is apparent that Convoy BT-6 was not a well regulated operation."

Ipitanga and Aratu

In addition to periodic forays of navy surface ships from the port of Salvador, Admiral Ingram had both a seaplane base (Aratu on the bay), and a land plane airfield (Ipitanga) made more fully operative in early 1943 when new PBM-3C and PV-1 Ventura squadrons became available. Previously, VP-83 had periodically used Aratu or Ipitanga as advanced stop-off points during its convoy coverage flights up and down the coast.

Several PBM-3 squadrons were based at different times at Aratu, Bahia seaplane base. VP-74, VP-203, and VP-211 all had the Martin Mariners operating from Aratu depending on the scope of U Boat activity off Bahia at any given time.

For most of the time in Brazil the PBM squadrons were based in Bahia and Rio. The harbor characteristics of Natal and Recife were not as conducive to successful takeoffs by PBM's. These large flying boats were somewhat underpowered and long surface taxiing as required at Natal caused considerable stress on the planes' engines and shortened the useful period between engine overhauls or replacements. In addition, Natal had PBY's, PV-1's, and later PB4Y's for convoy coverage.

Water which was a bit rough made takeoffs easier for PBM's. It is clear that the power requirements for a takeoff for a large flying boat from water (instead of land) imposes a heavy burden on the engines. Amerigo Vespucci, the Italian navigator for whom the Americas were named, sailed into the Baia de Todos os Santos in 1501, only 9 years after Columbus is credited with discovering the New World.

HISTORY OF SALVADOR DA BAHIA

The Portuguese King Joao (John) sent a group of colonists to Bahia in 1530 to establish a Portuguese presence on the eastern half of South America. The Portuguese and Spanish had a wobbly vacillating agreement on which portion of South America was to be a Portuguese colony and which portion would become a Spanish possession. This agreement had been arranged by the Pope of Rome whose offices played a dominant role in the Catholic world, and particularly in the Iberian Peninsula countries.
By 1544 Salvador da Bahia had become the capital of Brazil and it remained so until 1763 when the capital was removed to Rio. The Reconcavo sector of Bahia became the foremost agricultural area of

Brazil (sugar cane, tobacco and later, spices) at that time. Salvador is the oldest and most historic city of Brazil. The predominance of agriculture required the importation of African slaves in large numbers after many of the native Indians fled to the interior to avoid slavery. As a result, Bahia became a real melting pot in terms of skin color and ethnic background. Almost half the population is of African origin and even today one can find gradation from black to white and every shade in between due to extensive mixing of the white, African, and native Indian populace.

In 1624 the Dutch conquered Bahia but the Portuguese (with support and troops from Spain) returned the following year and recaptured the city. The Dutch then switched their aggressive attentions to Olinda and Natal. By 1640 the Dutch had conquered Olinda, built the city of Recife and taken Natal, but they did not again challenge the Portuguese in Bahia. Salvador da Bahia became (after Lisbon) the second largest and most important city in the Portuguese empire.

Over the past two centuries, Salvador da Bahia and the entire northeast of Brazil has lost its earlier dominant position in economic and governmental affairs in Brazil to the large power axis in the southern part of the country from Rio de Janeiro through Sao Paulo and Rio Grande del Sul.

The northeast is a relatively less developed area in economic terms but remains a great cultural and historic area of Brazil. Its benign climate and beautiful beaches have fostered great growth in the tourist industry with many Brazilians and Europeans vacationing in the areas from Bahia to Fortaleza.

The Ipitanga land plane base at Bahia was a home for VP-129, a Lockheed Ventura PV-1 squadron. The PV-1s were used to respond to specific U Boat sightings since their lack of range did not allow them to conduct lengthy barrier sweeps like the PBYs, PBMs, and later the PB4Y Liberators.

Just as in Recife and Natal the wartime Ipitanga Air Base has been converted into an international airport serving Bahia.

PEOPLE AND PLACES: SALVADOR - 1944

Colonial Salvador is famous for its many gold decorated churches and beautiful mansions inhabited by the Portuguese colonizers and their descendants. Because of the large number of African slaves brought in to do all the agricultural work for their white masters, the black African population grew to make up about 50 percent of the total population. While there was some assimilation due to interracial conjugal activity, blacks of Salvador maintained their basic African culture more so than any other area in the Brazil.

The following nine photographs show what Salvador looked like in 1944.

I-234; Lacerda Elevator and Cidade Alta from the dockside (Cidade Baixa)

In 1944 I stood on the dockside of the lower city (Cidade Baixa) area and took this photo looking up the cliff to the upper city (Cidade Alta) section of Salvador. On the left is the Lacerda elevator (Expresso Moderno) built in 1930. The cliff which separates the two sections of the city continues both to the left and right from the location of the elevator.

I-235; Cidade Alta from Bonde roundabout in lower city

This photo shows the cliff side buildings to the right of the elevator and the Bonde station at the dockside. The Bondes primarily served the commercial sector to the left of the elevator's entrance in the Lower City.

In 1944 there was a significant business district to the left of the bottom of the elevator and the Bondes went along the streets of Cidade Baixa.

I-236; View across Baia de Todos Santos from Cidade Alta

This photo, taken just north of the upper city exit of the Lacerda Elevator, gives the view across the Bay of All Saints (in a westerly direction) toward the land on the other side of the mouth of the bay. Note the Destroyer in the bay. When I took this picture I would have been pointing my camera along what is now the route of a ferry to what are now towns on the Ilha Itaparica, an island west of Central Salvador.

North of the city of Salvador, the smaller Bay of Aratu empties into the large Bay of All Saints. Aratu was the site of a seaplane base used by the US Navy and Brazilian air force during World War II. For a comparison n how the view from the upper city by the elevator looks today please note a similar contemporary photo in the section on Modern Salvador da Bahia.

I-237; Church and plaza - Salvador

The large Igreja in this photo faced a public square housing an open air market with festival booths. The inside of this and many Brazilian churches were replete with ornate and elaborate inner decorations which reflected the dominant position of the church which was in stark contrast to the material poverty of most of the population. The slaves and their descendants adapted to Catholicism while retaining much of their African cultural and religious heritage.

I-238; Carnival figurine

At a different portion of the Plaza we note in this photo the African figurine atop the temporary Carnavale booths. The signs advertise various merchants and shops including a tailor and a key maker among other things.

I-239; Closer view of Lacerda Elevator

I took this photo from the area of the dockside in Cidade Baixa near the base of the Elevator. The lower entrance to the elevator was a Bonde way station. Note the Bayer Medicamentos sign near the top of the elevator in Cidade Alta. This sign is emblematic of the problem US leaders faced in keeping Brazil in the Allied camp. Bayer was and is a giant German chemical company.

The Germans owned many types of industrial plants in Brazil, and ran many of the stores, hotels, and restaurants up and down the country. They also owned the major airline, Syndicato Condor, which operated throughout Brazil and to several of its neighboring countries. The Germans were also carrying out a well planned cultural infiltration in the schools, cinemas, and newspapers.

The Italian Fascists were also strong in southern Brazil due to the presence of some 3,500,000 first or second generation Italian immigrants who had come to or been born in Brazil. The farther south one went in Brazil, from Rio through Sao Paulo to Rio Grande do Sul, the more prevalent Axis sympathizers became. We were told that from Rio south it would be better to wear civilian clothes when visiting the cities.

President Vargas and his administration successfully countered the efforts of dissident German and Italian groups.

I-240; Passenger steamer - Bahia

The Brasileros did what appears to be a painstaking job in building this detailed model of the "Bahia", a coastal passenger boat. This type of boat depicted in this model was typical of many such vessels used to move people from city to city along the coast where a very large percentage of the population chose to live.

I-241; Street scene - Cidade Alta - Salvador

In February, 1944, we note in this photo that most of the strollers are wearing jackets even though it was summertime. The temperature in Cidade Alta would have been more moderate than that at Dockside which also was reasonably temperate in climate.The large sign, Sao Paulo, must indicate either a bank building or an insurance company because the sign says, “Secure for Life”.

I-242; A town square in Salvador

In this photo we see Wolff and Morales, two sailors of the group headed to Rio during Carnival time. Once again we were bumped off our flight from Recife and spent a second night of Carnival in Salvador.

Presumably the large building with the clock is a government building? The Suerdieck sign is atop what appears to be a bus or Bonde turn around station?

I-243; Family group at sidewalk cafe in Salvador

In this photo it looks as if this family has not yet been served with whatever they have ordered. The crowd in the background must have been watching a parade of some sort. The little girl's pointed cap must be part of her Carnival attire.

I-244; A Bonde junction - Cidade Alta

At the left center of this photo where two Bondes are stopped we can see some American sailors about to board. As usual the Bondes are being fully utilized. Note the large sign about Guraina (sometimes spelled Guarana), the Brazilian soft drink which was very popular.

I-245; Bonde no. 180 and sailors - Salvador

Cidade Alta, which is on a high bluff above the Dockside area of Cidade Baixa was also hilly in its own right. In addition to Wolff and Morales we see two other US sailors in the background. Since we had both land planes at Ipitanga and seaplanes at Aratu we had a significant number of navy personnel there. Salvador had been a center of commerce for centuries so it had a large business district. These were Bondes in both Cidade Alta and Cidade Baixa but I do not know whether or not one could ride the same Bonde between the two sections of the city.

20

Rio de Janeiro - 1944

God took seven days to create the world and
used two of those days to form Rio de Janeiro.

Brazilian Proverb

THE CIDADE MARAVILHOSA

The physical beauty of the "Marvelous City" is well known to people who have either visited there or have seen aerial photographs of Rio de Janeiro. The words Sugar Loaf mountain and Copacabana Beach are widely known and associated with Rio.

Most people of the world's populace refer to this spectacular city simply as Rio. Mention of Rio conjures up visions of a magical place with a benign climate, beautiful surroundings, and elaborately costumed people dancing in the streets, or of nearly naked people relaxing on the white sand of Copacabana Beach. Most of these visualizations are reasonably accurate. However, like other large cities (i.e. Los Angeles, San Francisco or New York), Rio today has certain areas which are poverty stricken. Those areas were much smaller and less apparent during the 1940's than they are today.

LOCATION OF RIO DE JANEIRO

Map No 13 (from reference J.W. Clement) which shows the eastern half of the Brazil of 1943 illustrates the position of Rio in the southeastern portion of the country. The size of the lettering of the names of the various cities is reflective of the dominant position of Rio relative to Salvador, Recife, Natal, and even Sao Paulo at that point in time.

During the 1940's Rio, with a population of 3,275,000 was both the governmental capital of the country and also the main financial, business, and cultural center of Brazil.

The paucity of the intercity and interstate highway system in the Brazil of the 1940's also is evident in this map. While there are some roads around Rio and other cities in the state of Minas Gerais and to and from Sao Paulo, there were practically no highways in the northeast, central, north, and western sectors of the country.

It is interesting to note that as long ago as the 1940's, the site of the future Brasilia as a federal capital of Brazil had been identified.

I-246; Map No. 13 - Eastern half of Brazil - 1943

The lines on the map depict rivers. Note the dotted square in the middle pinpointing future sites of Brasilia.

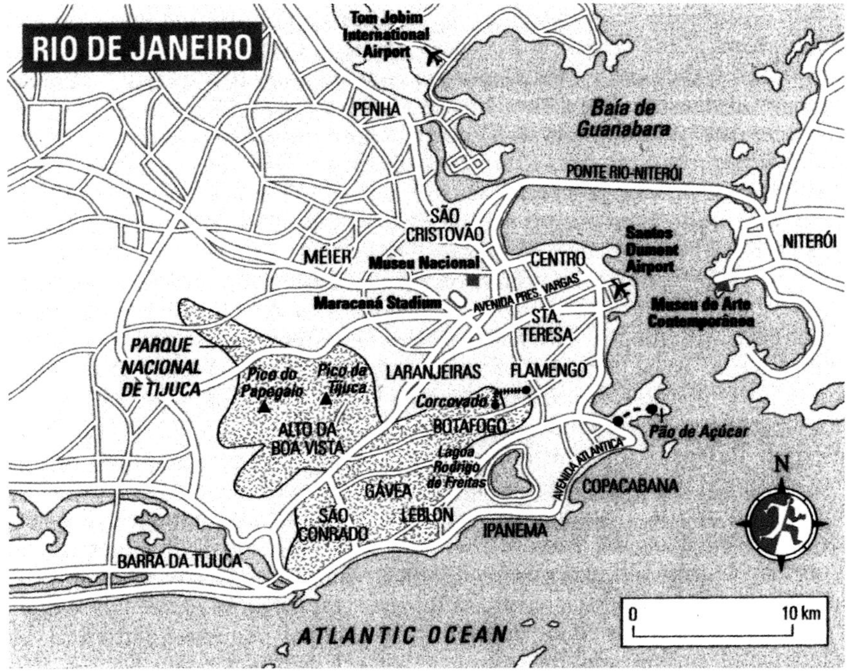

I-247; Map No. 14 - Rio de Janeiro

This is a modern map which shows more than what was in Rio during the war years.

This map shows how Rio is situated primarily on the west bank of Guanabara Bay and fronts on its southern side on the Atlantic ocean.

Guanabara Bay is huge (147 square miles) and it is easy to see how early explorers thought the bay was the mouth of a large river (the River of January), which it is not.

This map from the 5th edition of the Rough Guide to Brazil published by Rough Guides, Ltd, is reproduced with permission of the publisher.

TOPOGRAPHY OF RIO DE JANEIRO

The topography of Rio, consisting of a large beautiful bay opening into the ocean surrounded by green clad granite mountains interspersed with settleable sections of land fringed by white sand beaches provides the opportunity for many eye pleasing vistas. Add in a benign climate with no harsh winters and we really understand Rio's magnetic appeal for both residents and tourists. City leaders have accentuated the opportunity to view these areas by providing access to the tops of Corcovado, Sugar loaf Mountain, and Hunchback Mountain. Just as India was known as the "Jewel in the Crown" of Queen Victoria's India, Rio can be described as the Jewel of Brazil and indeed of the Western Hemisphere.

I-248; The view from Corcovado - 1943

As always, Pao de Acucar (sugar loaf) guards the entrance to Guanabara Bay.

The built-up area in the bottom center of the photo is the Bota Fogo sector of Rio. Note that there appears to be only a few high-rise buildings present in those days.

In subsequent decades Rio would expand westerly along the Atlantic shoreline. The mountainous terrain presented a challenge to this expansion of Rio which was met by innovative tunneling and highway construction techniques.

The following 4 photos (I-249-252) taken from a VP -211 PBM during a fly over in 1944 show the topography and beauty of the Rio of that time period.

I-249; PBM's over entrance to Guanabara Bay

In this photo we see 3 PBM's of VP-211 flying in from the Atlantic Ocean in a northerly direction entering the mouth of Guanabara Bay. Just to the right beyond the nose of the center PBM one can see the white sands of Copacabana Beach fronting on the ocean. A bit to the right of the lead PBM is Praia (Beach) Vermelha. On the right still further ahead is Pao de Acucar.

I-250; PBM's over Rio's center

In this photo we note 3 PBM's proceeding northward past the Santos Dumont airport toward the ferry route to the town of Niteroi across the bay. After the war a bridge was built to connect Niteroi and Rio.

I-251; PBM 211-P-1 near Santos Dumont Airport

Reversing course after circling the bay 211-P-1 proceeds southward toward Santos Dumont Airport. Santos Dumont has been cited as the first person to fly an airplane without the use of a tow rope. When his invention (the airplane) was used to bomb and kill people, Santos Dumont commited suicide.

I-252; PBM's Flying by Christ the Redeemer

On the way back toward the ocean in a southerly direction the PBM's pass by the front of the statue of Cristo Redentor on Corcavado. The view from the visitor's platform at the statue provides the full perspective of the city and its surroundings. The statue of Christ (100 feet tall) was completed in 1931. Its designers were led by Paul Landowsky, a French sculptor.

HISTORY OF RIO DE JANEIRO

The Rio area was first seen by white Europeans in January 1, 1502 when a few Portuguese sailing vessels arrived. Depending on which book one reads the discovering captain was either Amerigo Vespucci, Andre Concalvos or Graspar de Lemos. It appears that both latter captains, serving under Vespucci's command, were there?

It is of interest to note that up to date historians and archaeologists have found direct evidence that the Phoenicians had visited Brazil long before the time of either Christopher Columbus or the time of the Vikings who had visited the maritime provinces of Canada. Phoenician artifacts (drawings) have been found in Rio de Janeiro. It is now held that the Portuguese and Spanish knew that there were lands like North and South America long before the time of Christopher Columbus.

The Rio portion of the city's name came from the Portuguese explorer's mistaken belief that they had discovered a mighty river (the River of January). Actually they had entered a huge (147 square mile) bay surrounded by hills and small mountains which the native Indians called Guanabara (arm of the sea).
The Portuguese, because they were concentrating on Olinda and Salvador, did not attempt a settlement at that time and the Indians had things to themselves until 1555, when the French, who had been competing with the Portuguese in harvesting Brazil wood (for a red dye) from the coastal areas did make settlement in Rio. In 1565 the Portuguese returned in force to Rio and drove out the French.

In 1763 the Portuguese, because of the importance of mineral development in Minas Gerais (near Rio) and the growth it caused in Rio, moved the Brazilian Colonies capital to Rio de Janeiro from Salvador. In the 1700's importation of African slaves had resulted in the fact that the majority of Rio's populace was black or mulatto due to deliberate intermarriage to increase the "number of souls to be saved by the clergy."

In 1808, the King of Portugal, Dom Joao VI (actually he was Prince Regent but ruled for his widowed Queen Mother) fled to Rio to escape Napoleon's conquest of the Iberian Peninsula. He came with his court of 1500 people. Dom Joao stayed in Rio after Napoleon's defeat in 1815 and declared Rio was the new capital of the United Kingdom of Portugal, Brazil, and the Algarves (presumably including other Portuguese colonies around the world). Rio had become prosperous from the coffee trade by this time.

It was not until 1822 that Brazil became independent of Portugal. Dom Joao VI had finally been forced (in 1821) to return to Lisbon, and it was his son, Dom Pedro I, as Prince Regent, who led Brazil to become independent of Portugal.

Rio de Janeiro remained the capital city of Brazil until 1960 when the construction of Brasilia was completed and Juscelino Kubitschek, then President, moved the capital from Rio to the new city. Brasilia is about 800 miles northwest of Rio de Janeiro and about 800 miles inland. The location was chosen to promote more growth in the interior of the country and encourage more development and population growth there. The concept has been only partially successful.

During the first few decades most of the government officials would fly home to Rio on weekends and every other opportunity. In addition, the tremendous cost of building Brasilia resulted in decades of great financial and political problems for Brazil and horrendous inflation. For a concise and informative narrative on the struggles of Brazilian leaders and the body politic to advance their country to a true functional democracy, attention is directed to reference 8.

ALLIED FORCES IN RIO DE JANEIRO

There had been a long time friendly relationship between the US Navy and the Brazilian Navy starting as far back as 1914. The Brazilian Navy was pro-United States from the beginning of hostilities according to Morison (Reference 5). This was in contrast to the Brazilian Army whose officer corps contained a significant number of those with pro-Axis sympathies. In addition to the favorable previous relationship between the two Navies, the Navy Department made an excellent choice in selecting Jonas Ingram as Vice-Admiral in command of first, Task Force Three, and subsequently the Fourth Fleet in the South Atlantic. Admiral Ingram had formed close personal relationships with President Vargas and ranking officers of the Brazilian Navy and Air Force.

Since the Brazilian national government was at Rio de Janeiro, Admiral Ingram visited that national capital numerous times in his continuing effort to maintain a close working relationship with his Brazilian counterparts.

Within a few months time after Brazil declared war on the Axis Powers, US Navy squadrons began supplying the Brazilian forces with PBY's and

PV-1's (Hudsons) and informally training Brazilian pilots on their usage in the anti-submarine campaign. This training occurred at Rio de Janeiro and other bases on the coast of Brazil. When the Germans moved a number of U-Boats into the area between Rio and Florianapolis the joint US – Brazilian efforts proved very worthwhile.

In early 1943, Fairwing 16 dispatched VP-211 and VP-74 with some of their PBM 3 Mariner flying boats to Rio to extend joint efforts with Brazilian squadrons to counter U-Boats and scout for blockade runners and armed Axis surface raiders in that sector. Photo I-253 shows a PBM being beached at Galeao near Rio.

A striking example of how the Fairwing 16 squadrons and the Brazilian air forces cooperated in battle is the following story of the destruction of the U-199. The story also introduces one Alberto Martins Torres.

Alberto Martins Torres sinks the U-199

Reference 4 contains a detailed account of how VP-74's Mariners and Brazilian Lockheed Hudsons and PBY's carried out a running battle with U-199 during the month of July, 1943. In the initial battle on the 4th of July, a PBM Mariner in attempting to attack U-199 at night crashed at sea with the loss of all hands.

On July 31, VP-74 (P-7) again located U-199 off Rio. P-7 attacked the U-Boat and severely damaged its ability to submerge or maneuver but did not sink it. A subsequent attack by a Brazilian Hudson (Pilot – Sergio Candido Schnoor) further damaged the U-199. A Brazilian PBY on which cadet Alberto Martins Torres was second pilot then came on the scene and with Torres at the controls made a depth charge attack on the U-199 and sank the U-Boat.

After sinking the U-199, Torres circled his PBY close over the German survivors in the water and using a bull-horn told them in perfect German that a surface vessel was on its way to retrieve them from the sea. One can only imagine the incredulity of the German sailors on hearing a voice from the PBY which had just destroyed their U-Boat addressing them in German.

Alberto Torres was the son of a Brazilian Consul who was serving in Brazil's legation in Washington, DC when Alberto was born in Maryland. This gave Alberto dual citizenship. Alberto's father subsequently was assigned to diplomatic posts in Europe, including Germany, and as a result Alberto learned English and German as well as other European languages.

FORMATION OF THE FIRST BRAZILIAN FIGHTER SQUADRON

In 1943, the US Army Air Force started a formal training program for Brazilian fighter pilots to enable formation of the Brazilian fighter squadron which had been promised by President Vargas in January, 1943. The Brazilian pilots and ground crews, including Alberto Torres were sent to the USA for training and were accompanied by a specially chosen USAAF pilot by the name of John Buyers.

I-253; PBM being beached at Galeao, Rio

Galeao was inside Guanabara Bay. VP-211 and VP-74 both had PBM's operation out of Galeao Seaplane Base at certain times. A Brazilian squadron of PBY's also patrolled from Galeao. Beach crew duty was more pleasant than Quonset Point Naval Air Station.

John Buyers

The US Council of Churches sponsors missionaries in Brazil. John Buyers was born in 1920 in Brazil where his father was a long serving Methodist missionary in Rio, Minas Gerais, and Sao Paulo for about 60 years. Having American parents and being Brazilian born he also had dual citizenship and dual language capability. Most of John Buyer's years before high school days were spent growing up in Brazil. He came to the USA for high school and college and then became a USAAF cadet pilot in 1941. As soon as he finished flight training and became a commissioned officer his language capabilities became of great interest to both USAAF commanders and General Eduardo Gomes of the Brazilian air force. At Gomes' recommendation, Captain John Buyers became the US liaison officer to the Brazilian Air Force.

The Brazilians were to be trained to fly P-47 Thunderbolts. John Buyers joined the Brazilian 350th Fighter Squadron as they carried out their training in the USA prior to flying to Italy to aid in the Italian campaign. The Brazilian P-47 squadron performed very well in Italy as a part of the 350th fighter group. When the war ended they flew back to Brazil. On arriving above Rio they buzzed low over Copacabana Beach in a victory flyover, a proud day for Brazil, Alberto Torres and comrades, and John Buyers. I-254 shows John Buyers on the wing of his first Brazilian Fighter Squadron P-47 Thunderbolt while in Italy.

I-254; Captain John Buyers: USAAF pilot assigned to first Brazilian fighter squadron in Italy in 1944

Right after the war, John Buyers spent about 6 months in Brazil before returning to the Pentagon for about 3 more years of active service. Then he returned to Brazil, met a Brazilian lady near Maceio, got married and decided to stay in Brazil. He worked on construction projects for Texaco Oil Company, and then got involved in his in-laws sugar producing operations prior to retirement. He has written two books, one about the history of the Brazilian fighter squadron and the other about the 350th USAAF fighter group, in which the Brazilian squadron served. These two books have been published in Brazil in Portuguese and hopefully will be published in English.

BRAZIL'S EXPEDITIONARY FORCE (FEB)

In addition to the Forca Aerea Brasileiro (FAB), the Brazilian government, at the urging of its skillful foreign ministor (Oswaldo Aranha), convinced President Vargas to commit Brazil to the supply of ground forces to the European theatre of war.

During the January 28th, 1943 meeting of Vargas and FDR at Natal, Vargas promised to send 3 army divisions to Europe. Both the Forca Expenditionary Brasileiro (FEB) and the FAB were Brazilian ideas as they felt that the effort would have positive post-war effects for Brazil. FDR, of course, encouraged Vargas in this belief.

Largely because of wide-spread physical fitness and oddly enough, dental health problems, the Brazilians ended up with only one division of troops being sent to join Mark Clark's fifth Army in the tough Italian campaign.

The Brazilian army, which had not originally been very sympathetic to the allied cause, indeed there were many German leaning officers in the Brazilian Army prior to the U-Boat's sinking of Brazilian troopships in 1942, also now favored full cooperation with the Allies.

The 25,000 or so Brazilian troops fought well in Italy. they particularly distinguished themselvs at the Battle of Monte Castello where they fought alongside the U.S.'s famed 10th Mountain Division.

Unfortunately, U.S. foreign poicly toward Bazil since World War II had not capitalized on all the positive aspects of our joint military efforts during World war II.

ITALIAN CAMPAIGN – FIRST BRAZILIAN FIGHTER SQUADRON

The hills and mountains of northern Italy plus the military skill of German Field Marshal Albert Kessering and his forces made the Allied effort to drive the Germans out of Italy a difficult task. There was a need for effective use of fighter bombers like the P-47's flown by the Brazilians to support the ground forces battling their way up the Italian peninsula. Together with their three companion U.S. fighter squadrons (345th, 346th, and 347th) the 1st Fighter Squadron, Forca Aerea Brasiliera (FAB) as members of the USAAF 350th Fighter Group played a key role in the Italian campaign.

The following series of photographs are of the 1st FAB squadron personnel; camp; and equipment in northern Italy.

I-255; Camp - Tent City Camp 1st Brazilian Fighter Squadron

Like their American allies back in Natal and Recife, the personnel of the 1st FAB squadron bivouacked in tents in northern Italy. Here in this photo we see 3 P-47's circling for a landing and the Brazilian flag flying over the camp.

I-256; P-47 Thunderbolts being serviced

In photo I-256, three P-47's are being serviced by Brazilian mechanics. The squadron's emblem, a fierce looking bird firing a cannon while holding a shield with a drawing of the Southern Cross constellation on it is emblazoned on the cowling of the engine of the P-47. The words "Senta a Pua" on the emblem translate to "sock it to them" or "knock them down".

I-257; Rest and Relaxation with Ceasar

Five pilots of the 1st FAB squadron on a warmer day in Italy with their mascot, a stray dog who wandered into Tent City.

I-258; Nineteen pilots of FAB 1st Brazilian Fighter Squadron

Since they are wearing summer type flying suits and the plane is not painted in battle colors, this photo was probably taken after the Italian Campaign when the squadron had returned to Rio.

By virtue of the authority vested in me as President of the United States and as Commander in Chief of the Armed Forces of the United States, I have today awarded

THE PRESIDENTIAL UNIT CITATION (AIR FORCE)

FOR EXTRAORDINARY HEROISM

TO

1ST BRAZILIAN FIGHTER SQUADRON

BRAZILIAN ARMED FORCES

The 1st Brazilian Fighter Squadron, Brazilian Armed Forces, distinguished itself by extraordinary heroism in connection with military operations against an enemy of the United States in the Mediterranean Theatre of Operations on 22 April 1945. By heroic services involving utmost gallantry and a display of consummate skill in armed reconnaissance and fighter-bomber attacks, and by demonstrating superb tactical coordination with the Fifth Army, they contributed directly to the Allied crossing of the Po River. They destroyed vast quantities of enemy materiel and vehicles thus preventing the enemy from escaping to safety behind prepared defenses. By discovering a skillfully concealed and heavily defended enemy motor pool near Nantova, Italy, they destroyed at least 45 vehicles and doubtlessly immobilized many more. By harassing enemy pontoon barges on the Po, they helped to thwart their retreat, leaving many elements of Germans with no means of escape. By their vigilant air cover of road nets and prepared battle positions, they destroyed many other vehicles, including armored field pieces, and harassed trench positions. The casualties that they suffered reduced their pilot strength to about one half that of the United States Army Air Force squadrons operating in the same area, but they flew an equal number of sorties, performing tirelessly and beyond the normal call of duty. The maintenance of their aircraft was highly efficient. They met serious weather difficulties with excellent planning and navigation. By the most capable employment of the camera, they photographed the results of their attacks and contributed to the pictorial record of a historical campaign. Eleven missions of 44 sorties were flown destroying nine motor transports and damaging 17. Additionally, they destroyed the facilities of a motor pool, immobilized 35 horse vehicles, damaged a road bridge and a pontoon bridge, destroyed 14 and damaged three enemy-occupied buildings, and attacked four military positions and inflicted much other damage. The professionalism, dedication to duty, and extraordinary heroism demonstrated by the members of the 1st Brazilian Fighter Squadron are in keeping with the finest traditions of the military service and reflect the highest credit upon themselves and the Armed Forces of Brazil.

Ronald Reagan

I -259

This somewhat delayed U.S. Presidential Citation (I-258) describes some of the heroic efforts by the squadron in the Mediterranean theater of war. Since it was issued by President Reagan. the citation was made in the 1980's. It is unkown to the author as to whether or not any citations were given to the BEF (Brazilian Expeditionary Force) solders.

21

People and Places – Rio, 1944

Best duty post outside the USA? Rio!

A widely held opinion.

In the Atlantic Fleet Air Force of the US Navy there was a natural tendency for naval personnel to hope for posting to land bases or home ports which would offer the best "Liberty" or shore leave opportunities. In the USA that was either Floyd Bennett Field in New York City or an appropriate facility near the individual's hometown. In Fairwing 16 in Brazil, posting to Rio de Janeiro won hands down. However there were not a lot of duty slots at Rio. Nonetheless, many Fairwing 16 personnel did, after serving an appropriate amount of time in Brazil, get to go on 7 day leaves of absence to that great city.

Early in March, 1944, after I had been Brazil for nine months, I was informed that I had become eligible for a seven day leave in Rio. Having recently returned to Natal from a sojourn on Fernand de Noronha, I looked forward to the visit to Rio de Janeiro with great anticipation. I was not to be disappointed.

While I would not be allowed to take one of the navy's Kodak Medalist cameras with me I had been fortunate in getting my mother to get my miniature Speed Graphic to me in Natal. A.E. "Red" West had gone on leave to his hometown in Illinois so I convinced my mother to send the camera to Red's home and he brought it back to Brazil to me when he returned from his leave.

So on February 18th, 1944 I joined three other sailors from Hedron, Fairwing 16 as we boarded a Naval Air Transport Service (NATS) DC-3, fully expecting to arrive in Rio that evening for the start of carnival time.

Unfortunately, we were all four bumped off of the NATS flight in Recife. The next day we got on another NATS plane but once again we were bumped off at Salvador/Bahia so we spent another night of carnival in Bahia. At least this did give me a chance to visit and photograph people and places in Salvador.

Finally, on February 22nd, three of us boarded a third NATS plane for our flight to Rio. So we got to Rio just as Carnival ended. The fourth sailor in our group, Moe Littman, got on another plane in Bahia which had problems and had to land in NIteroi across the bay. He finally joined us at the Luxor hotel on Copacabana the next day. Presumably Moe spent his time in Nitreoi waiting for the ferry to Rio in his usual activity; carefully studying horse racing forms and reports.

The scarcity of seats on NATS planes worked to our advantage later as we didn't have to come back to Natal until March arrived because we could not get space on any planes

The following series of photos illustrate why Rio was such a favored port of call for American servicemen. Once again the irony of Chief Sander's words to us as he informed us that, "you lads are going to a hot place" rang in our ears as we enjoyed a visit to the premier liberty town in the western hemisphere.

I-260; The USO club in Rio de Janeiro

Of all the Brazilian cities, Rio had the largest USO club for servicemen. Ironically since Rio had so many other attractions, most of the sailors who went there on leave did not spend much time at the USO. However, the men stationed at Galeao Air Base near Rio probably did frequently use the USO facilities.

During our visit on leave we did not even know where the USO was located and did not bother to find out. The photo above shows 10 sailors and a couple of soldiers at the entrance to the USO.

As noted in his writings, Billie Goodell did go into the USO during his Christmas leave (1942). However that was due to the fact that he had received a kind letter from a young American expatriate girl who was a volunteer at the USO and had helped collect and send Christmas gifts to VP-83 personnel at Natal.

It appears that the size of the various USO clubs was not related to the number of servicemen present.

I-261; Copacabana Beach - February 1944

I took this photo in a southwesterly direction from the balcony of the Hotel Luxor which was where most Navy personnel stayed while on leave in Rio. Note the mosaic tile sidewalk typical of Portuguese cities. The weather was fine during the midst of summer in the southern hemisphere due to ocean breezes.

I-262; Copacabana at about high noon

It was customary for Brazilians to spend the morning hours on the beach but between 12 noon and 1pm the majority would depart (probably for lunch and siesta). As shown in this photo very few would remain on the beach in the afternoon.

I-263; Duas Moc̲as from Sao Paulo

We met several fine young ladies on Copacabana Beach. The two pictured here with the author were vacationing from Sao Paulo. I cannot recall their names. At that time, young ladies of quality were always chaperoned carefully by family members or domestic employees.

I-264; Jim Tortorice and Friends on Copacabana

Jim Tortorice was a storekeeper at Natal and a popular fellow. He had a truck at his disposal at Parnamirim. In photo no. 264 we see him, one Bill Rowan (originally from Saratoga Springs, New York) and two young ladies. One of the young ladies was probably one Anna Maria Perglia (spelling of her last name may not be accurate) of Rio whose father was the manager of the opera house in Rio. While Jim was in Rio, Anna Maria and her family took him to a performance at the opera.

Jim Tortorice spent 19 months at Natal's Parnamirim Air Base (May 1943 until October 1944) and subsequently served for 12 months on the USS Laertes, a repair ship in the Pacific theatre of war. Today he lives in Clairton, Pennsylvania with his family. Jim had a book of photos from Brazil but he sold it to a collector.

I-265; Luxor Hotel

This was a comfortable well appointed hotel in the 1940's. It is still there but it has been modified and has a new name as of 2008. In this photo note the "Woody" Chevrolet station wagon and the bus going to Castelo-Lebloa. In 1944 the Luxor claimed to be "a luxurious hotel fronting on Copacabana". Thousands of U.S. service personnel stayed at the Luxor while on leave during the war.

I-266; Two young ladies from Ballet Londres with sailors

These young ladies who were staying at the Luxor were from Uruguay. From the left the sailors in this photo are: Littman, Wolff and Boyd. They and I had finally made it to Rio just as Carnival was ending.

I-267; Maria Dulce

This photo is of a young lady from Belo Horizonte who was visiting her cousins in Rio. One of her cousins who lived in Rio was named Dulce Maria and the other was Lupe. Dulce Maria and Lupes' father was a medical doctor. They all spoke good English. When I got back to Natal, Maria Dulce wrote me a letter from Belo Horizonte with postcards with one marked with an x to locate where her home was. She and her cousins were charming company and they appeared to come from good families. Our evening contacts with them were chaperoned.

I-268; Avenida Rio Branco - Rio

This photo of a main street in the central shopping area, Rio Branco Avenue, shows the typical broad mosaic tile sidewalks favored by the Portuguese. Just past the Colombo sign advertisement we see a convertible powered by a charcoal fueled methane powered car following another vehicle with the same combustion system.

I-269; Close-up charcoal/methane fueled car

In this photo we see the two tank system burning charcoal used to generate methane to fuel the engine in a car in Rio. I leave it to my auto buff colleagues to elaborate on exactly how these systems functioned. It is most likely a "Starved Air" combustion system producing methane.

I-270; Restaurante e Bar - Balalaika - Rio

On the Avenida Rio Branco we see in this photo what must be a Russian influence with the name, Balalaika. Note in the lower right hand corner, the two tank setup on the back of passing automobiles.

I-271; Unusual House - Avenida Atlantic

There were many fine homes along Avenida Atlantic which paralleled and was next to Copacabana Beach. The one shown in this photo seems to be of unusual architectural design.

I-272; A "Civilian Stroll" on Avenida Rio Branco

Since we had been advised that wearing civilian clothes in Rio was still a good idea we did so as shown in this photo. While there I went into a store to buy some souvenirs and used my best Portuguese lingo to do so in order to get the best price. I like to think that my speech was good enough that they did not realize I was an American.

22

Modern Natal

Progress but nostalgia for the Ribeira.

Personal perspective of the author

GROWTH AND URBANIZATION

The wartime city of Natal (population about 50,000), had a typical friendly small town flavor and ambience which American service men enjoyed. Over the past 60+ years the city population has increased to around 800,000 and its geographical area has greatly expanded. Like similar American cities, the city limits have expanded to include villages well outside the Natal of 1945. Natal is now a metropolis.

Alecrim used to be a small village adjacent to Natal. Now Alecrim is part of metro Natal. The Redinha area on the north side of the Potengi River and across from the Ribeira area of Natal was sparsely populated and accessible by boat in the 1940's. Redinha is now more developed and is now easily accessible as part of greater Natal via a new suspension bridge from the Ribeira area.

The state of Rio Grande do Norte, of which Natal is the capital and seat of government has grown to nearly 3,000,000 inhabitants currently. As a result Natal has many government offices and resident employees. Natal is also the educational center of the state and has several universities within the city.

The state and Natal benefit from a thriving combination of agriculture, energy production, seafood harvesting, and tourism.

Sugar cane, fruit and nut production, Potyguar shrimp farms along the coast, petroleum from 5,668 oil wells and 27offshore oil platforms, unspoiled fishing villages, and uncontminated beaces and sand dunes all contribute to the economy of Rio Grande do Norte and its capital city. The construction of large reservoirs in the interior and wind farms along the coast have aided development.

Clearly, Natal is no longer a small town type of city like it was in the early 1940's. The Ribeira area is no longer the main business district for stores and small cafe-bars. Regretably much of the Ribeira area has been allowed to become an unattractive and somewhat blighted section of Natal.

Quite a few riverfront areas in the USA have suffered the same fate. Some of the U.S. cities have in the past three decades, revitialized thier waterfront areas and made them into attractive busy places with features such as military museums, aquariums, and upscale hotels and restaurants. Boston, Baltimore and the city nearest my country home, Wilmington, Delaware are three U.S. cities which have recently successfully renovated and upgraded their waterfronts.

The following fifteen photos illustrate how dramatically Natal has grown since World War II.

I-273; Aerial of Port of Natal, former RAMPA and new bridge to Redinha

This photo (credit Eduardo Maia) shows the dockside Ribeira area and the Natal end of the new Ponte de Todos Newtown Navarro. The bridge, which originates on the ocean side of the Ribeira area, is named for a noted local artist, journalist and writer. Just beyond the ocean freight container ship and toward the mouth of the Potengi are the Pan Am Archway building and a U.S. Navy ramp area of World War II.

Further on toward the point where the river opens up into the ocean is the place where the Germans had built their seaplane base prior to World War II. The U.S. Navy forces took over the German buildings, nose hanger, and other facilities in early 1942 and made it part of the overall RAMPA seaplane base.

Moving further inland in this photo and just adjacent to the first cluster of small ships one can see a long, multi-story, tile roofed, tan colored building. This was a significant building during World War II. In order to enter the famous Wonderbar brothel, one passed through this particular building.

I-274; Ribeira shoreline from river showing old ships and Wonderbar location

During a recent visit to Natal, Fred Nicolau reprised my 1944 boat trip from the Ribeira area to Redinha and took the following photo of the Ribeira shoreline. While the building which housed most of the Wonderbar is gone there are some buildings of interest which are still there. Just to the left of center in the shoreline photo a long, tan colored, multi-storied building with an ornate roof can be seen. The Wonderbar balcony used to be between that building and the water's edge.

I-275; Close-up of Ribeira shoreline showing former Italian Consulate building and treed area where Wonderbar stood

This photo (credit Fred Nicolau) is a close-up of the water front showing the referenced multi-story building in the center of the photo. There are trees now in place of the Wonderbar building and its balcony from which Billie Goodell's shipmate climbed down a rope to escape the Marine Shore Patrol in 1942 during the escapade described in Billie's anecdote entitled the Wonderbar Excursion. In the 1941-42 period the large, tan colored, multi-storied building with the ornate roof was owned by the Italian Vice-Consul to Brazil at Natal, one Mr. Lettieri. He operated a dry goods store on the first floor of that 3 story building on Commerce Street (now Chile street) and one could pass through there to the Wonderbar at river's edge. Mr. Lettieri was arrested sometime after December, 1941 and charged with espionage for the Axis Powers. That large building had previously been the Governor's office, hence the ornate roof and large size. The building now houses government offices.

I-276; Aerial of Ribeira, Pan Am Archway building and former U.S. Navy RAMPA

The Pan Air Archway building is in the bottom center of this photo (credit Eduardo Maia). The original 1942 Pan Air do Brasil pier remains to the right of the Pan Air Archway building with its control tower. Also to the right of the Archway building are three white conjoined single story buildings and attached to these buildings is a two story building with wrap around corner windows on the second floor. In the early 1942 photo I-15 (chapter 2) this two story building with wrap around corner windows can be seen. In that referenced early 1942 photo there are very few buildings behind and to the left of the referenced two story building. That inland area then looked like mostly open land. In this recent photo we note that the area in back of the Archway Building has filled in with many buildings so the Ribeira area did expand across the peninsula toward the ocean since the 1940's. Unfortunately, the dockside Ribeira area nearer to the river has fallen into disrepair at many locations.

I-277; Aerial of main dockside with ocean going container ship, part of Ribeira, and high rise buildings at edge of Cidade Alta

The more inland upriver dockside area shown in this photo (credit Eduardo Maia) has been well maintained. In the upper right of this photo one can see some of the high-rise buildings which dominate the Cidade Alta area and the expanded metropolis of Natal to the south and west of the Ribeira area.

I-278; Aerial of Praia do Meio looking northward toward river, Praia do Forte, and new bridge

In my 1944 photo from the Beach USO club on the hillside south of the Ribeira area looking northward toward Fort dos Reis Magos (photo I-41) one could see a broad expanse of open beach area. The development of that area is noted in this photo (credidt Eduardo Maia) which shows a variety of new buildings have been built out onto the previously open beach area since the 1940's. The beach front road has also encroached on what had been an open beach area. In my 1944 photo the palm trees once stood as solitary inward blown sentries on the wide open beach area. Fortunately, modern Natal still has miles and miles of beaches starting at Ponte Negra section and on southward which are accessible by the Via Costeria (coast road). These fine beaches are next to the Dune Park (a large urban park). On the north side of the Potengi River at Redinha and Genipabu a second very long series of sandy beaches stretches northward for 250 kilometers almost to the border of the neighboring coast state of Ceara. One of the major attractions to the more adventurous tourist is to rent a “Beach Buggy” for a lengthy excursion of these beaches and intermittent palm grove oases.

I-279; Aerial of new bridge from above Redinha eastward toward the ocean and Forte

Looking eastward over the Redinha end of the new bridge in this photo (credit Eduardo Maia), we see two causeways or breakwater walls jutting out on either side of the mouth of the Potengi. The breakwater wall from Redinha ends in the ocean but the one from the RAMPA area of Natal leads out to the Forte dos Reis Magos, making that historic attraction readily accessible.

I-280; Aerial looking south above Via Costeria toward Ponte Negra beach

Natal has also spread out southward along the coast and beaches all the way to the area known as Ponte Negra as can be seen in photo I-280 (credit Eduardo Maia). In the 1943-44 period the USO had a beach club between what was then the southernmost portion of Natal and Ponte Negra area. The last two photos in Chapter 3 show what the beach below the USO beach club and the Ponte Negra beach looked like in 1943-44.

I-281; View from southwest showing Nordestao Supermarket, Midway Mall and high-rise buildings

Greater Natal has expanded dramatically to the south and west of the old Cidade Alta area as we see in this photo (credit Eduardo Maia). In the center, the Midway Mall, a large enclosed shopping mall dominates the scene. Alcides Araujo and his in-laws (the Pinheiro family described in Chapter 13) were the proprietors of Casa Rio during World War II. Alcides and his son, Flavio, now operate a large store in the Midway Mall. The building with the sign Nordestao is a grocery supermarket. As the saying goes, "everything is up to date in Natal". The many high-rise residential buildings shown in back of the Midway Mall illustrate how the population density increase in Natal has been directed.

I-282; Aerial from above government offices and sports complex south of 1940's Natal

An aerial view from a further distance to the southwest of Old Natal (credit Eduardo Maia) shows additional elements of modern Natal. Here we see in a major sports complex both a large soccer (football) stadium and a basketball arena. The sports complex is surrounded by the many office buildings housing the state of Rio Grand do Norte's governmental employees. Natal is the capital of that state. The major divided highway on the right in the photos is the main road from the city of Parnamirim into Natal.

I-283; Close-up aerial of Parnamirim – Natal dual highway with state office campus entrance on left

This photo (credit Eduardo Maia) is a closer view of the major intersection on the road from Parnamirim and a second major highway. Presumably the major highway from Parnamirim to Natal approximately follows the old 1940's road from Parnamirim Air Base to Natal. In Chapter 2, Marshall Jamison described some of the perils of navigating the primitive old Parnamirim to Natal road.

I-284; Marshall Jamison sitting on a remnant of the original 1942 road from Parnamirim (Credit Marinho Neto)

During Marshall's visit to Natal in 2007, an aficionado, who is one of a group at Natal who are working to memorialize the WWII events there, escorted Marshall to Parnamirim to visit "his" former ACFC base. That base is now occupied by the Brazilian Air Force and is known as Base Aereo Natal (BANT). This WWII road, which parallels the new highway BR-101, is reputed to be the first asphalt paved road constructed in Rio Grande do Norte. Marshall and a friend also visited the old Air France hanger area at Parnamirim.

I-285; Marshall Jamison at Parnamirim airport (now Augusto Severo Airport) alongside a B-25 (Credit Marinho Neto)

Marshall enjoyed his visit to the Augusto Severo airport which now encompasses the old Parnamirim air field. In this photo we see Marshall next to an old World War II airplane typical of the many he helped get through Natal to the various theatres of war. While he has fond memories of Natal and its people, he is not comforted when he remembers all the fine young men (and women) who passed through Natal during the war, many of whom would be lost in combat. It was an emotional occasion.

I-286; Marshall Jamison with the Commanding Officer of BANT and his staff

While Marshall and friend were in the old Air France hanger at Parnamirim they were approached by a Brazilian who told them the Base Commander (CO) wanted to see them. When they reached the large office of the CO he stood and ordered some twenty officers of his staff to stand and salute Marshall with the honors of the Brazilian Air Force. The Base Commander, Colonel Carlos Eduardo da Costa Almeida, told his officers that they were saluting the first CO of the air base at Parnamirim.

I-287; Luxury high-rise residence buildings in Natal

Immigration from Europe and tourism are also significant contributors to the growth of Natal. Many Europeans have discovered the benign climate, ocean side location and friendly people of Natal so many retirees from Europe have migrated there over the past few decades. In addition to the ocean front condominiums many high rise luxury residences continue to be built to accommodate immigrants. In this photo (credit Eduardo Maia) shows typical new residential construction in Natal. The momentum of European immigration and tourism is reflected in the fact that non-stop daily air service from Lisbon to Natal has been established. So far Natal has dealt with its growth reasonably well but like most expanding cities, its previously excellent water supply and wastewater treatment systems are struggling to cope with the rapid growth.

CAN THE RIBEIRA BE REVITALIZED?

As was shown in photos of Natal in 1943-44 (chapter 13) the Ribeira section of town was the "downtown" area of the city at that time. The buildings were all well maintained and many stores of various kinds and café-bars (and three brothels) were there. On the weekends many residents from outlying areas would gravitate to the Ribeira to shop, dine and drink, and be convivial (Note photo No. 146). Unfortunately, just as with many U.S. cities, as urbanization and suburbanization ensued since 1945, the river front (Ribeira) areas were neglected, businesses moved away, and buildings deteriorated. This is a problem for Natal just as it was for Boston, Baltimore, Wilmington, Delaware and other coastal U.S. cities.

However, it also offers a great opportunity for the entrepreneurs and government of Natal and Rio Grande do Norte if they choose to emulate what has happened at the three U.S. cities mentioned. By forming dedicated corporate foundations, the riverside (Ribeira) areas of these cities have been greatly rejuvenated and turned into attractive business-residential tourist sectors containing enclaves which have improved the local economies and attracted many tourists. There is a preliminary indication that such a rejuvenation effort may be undertaken for the Ribeira area of Natal.

CHANGES AT PARNAMIRIM

Parnamirim Air Base still contains a few of the many buildings which were constructed there by a joint Brazilian – American effort. The airfield now contains the Auguste Severo airport which serves as a regional airport. The Brazilian Air Force also maintains a base at Parnamirim designated as Base Aerea de Natal (BANT). There are indications of developing capacity problems at the existing regional airport.

Parnamirim proper, the area surrounding the wartime air base, has grown to become a small city. The village of Macahyba has also grown sufficiently in population that it is incorporated and has a mayor. The mayor of Macahyba (Salomao de Oliviera), was made an honorary member of VP-83/VB-107 and attended a squadron reunion in 1997.

23

Modern Recife and Olinda

Recife has grown in size and number of inhabitants since 1945 and is so closely connected to Olinda today that it has become one large metropolitan area with a population of about 2,000,000. Olinda still maintains an identity of its own due to its colonial charm and hilly topography but for all practical purposes, Recife tends to be dominant. Recife is frequently the first port of call for ships and planes from Europe due to its location and excellent port facilities.

ECONOMY OF RECIFE AREA

Since Recife is the capital of the state of Pernambuco (state population of 7,900,000) the city has extensive state government offices and employees. Because of its strategic location, climate, and historical heritage it is a focal point for tourism. Its many venerable churches and museums also are attractions to tourists. Olinda, with its carefully preserved colonial churches and buildings is also a major tourist magnet.

While there is not a large amount of heavy industry in Recife proper, the sugar fields, sugar mills, and distilleries in the nearby inland area provide an industrial base, particularly when supplemented by the cattle industry also just inland from Recife. About 24 miles south of Recife at Porto de Suape, a large amount of build-up of industry has occurred since the 1940's.

About a 40 minute drive south of Recife, on the coast is Porto de Galinho which has developed into a noted beach resort. The ironic name of this now thriving town refers to "Angolan Chicken" (galinha), which is related to a ruse employed by slave owning sugar plantation barons in dealing with the outlawing of the importation of slaves into Brazil which took place in 1850. The importation of slaves had been prohibited starting in 1850, but the continued use of slaves was not curtailed for several more decades. The sugar barons continued to bring slaves into Brazil from Angola/Africa by labeling the shipments as being "Angolan Chickens".

Modern Recife, with its many islands constructed by Dutch invaders and colonizers and its numerous canals and 39 bridges, stands as a monument to the geotechnical engineering skills of the Dutch pioneers of the 17th century. Fortunately the Portuguese Brazilians and their antecedents have maintained the island configurations constructed by the Dutch. Not all the Dutch left after the Portuguese recaptured the area so there are citizens of Recife with Dutch forebears.

Recife has expanded dramatically in several directions since the 1940's. In Boa Viagem the growth has been largely vertical. Many high rise buildings have been built along the beach front and also inland as far as suitable ground allowed. On the mainland of Boa Vista the city has spread out north, south, and west. Presumably most of the area just west of Boa Vista proper has been modernized by replacement of the modest small homes depicted in my 1944 photos of the "Suburbs" with newer homes and businesses.

The entire northeast coastline area of Brazil from around Maceio north through Recife to Joao Pessoa, Natal, and Fortaleza has experienced a large wave of immigration from European countries (particularly from Italy, Spain, Portugal, France, and the low countries) during the past few years. There are probably a number of reasons for this renewal of immigration to Brazil. The advent of the Euro as a common and stable currency plus a favorable exchange rate and the lure of sunshine and warmth by a beautiful seashore certainly have been factors. The European immigrans have acquired a substantial amount of real estate in the northeast. Since Recife is the main port of entry in the northeast, the city has prospered from this immigration of Europeans.

VIEWS OF MODERN RECIFE AND OLINDA

My Brazilian friends have furnished me with the following recent photographs of Recife and Olinda. Participating in obtaining these photos were Fred Nicolau of Rio Preto, Sao Paulo State, the tourist agency of the state of Pernambuco known as Empetur, and Hans Von Manteuffel of Recife.

I-288; Boa Vista, Central Recife, and Recife Island (credit Hans von Manteuffel)

This aerial photo was taken from a westerly perspective above Boa Vista (the peninsular mainland) looking eastward over Ilha San Antonio (central Recife) toward Recife Island and the ocean. Ponta Sta Isabel, in the left center of the photo goes from Rua Aurora over the river Capibaribe to Ilha San Antonio (the central business district). In the top left center, the Ponta Buarque de Macedo allows access to Recife Island and the dock areas.

I-289; Rua Aurora (credit Hans von Manteuffel)

Taken from Ilha San Antonio on the east side of the river Capibaribe this photo shows that Rua Aurora on the riverfront is still as picturesque as it was in 1944 when I made a similar photo (see photo I-202).

I-290; Aeroporto Internacional dos Guararapes – Ibura Field) (credit Hans Von Manteuffel)

What was Ibura Field in 1944 has been expanded to become Recife's airport. In the background of the photo we note the many high-rise buildings of Boa Viagem and the South Atlantic Ocean. Boa Viagem is about 1.5 miles from Guararapes. It looks closer in this photo because Hans used a telephoto lens on his camera.

I-291; Modern Boa Viagem Beach (credit Hans von Manteuffel)

As the photo taken in a westerly direction from over the ocean shows, Boa Viagem is no longer a quiet almost rural area with small tiled roof homes lining the beach front. The benign climate, ocean breezes and sunshine have attracted dozens of high rise hotel (and condominium) buildings for the lengthy seasons in the sun.

I-292; Carnival Dancer at Recife (credit Hans von Manteuffel)

This photo shows that the Carnival costumes in Recife have become more elaborate than most of those prevalent in 1944. The bright smile and exuberance of the beautiful young lady personifies the *elan* vital of Recife's and Brazil's citizens, particularly at Carnival time.

I-293; View from Olinda Toward Recife (credit Hans von Manteuffel)

By contrast, the Olinda area, just north of Recife on the ocean is mostly a hilly area. This view photo from the hills of Olinda looking southward toward Recife shows that these two cities are now contiguous. Olinda has, because of its unique old architecture, hilly streets and artistic contents, developed into a tourist attraction in its own right, particularly at Carnival time. It is famous for both music and art traditions and has the third most popular Carnival period in Brazil, behind Rio and Salvador. Some have called Olinda, “The Greenwich Village of Brazil”.

Modern Salvador da Bahia

In Salvador lies the African soul of Brazil

Brazilian Proverb

In no other city of Brazil is the mixture of African, Amerindian, and European races so clearly apparent as in Salvador. All shades of color, black, brown, coffee colored, and white faces are seen. Of the 2,700,000 residents of Salvador, more than 50% are Mulattos, only 530,000 are white and 450,000 are black . This racial mixture does not appear to be any problem for the Salvadorians. The religions are also blended and the result is a number of believers who worship Catholic saints albeit with Afro-religion names. Canomble is an African origin religious form of worship via song and dance and animal sacrifice with cultish overtones which is practiced by groups of Salvadorians to a limited but significant degree.

Salvador has also been called the artistic epicenter of Brazil. Many writers, poets, musicians, and composers are either Salvadorian by birth or residence. (Tom Jobim of the Girl from Ipanema fame for one). In addition many insist that the Carnival festivities in Salvador are the most impressive of all because of the unique music and dance.

The city has expanded outward in all possible directions in the past 63 years. The Lacerda elevator is still the shortest connection between Cidade Baixa (the dockside commercial center) and Cidade Alta, the older colonial area which sits on a bluff over 200 feet above the Cidade Baixa. Cidade Alta (upper city) contains many historical buildings and government offices.

ECONOMY OF SALVADOR

Salvador, which was the early capital of Brazil for two centuries before the capital was moved to Rio de Janeiro is still the capital of the state of Bahia which has a population of 13,000,000. As a result the city contains many state government employees and offices.

The Reconcavo or plantation zone is still a large part of the Salvadoran economic base. Bahian cigars are considered by some aficionados to be at least equal to the best Cuban cigars. Spices and fruits also continue to be important products of the area.

The Centro Industrial de Aratu, an industrial park north of Salvador which sprawls around the Bay of Aratu is three times the size of the city of Salvador and is home to 100 industrial firms. Petroleum and chemical production are included in the industrial base of the area. Ford has a large automobile assembly plant in Bahia.

MODERN SALVADOR'S REVITALIZATION

Like several other Brazilian cities, Salvador is a blend of the old and the new whose configuration, appearance, population and culture are an accurate reflection of the previous 500 years of history at that location. The full name of the city is City of Salvador in Bahia of All Saints. This names describes the city's location and its strong religious background and heritage.

I-294; View Across Baia de Todos Santos from Cidade Alta

VIEWS OF MODERN SALVADOR

The following five pohtos supplied by Brazilian friends Christian Fehr and Roberto Costa Pinto show how Salvador has grown since 1944.
In this contemporary photo (credit Christian Fehr) taken from alongside the upper exit of the Lacerda elevator looking across the Baia de Todos Santos we note the large Mercado Modelo building in Cidade Baixa and the new high rise buildings to the right. That row of high rise office buildings is the edge of a greatly expanded commercial business area spreading out to the north.

Apparently, the Mercado Modelo, a large covered arts and crafts market, has been built since 1944 because I do not remember it being there in 1944. My 1944 photograph photo from almost the same perspective, shows that several buildings near the bottom of the elevator have been removed to provide space for more roadways servicing the Mercado Modelo.

I-295; Dockside of Cidade Baixa – Lacerda Elevator and Cidade Alta from Forte do Mar

This photo (credit Christian Fehr) taken from the Forte do Mar shows that the immediate surroundings on the bluff between the Cidade Baixa and Cidade Alta have not changed greatly since 1944. The Bayer sign of 1944 alongside the upper exit of the Lacerda Elevator is no longer there. Bayer is a large German chemical company.

I-296; Aerial view of Salvador from above Forte do Mar

This photo (credit Roberto Costa Pinto) is an aerial view of Salvador from above the Forte do Mar which is now the Customs House. The new hi-rise office buildings of the Cidade Baixa commercial area are visible on the left and the area of government office buildings and part of the Cidade Alta are shown in the upper portion of the photo.

I-297; Aerial view of southern tip of Salvador

The extent of the expansion of Salvador to the south is illustrated in the aerial photo I-297 (credit Roberto Costa Pinto), which shows the southern tip of the Salvadorian peninsula with the typical colonial era fort and the many new buildings just north of it.

I-298; The Pelourinho Sector

Cidade Altas restored Pelourinho is the historic heart of Salvador. (Credit Roberto Costa Pinto).

Modern Salvador is, for the most part, considerably improved since the days of World War II, largely because of the leadership of a senator and former governor of the state of Bahia, one Antonio Carlo Magalhaes. That gentleman led the effort to rejuvenate the Pelourinho (PELO), the heart area of the Cidade Alta which contains the largest colonial city sector in the venerable city of Salvador and in the country. The PELO, 300 years ago, contained the mansion homes of the young sugar barons (Portuguese aristocracy), wealthy traders and clergy, as well as many of the 34 colonial era churches of that sector. In addition it contains, as its name implies, the Pillory or whipping post where slaves and criminals were punished with the lash.

Starting in the late 1800's the PELO area buildings were allowed to decline and deteriorate and be transformed into tenements and homes for prostitutes and criminals. The widespread rejuvenation of the PELO area began in the latter part of the 20th century with encouragement from the United Nations UNESCO agency which had declared PELO to be a World Heritage Site.

Today the Pelourinho sector is the largest colonial city centre in Brazil and is a major tourist attraction with its colorful buildings and streets and many shops and cafés. Many of the people of Salvador go to church for mass and then fan out into the PELO streets for an evening of drinking, chatting, dancing, and music late into the night.

25

Modern Rio de Janeiro

This thick brew of Cariocas pursues pleasure like no other people: beaches and the body beautiful; samba and cerveja: football and cachaca (rum).

From the Book – Brazil, Lonely Planet Survival Kit, Lonely Planet Publications

The overall natural beauty of Rio de Janeiro remains largely unimpaired as we see in photo I-299 (credit Roberto Costa Pinto). This most famous vista from above and behind the statue of Christ the Redeemer on Corcovado facing over Guanabara Bay past Pao de Acucar with the Atlantic Ocean as a backdrop shows how unique topography contributes to the continuing mystique of Rio. But there are "growing pains in paradise".

Over the past 63 years the population of Metro Rio has grown to 14,400,000 inhabitants with 6,000,000 Cariocas living in Rio proper. Despite the population growth, Rio is no longer the federal capital nor the economic center of Brazil even though the intelligentsia of the city still claim to have a major influence on the country's direction. Their claim has merit in that Rio is the headquarters of Redo Globo, the dominant television network of Brazil. Roberto Marinho, the owner, is very influential in Brazilian politics due to his control of Redo Globo.

ECONOMY AND LIFESTYLES IN RIO

While there has been some industrial growth in Rio since World War II it has been small compared to the tremendous increase in the industry, economy, population and physical size of Sao Paulo. Sao Paulo is the third largest city in the world, about 37 miles wide with 17,000,000 inhabitants. Sao Paulo recently experienced a 100-mile long traffic jam.

Fortunately for Rio de Janeiro, its topography and other political and socio-economic factors have constrained its population growth to some degree. See photo I-300 for an aerial view of part of Sao Paulo.

As noted in the quotation, the pervasive lust for life of the Cariocas helps them maintain a collective mental equilibrium despite the problems they have in dealing with a large influx of poor migrants from other parts of Brazil. Roughly one third of Rio's inhabitants are poor people living in shanty towns on the steep hillsides above the affluent beach-side communities.

Tourism is a major element in Rio's economy. The growth of the tourist trade prompted an expansion of accomodation facilities which in turn created a need for more service workers (migrants).

These circumstances caused the development of two distinct life styles in Rio. The affluent Cariocas live well in material ways while those in the shanty towns struggle for the basic necessities to sustain life. The motto on the Brazilian flag is "Ordem and Progresso:. Democratic order has now been firmly established and progress haas been made . The distinct two class system prevalent in Rio typifies the large remaining challenge to the Brazilian political system.

I-299; Panorama of Rio - (Credit Roberto Costa Pinto)

This was made from photos taken from atop Corcovado mountain the area near the statue of Cristo Redentor. On the left across the Guanabara Bay from the Santos Dumont Airport lies the neighboring city of Niteroi which is now accessible by a bridge from Rio.

Pao de Acucar (Sugar Loaf) mountain is the center of the Panorama. Behind and a bit to the left of Sugar Loaf is the Botafogo section and Praia (beach).

Copacabana beach is just to the right of Sugar Loaf Mountain.

In the 1940's Copacabana was the most famous beach in Rio . It is still well known but other Rio beaches have become prominent. Just to the right of Copacabana the beach front of Ipanema appears. During the 1950's as Copacabana residential and beach areas became more crowded the Ipanema sector was expanded to accommodate popuation growth.

In subsequent decades (60's and onward) the continuing growth in population sparked the development of new residential and beach front properties in a west-southwest direction.

On the right side of the panorama fronting on the Atlantic ocean, Leblon sector and Leblon beach can be seen. Further to the right, but not visible in the photo are the newer communities known as Gaveao and Sao Conrado and Barra Da Tisuca (the Barra). The Barra is the enclave of the very wealthy "Upper Crust" of Rio society.

I-300; Aerial view of Sao Paulo (credit M.C. Pinheira)

This photo shows only a portion of the huge metropolis which is now the epicenter of the Brazilian economy. As a growing center of industry and business it has attracted immigrants from many countries.

FAVELAS

Parallel to the steady growth of the affluent beachside communities, the surrounding hills and mountainsides experienced a different type of development. Population pressure and economic necessity brought a large influx of poor migrants to Rio seeking employment. These folks needed a place to live, a roof over their heads, and ready access to the Oceanside areas which offered domestic employment. The result has been a plethora (500 or so) of shanty towns precariously perching on the steep sloped hillsides just inland and above the several beachside enclaves.

The juxtaposition of the shanty towns and the modern high-rise condominiums and offices is apparent in photo I-301 (credit Margi and Gerard Moss). This photo is of the area between Ipanema and Leblon and shows a position of Lagoa Rodrigo de Freitas.

The Favelas are hotbeds of poverty, crime, drug trafficking and abuse. Gangs of youths toting automatic weapons to control the drug trade are a menace. Shootouts between rival gangs and police versus gangs are a problem.

These developments are symptomatic of Rio's and indeed Brazil's most pressing sociological political problem; a reasonable distribution of wealth, health services, and education between the two distinct classes, rich and poor. The climate, music, Carnival and the beaches (which are democratic and integrated) are the safety valve outlet that mitigates the class problem to a significant degree. Currently a new mayor of Rio has been on a campaign to alleviate the difficulties of the Favelas. In fairness it should be noted that large cities in developed countries also have problems with the narcotics trade and with frequency of homicides. Washington, D.C., the murder capital of America, has a homicide rate in the same league as that of Rio.

Just as with the decrepit, dangerous, impoverished barrio sectors which exist in other major urban areas of the world, one wonders who owns the Favela shacks and collects the rent? One also wonders about the structural stability of these houses during periods of heavy rainfall?

A closer view of this particular Favela is provided by photo I-302 (credit Margi and Gerard Moss). This would appear to be one of the better constructed Favelas.

Land in the beach front communities of Rio has become increasingly expensive for obvious reasons. It is somewhat surprising to note that both properties and land in the Favela areas have also become expensive. This development of high prices for real estate in Rio has deterred overseas migration from Europe and encouraged more European migration to the less crowded cities and beachfront areas in Northeast Brazil.

The cities of the northeast (Salvador, Maceio, Recife, Natal, and Fortaleza) have all grown large enough to provide big city conveniences They all also have benign climates, long stretches of ocean beaches and less of a class structure problem than Rio.

Despite Rio's growing pains all of its oceanside areas still are very popular with many tourists as well as with local inhabitants. Copacabana beach is still popular despite occasional crowded conditions. The Luxor Hotel of 1940's fame is still there but it has been modernized in 2008 and its facade has changed as we see in photo I-302. The Luxor is now the Golden Tulip of Copacabana and has new owners.

I-301; Moutainside Favela above high-rise condos and office buildings - Rio

This shows the Ipanema - Leblon area near Lagoa Rodrigo de Freitas in Rio de Janeiro (credit Margi and Gerard Moss).

I-302; Close-up aerial photo of mountainside Favelas - Rio

This shows how these Favelas are perched below the steep slope of the mountains and above the more affluent sections of Rio de Janeiro (credit Margi and Gerard Moss).

I-303; The Luxor Hotel (2008)

The U.S. Armed Forces in Brazil in the 1940's had both Army Air Corps and Naval air Transport (NATS) planes flying regularly up and down the Brazilian coast including stops at Rio. For rest and relaxation (R & R) purposes both the Army and Navy personnel, after a prescribed time of service in Brazil, would be granted one weeks leave in Rio de Janeiro.

Apparently a formal arrangement had been made with the Luxor Hotel on Copacabana Beach to accommodate U.S. service personnel on R&R leave. Photo I-265 in chapter 21 shows what the Luxor looked like in 1944.At that time the hotel rooms all had balconies overlooking the beach. Since then the Luxor has been taken over by the Golden Tulip hotel chain and he building has be renovated as we see in photo I-303 which was kindly supplied by the Golden Tulip people.

A GAROTA de IPANEMA

Many Americans are familiar with the classic Bossa Nova song, "The Girl from Ipanema". Those who have had the good fortune to visit Rio in recent years also most likely visited or stayed in the Ipanema sector which is just west southwest of Copacabana Beach fronting on the Atlantic Ocean, as does Copacabana.

As Copacabana residential and beach areas became more crowded after the 1950's, Ipanema became the area where the upper middle classes moved to have more elbow room. At first exclusive and expensive homes were built but some of them soon gave way to multi-story apartment buildings to maximize real estate returns and cope with population pressure. From the 1960's on, the smaller apartment buildings were largely replaced by the typical high-rise buildings on or near the beautiful beach.

In the 1960's, Ipanema, paralleling events in the USA, temporarily mimicked the bohemian atmosphere of Haight-Asbury with hippies, rock and roll, long hair, drugs, and free love becoming prevalent. During this period one particular bar in Ipanema was the favorite hangout of a classically trained pianist and composer named Antonio Carlos (Tom) Jobim (a native of Salvador da Bahia) and his drinking buddy, one Vinicius de Moraes, a poet and former diplomat. A beautiful young schoolgirl happened to walk by the open doorway of the bar regularly on her way to school. Apparently her daily walk served as a real eye-opener, both for Tom Jobim and Vinicius de Moraes, after Tom called her to Vinicius' attention.

Inspired by the beauty of the young girl, the two drinking buddies composed and wrote the lyrics to that classic Bossa Nova (new thing) song, "The Girl from Ipanema". Subsequently, the famous Bahiana guitarist, Joao Gilberto, who was a prime mover in the genesis of Bossa Nova, recorded his version of the "The Girl from Ipanema" using his original, self invented style of guitar which mixed cool jazz and a modulated form of samba. Joao Gilberto's' wife, Astrud, made a recording of the song which is reported to be the most famous recording ever produced in Brazil.

The world outside Brazil became fully aware of the Bossa Nova when Tom Jobim mesmerized New York's Carnegie Hall audience in November, 1962 with his rendition of "The Girl from Ipanema".

While Tom Jobim and his pal Moraes are gone, the "The Girl from

I -304; Heloisa (Helo) Pinheiro (Credit Helo Pinheiro)

Ipanema", one Heloisa (Helo) Pinheiro, is now a middle aged mother of four children. The street down which Heloisa walked is now named after Moraes and the bar is named A Garota de Ipanema.

For some years Ipanema replaced Copacabana as the "In" place of Rio with the fanciest shops, jewelry stores, cafes and bars. It was the Rodeo Drive, Beverly Hills of Brazil.

Helo Pinheiro opened a clothing boutique in Ipanema, logically titled "The Girl from Ipanema" where bikinis are the main item of commerce. In 1987 Helo became a Brazilian Playboy Playmate and in 2003, both she and her daughter, Ticiane did a Playboy pictorial.

CARNIVAL IN RIO

Festive activities in Rio climax at Carnival time. From the Friday before Ash Wednesday to the following Thursday the city erupts in song, music, dance, drink and a generalized celebration of life. There are many organized parades with elaborate costumes and demonstrations of the samba.

Though the formal Carnival time occurs for those few days just before Lent begins, tourist oriented Carnival shows are held all year round. While the Carnival festivities in Rio are the most glitzy and spectacular, the other cities, Salvador, Recife, Olinda, Natal, etc., offer their own unique forms of parades and spectacles. Many foreign tourists descend on Rio during Carnival. Tourism is a year round major industry in Rio which is understandable due to the sheer physical beauty of the area. The Cariocas have done a fine job in organizing facilities which promote tourism.

A SANCTUARY CITY

Many motion pictures involve a climactic scene wherein the villain of the work is depicted as escaping to or trying to escape to Rio to avoid capture. This device is used because Brazil typically had not extradited criminals or alleged criminals. This is one case wherein truth and fiction coincide as some criminals from developed countries have found asylum in Rio or other areas of Brazil. A most notable case was that of one Ronnie Biggs, one of the crooks who pulled off the "Great Train Robbery" in Britain (30 million pounds sterling in today's valuation). Bigg's was caught and convicted but escaped from prison, fled to Rio and has lived there in a fashionable area since the 1960's. As Brazil has become more active on an international trade basis the country has signed extradition treaties with various countries.

EPILOGUE

A normal tour of duty in Brazil had been about 18 months, so it came as a surprise when I was notified on July 17th, 1944 that I was to be transferred stateside into Photographic Squadron 2 (VD-2) at Norfolk, Virginia. On the 24th of July, I flew in a Naval Air transport (R4-D) from Recife to Natal, thence on the 25th from Natal to Zanderey, Dutch Guiana (a 10 hour flight), and on to Miami (a 13 hour flight). Thus it took 24 hours to get form Recife to Miami contrasted with the 30 days it had taken to get from Gulfport Mississippi to Recife by sea during the previous year.

While I knew at that time that I had been very fortunate to serve overseas in Brazil, it would be many years later before I fully realized just how lucky I had been.

A Warm Welcome to Norfolk Naval Air Station

My flight from Miami to Norfolk Naval Air Station got in about 9:30 at night. That installation had grown significantly since I had left for Brazil so I stood waiting for the Navy inter-base bus to take me from the airfield to my barracks. Two nice looking WAVES came by and stood next to me and struck up a conversation by asking where I had come in from.

When the Base Bus arrived they insisted on helping to get my parachute bags onto the vehicle. After we sat down they introduced themselves (one was named Ivy McNeal) and they then volunteered to do my laundry. Since I was still a bit shy I didn't take them up on their offer but after finding that the Navy's laundry service on base took at least a week, I could see why their offer was a real act of kindness.

Service in VD-2 – 1944/45 and Several Defining Moments

There were quite a few photographers (both male and female) in VD-2 to cope with all the needs of the Air Station, the local Fleet Air Wing, and to serve as a personnel pool for the Air Force Atlantic Fleet as well as all the new ships being commissioned at the local shipyards.

Since I still had a yen to go to sea, I volunteered twice to go onto new aircraft carriers as a crew member when they were scheduled to go on their shakedown cruises prior to duty in the Pacific. One of these was the Antietam and other was the Midway. This was just about the time that the Kamikazes were becoming active so once again one could well ascribe to me the saying that "when we are young and foolish we do foolish things." For various reasons, sailors returning from Pacific fleet duty were given priority on assignment to new carriers. On both occasions when I volunteered for new carrier duty I was bumped aside by other photographers who had returned earlier from service in the Pacific Fleet.

After I had first arrived at VD-2 I had been granted a 30 day leave. During that leave I had the good fortune to begin a courtship of a fine young lady from my hometown village. As our relationship grew I lost my interest in volunteering for aircraft carrier duty.

Following a six month tour of duty in VD-2 I was transferred to Richmond, Florida Naval Air Station, Hedron, Fleet Air Wing 2 (a blimp air wing) in early February, 1945.

The young lady from my hometown and I were married in April, 1945 and we have been blessed with four children who have brought great cheer and love to our lives. In 2011, we celebrated our 66rd wedding anniversary. I was discharged from the Navy in October, 1945.

After I was discharged from the Navy a few months after the war ended, we moved back to our home town of Yorklyn, Delaware. At first I planned to follow a career in photography. Two of my U.S. Navy friends owned photography businessess and wanted me to work for them. One lived in Durham, North Carolina and the other one had a business in Chicago. We decided that we did not wish to leave our hometown area at that moment. Due to the G.I. Bill's availability we decided that I should go to the University of Delaware to study engineering. That proved to be a wise decision and a very defining moment in our lives.

Reflections on the War and Subsequent Events

Most, but not all of the things that occur during and right after a large scale war are bad, indeed horrific. The bad things, the death and injuries of tens of millions of people around the globe were indeed terrible. However, a few good things did result from World War II.

One of the good things that came out of World War II was the GI Bill of Rights. This program enabled many of my fellow servicemen and women and myself to obtain a college education, something which probably 90% of us would not have even envisioned being within our reach before the war.

The GI Bill was formulated by the generation of our parents because they were in charge of government polices at that time. So hats off to our parent's generation. Many of them had served in the military in World War I. They had endured raising children during the Depression and then borne the hard work on the civilian front and the pain of sending their young offspring off to a terrible war. My generation has been described as the "Greatest Generation", and I had a lot of comrades and shipmates who certainly fit that description. But let us remember, the "Greatest Generation" did not materialize from thin air. It was born and nurtured by caring, hard working people, with a strong set of moral, spiritual and family values and an education system that, sadly, was better in many respects than the one we have today.

After obtaining a degree in Chemical Engineering I enjoyed a 12 year career with a multi-national chemical company in that discipline before a subsequent 33 years of work in environmental engineering. During that career I visited and worked with many people from the Northern Hemisphere portion of the Americas. We also lived in England for several years when I was assigned to work in Europe.

My experience in life and knowledge of history causes me to suggest that there are several generations of people who need to reflect not only on the events of World War II and its aftermath (the Cold War) but also on its basic primary causes. This needs to be done to help avoid future conflicts. The generations I refer to are: the "Baby Boomers" who are the offspring of World War folks; and Generation X, the children of the Baby Boomers. Clearly this includes much of our adult population.

The period between 1919 and 1939 was largely a 20 year armistice in an unfinished conflict mostly between the French, British, Italian and Russian empires on one side and Germany, Austro-Hungary and Turkey on the other. While Russia played a less than definitive role in World War I, the Soviet Union would play a large role in WWII, (thank goodness).

The treaty of Versailles (an act of savage revenge) was a principal cause of the armistice of 1919 becoming a temporary cessation of hostilities. It was a vindictive, self defeating treaty based on hatred which had been fathered primarily by Georges Clemenceau of France, who was aptly called the "Tiger of France". Unfortunately, Lloyd George of Britain could not or would not counterbalance Clemenceau, and at the time of the crucial treaty negotiations, Woodrow Wilson was in ill-health and unable to prevent the disastrous form and content of the Versailles treaty. Wilson was also hampered by an isolationist Congress and an ill-informed public. That treaty prostrated the German economy and people and created the climate that allowed a mentally and physically diseased personage (Adolf Hitler) to gain power in Germany. The disastrous economic condition of Germany in the 1920's was a major cause of the Great Depression.

Only later did Winston Churchill, that greatest figure of the 20th Century enunciate his memorable phrase: In War, Resolution; in Defeat, Defiance; in Victory, Magnanimity. The Allied Powers at the end of World War I failed to be magnanimous in their terms for peace and the eventual result was World War II.

The Versailles Treaty terms should be contrasted with the Truman Plan for Greece and Turkey and the so called Marshall Plan for both the defeated and victorious European nations of World War II, and the enlightened policies of General MacArthur in defeated Japan. The USA, under Harry Truman, was magnanimous in victory with very positive results for all free people.

Unfortunately, President Roosevelt, who had done many great things in his years in the White House, was a dying man in the last critical year of World War II when negotiations with that great monster of the 20th century (Joseph Stalin) on the shape of the World after 1945 was being decided. The Cold War lasted so long and cost so much because our leadership on the world geopolitical stage had been naïve regarding the nature and intent of Stalin and the Communists before Harry Truman became president and got up to speed.

The Soviet Union was indeed an "Evil Empire" wherein the 2 million members of the Communist Party (the latter day "aristocrats") had led the Russians in conquering and subjugating many of the other countries around Russia such as the Ukraine, Georgia, the former Baltic republics and eleven other small countries. Those 14 other countries did not voluntarily join with Russia to from the Soviet Union, they unwillingly surrendered to overpowering force of arms. The Soviet Union was a "Continental Empire" in contrast to the "Colonial Empires" of the Western European nations. As a result the inhabitants of the 14 non-Russia Republics were forced to endure decades of harsh lives similar to those endured for centuries by the long-suffering people of Russia proper.

Why review these events in a book such as Fairwing-Brazil? Hopefully those who may read this book will realize that a study and knowledge of factual history is an essential part of citizenship in a democracy and will be stimulated to not only study historical events themselves but also do something about improving education in history for students at all levels of formal education. At the present time the history intelligence quotient of our younger generations is astoundingly poor and this does not bode well for the future well-being of our country unless changes are made. Given the resilience and basic common sense of the American people I am confident that this situation will be addressed in the near future.

Recommended reference works

In writing this book I had the opportunity to study a series of books on the 20th century and both phases of the World War (1914-1918 and 1939-1945). The most impressive and informative work that I studied was "The War of the World – Twentieth Century Conflict and the Descent of the West" by Niall Ferguson, Penguin Books, ISBN: 1-59420-100-5. This monumental work should be required reading and study for every high school senior or first year college student in our country. Professor Ferguson provides a wide ranging but incisive analysis of the causes and effects of all the wars of the 20th century. He includes much information not previously brought to the attention of mankind.

The book "Brazil, Past and Present" (Reference 20) is notable both for up-to-date perspectives of Brazil and also for truly outstanding photos and historical commentary.

The Rest of Brazil

Description of the several other cities and sectors of the vast country of Brazil are beyond the scope of this book. Sao Paulo, Brasilia, Manaus, Fortaleza, Belem, etc., and the Amazon, Mato Grosso, Iguacu Falls areas are all interesting places. The reader is referred to references 2, 8, and 20 for information on these locations in Brazil.

APPENDIX A

HISTORIC PARALLELS: ESTADOS UNIDOS DO BRASIL – UNITED STATES OF AMERICA

There are similarities in the flow of historical events which have and are taking place in the United States of America (USA) and the Estados Unidos do Brasil.

Before the European nations started their competing efforts to exploit the natural resources of the new world, the various native tribes in both American continents had engaged in tribal warfare to enlarge their own territories.

European Explorers of both American continents

When the European explorers first came their purpose was to establish enough presence to facilitate acquisition of raw materials for shipment to their own countries. Subsequently the facile availability of land and resources in the new world and the repeated tribal wars and religious persecutions periodically occurring back home in Europe resulted in waves of immigration to the new world and the establishment of permanent colonies.

As the new world colonies in both continents grew they developed their own ambitions and priorities. They eventually sought and achieved independence.

The Evolution of Slavery

The European colonizers in Brazil had first enslaved the indigenous natives to provide the labor for the agricultural system. Soon the natives either revolted or fled into the interior wilderness, so the Europeans imported slaves from Africa. In North America the colonizers were not able to enslave the native Indians (they also fled into the interior) so they also resorted to importation of African slaves.

The collective conscience of much of the populace in both the USA and Brazil eventually recognized the horrendous evil of slavery and took steps to abolish that abominable practice. It is interesting to consider the quite different procedures by which the USA and Brazil curtailed the practice of slavery.

Slavery in the USA

Slavery existed throughout both the northern and southern area of the United States during the 1700's and early 1800's. However the use and number of slaves in the south was much greater than in the north which had developed a greater industrial economy than the south. The agricultural economy of the south had grown substantially and profitability hinged on the availability of slave labor.

As the USA expanded westward the question of whether the new states would or would not permit slavery reached the boiling point and the Civil War was the result. Prior to the start of the Civil War there were about three million slaves in the USA.

Because the British Government had peacefully ended slavery in its West Indies colonies by buying the slaves from their owners ($400 per slave) in 1833, it was suggested that similar arrangements take place in the USA. That would have cost over <u>one billion dollars in taxes</u> which was a huge sum at that time. Because the practice of slavery in the USA was not ended via negotiation the Civil War ensued. The Civil War resulted in the expenditure of <u>six billion dollars in taxes</u> and the death of 600,000 people. The terrible slaughter of the Civil War entailed more deaths than the total for all the wars in which the USA has engaged since those bloody and fateful days of 1861-65. Nonetheless slavery had to be ended.

Slavery in Brazil

Brazil also had a largely agricultural economy during the 1700 and 1800 periods. Perhaps influenced to some extent by the Civil War in the USA and by a growing collective conscience, in 1871 the King Pedro II agreed to the Ventre Livre (Free Womb) law which mandated that the children of slaves would be born free. In 1885, the Brazilian Sexagenarios Law freed all slaves who were over 65 years of age. Finally, in 1888, the Princess Isabel signed the Aurea Law ending all slavery . Though slavery had persisted in Brazil for 23 years longer than in the USA, its demise in Brazil was more peaceable.

Lincoln's Valiant Efforts at Conciliation

Even as great a person and leader as Abraham Lincoln had not been able to prevent the Civil War or to mitigate its impact and aftermath as much as he hoped to.

By February of 1864 the North was in turmoil because of the prolonged war and the failure to finish it. President Lincoln, who by then was tremendously unpopular in both North and South, proposed offering a 400 million dollar reimbursement to the Confederacy to have them cease hostilities and end slavery but his cabinet unanimously opposed it and the war continued. The assassination of President Lincoln enabled the radical faction of the Union North government to carry out a vengeful Reconstruction process which devastated the South resulting in 100 plus years of regional animosity.

Civil war in Brazil

Brazil also had a short Civil War in 1930 but it was not caused by the slavery issue. The country had evolved from a colony to an empire to a monarchy and finally to a republic with a constitution in 1891. By 1894, the two states of Minas Gerais (the Rio de Janeiro area) and Sao Paulo alternately dominated Brazilian politics and government. Quarrels between these two states fueled by the effects of the world-wide depression and dispute over the Brazilian constitution erupted into a brief civil war in 1930. The federal forces from Rio de Janeiro (Minas Gerais state) quickly defeated the Paulistas from Sao Paulo and Getulio Vargas became president.

The Paulista forces included many of the descendants of the thousands of American Confederates who had emigrated to Brazil at the conclusion of the American Civil War.

Depression Induced Changes in Brazil (1929-1941)

Getulio Vargas, as president of the Republic, centralized the power of the Brazilian government and introduced government programs mandating: a minimum wage; a social security system; trade unions; and state schools; in effect a "New Deal " for Brazilians. But then, in 1937 he consolidated his own power and established a dictatorship which lasted until 1945 when he was deposed.

Depression Induced Changes in the USA (1929-1941)

In the USA, the Depression did not result in a dictatorship but FDR became a perennial president. By winning four elections over a twelve year period he would have lead the country for at least 16 years if he had not succumbed in 1945. FDR also centralized power and directed passage of more enlightened labor laws. He managed to mitigate some of the faults of an unbridled "laissez faire" capitalist system and in so doing saved the "free enterprise" capitalist system from its own excesses.

Brazil Struggled to Maintain a Democracy

Brazil had a much more difficult time in perpetuating a modern democracy. Vargas was re-elected president in 1951 but the power struggles overcame him and he committed suicide in 1954.

The battles between the competitive forces of nationalism, conservatism, and overt leftist populism between 1954 and 1964 culminated in a military coup that reestablished a 21 year military dictatorship in 1964. For a few years the generals were able to improve economic conditions but they also eliminated rights, suppressed political parties, and tortured political prisoners. By the late 1970's widespread renewed civic activism emerged and in 1984 the military was forced by the Congress to hold elections which resulted in a civilian being elected president A new constitution was adopted in 1988 and in 1989 democracy was firmly installed in Brazil.

It had taken much longer for Brazil to become a permanent democracy but Brazil has now emerged as the most important country in South America and as a significant force in world affairs. The promise of the motto on the Brazilian flag, "Ordem e Progresso" has finally begun to be fulfilled.

[Editorial Note: During World War II, the Brazilian currency was captioned: "The United States of Brasil", but now the official name of the country is; "Federative Republic of Brazil"]

APPENDIX B

S.K Taylor, War Hero, Educator, Dies*

With the death of Samuel K. Taylor, 91, the Lakeway Area has lost a decorated war hero and a man who dedicated his life to education.

First Lady Eleanor Roosevelt pinned the Distinguished Flying Cross on the World War II aviator for his service. The Maryville College graduate retired a full commander in the U.S. Naval Reserve.

But, it was in the realm of education that Taylor, who received his master's degree from the University of Tennessee, made his mark as a teacher and administrator.

"To me, he was the perfect example of a Southern gentleman," former Superindendent of Hamblen County Schools Herbert Harville said. "The kids at the schools were he served just loved Mr. Taylor and he had the same love for all the children."

Taylor was a teacher for 30 years. He was principal at Fairview-Marguerite School and Whitesburg High School. He also served as assistant principal at West High School for 15 years.

As a lifelong teacher, Taylor tried to live his life by a favorite passage from Shakespeare's Hamlet, according to his daughter -in-law Alice.

"To thine ownself be true, and it must follow, as the night the day, Thou canst not then be false to any man."

Director of Hamblen County Schools Dale Lynch said Taylor was one of the first educators he met when he came to Hamblen County.

He embodies a great professional," Lynch said. "He always cared about people"

One of his former students, Hamlem County Commissioner carry Baker, remembers his principal as a fair but firm man.

"He ran an excellent school and no students ever spoke ill of him." Baker said. "He epitomized the old Southern Gentleman. I had the highest regard for him and he was an instrumental person in my life."
Taylor's passion for Hamblen County education carried over to his family.

His wife of 64 years, Cora Pattie Menefee Taylor, was a librarian in the school system and his sons Samuel III and Andrew are a principal and teacher, respectively, in the county school system.

In addition to his career as an educator, Taylor was a dairy farmer for many years. He served as president of Hamblen County Farm Bureau and was a member of the board. That passion was passed on to the Taylor's middle son Scott who followed his fathers path into farming.

The couple also have a daughter Susan Taylor Bryant, a financial adviser in Knoxville.

Retired educator Edwin Goan remembers Taylor as a compassionate gentleman of many talents. "He touched a lot of lives in Hamblen County," Goan said. "He's done it all. He's a true American."

Taylor was a lifelong member of the Ruritan Club and of Creech's Chapel United Methodist Church.

He served on the Morristown Education Association, Retired Teachers Association, Phi Delta Kappa educational fraternity and the Holston Conference United Methodist Church Financial Committee.

He was a just a great gentleman, an excellent person to work with," Harville said.

*From the Hamblen County, Tennesee newspaper. - 2009

Editorial Note: this story shows what is meant by the phrase - "The Greatest Generation".

Sources and Bibliography

1. Blair, Clay, Hitler's U-Boat War, Volume I, The Hunters, 1939-1942; Volume II, The Hunted 1942-1945, (Edison, New Jersey: Castle Books)

2. Cleary, Jenkins and Marshall, Brazil – The Rough Guide, Fifth Edition (London: Penguin Group, Rough Guides, LTD.) www.roughguides.com

3. Dimitri, Ivan, The Flight to Everywhere, New York, NY, Whittlesley House, McGraw Hill Book Company, Inc.,

4. Carey, Alan C., Galloping Ghosts of the Brazilian Coast, (New York, NY) I Universe, Inc

5. Morison, Samuel Eliot, History of United States Naval Operations in World War II, Volumes I, The Battle of the Atlantic, September 1939 – May 1943, and Volume II, The Battle of the Atlantic Won, May 1943 – May 1945. (Boston, Mass, Little, Brown and Company)

6. Smith, Dr. Clyde, Jr., Trampolin Para A Vitoria, (Natal, Brazil - Volume I in Portuguese) Universidade Federal do Rio Grande do Norte

7. Smith, Dr. Clyde, Jr., Trampoline to Victory, Volume II, Impresso Mo Brasil, (English and Portuguese)

8. Draffen, McAsey, Pinheiro and Jones, Brazil – A Lonely Planet Travel Survival Kit, Third Edition, (Oakland, CA: Lonely Planet Publications),

9. Newcomb, Richard F. – Abandon Ship, the Saga of the USS Indianapolis, the Navy's Greatest Sea Disaster, New York, NY: Harper Collins)

10. Command History, Fleet Air Wing Sixteen, US Naval Historical Center

11. Wilson, Richard A., Patrol Squadron 83 (VP83), Patrol Bombing Squadron (VPB107) U.S. Navy, Air Force, Atlantic Fleet, Chronology and Narrative of Personnel and Flight Operations, self published.

12. Wilson, Richard A., History of VP83, VB107, VPB107 in the South Atlantic Ocean WWII, self published.

13. McCullough, David, Truman, (New York, N.Y., Simon and Schuster)

14. The Historical Society of Ascension, Ascension at War. Introduction by J.A. Cant, April, 1943. A British publication.

15. Ferguson, Niall, The War of the World, London: UK, Penguin Press

16. Ragnarsson, Ragnar, U.S. Navy PBY Catalina Units of the Atlantic War (Westminster, MD: Osprey Direct)

17. A Group of Fourteen Brazilian Collaborators, Brazil Guide, (Sao Paulo, Brazil: BEI) bei@bei.com.br

18. Tuohy, William, The Bravest Man I Know, (Gloucester, UK, Sutton Publishing)

19. Agnew, Donald H; Kinney, W.A.; American Wings Soar Around the World, (Story of the U.S. Air Transport Command, National Geographic Magazine, July, 1943, p. 57 to 78)

20. Ceccato, Beppe, Brazil (Past and Present) Edizioni White Star, Italy ISBN 88-8095-391-5; (whitestar@whitestar.it)

21. Carter, William, Why Me Lord? Book by a naval officer serving on U.S. Merchant Marine ships on Murmansk Run.

LIST OF ILLUSTRATIONS

(Photographs, Maps, and Figures)

I - No.	Subject	Source
150.	Casino - Grande Hotel	JRH
151.	The 5 and 10 Cent Store	JRH
152.	The Leather Goods Store	JRH
153.	Confeitaria Avenida	JRH
154.	J. Tortorice and Friends - Ribeira	J. Tortorice
155.	Jangada Ashore	JRH
156.	Jangada Afloat	JRH
157.	Igreja Bom Jesus	JRH
158.	Teatro Carlos Gomes	JRH
159.	Grupo Escolar Augusto Severo	JRH
160.	Christmas in Natal - 1943	JRH
161.	Fortune Teller at Christmas Festival	JRH
162.	Young Lady of Photo Shop	JRH
163	Bonde at Top of Hill	JRH
164.	Guinora and Officer at Casa Rio	JRH
165.	Alcides Araujo, Giomar, Guinora and Soldiers	JRH
166.	Close-up of Guinora Pinheiro	JRH
167.	Jim Tortorice - Store Keeper	JRH
168.	Rosa Pinheiro, Daughters and Granddaughter	JRH
169.	Plaza Pius XII - Natal	JRH
170.	Suburbs of Natal	JRH
171.	Small Suburban Home - Natal	JRH
172.	The Abacaxi Stand	JRH
173.	Alecrim, Rio Grande do Norte	JRH
174.	Armazem Potyguar - Alecrim	JRH
175.	USAAF Ceremony - Alecrim Cemetery	JRH
176.	U.S. Navy Ceremony - Alecrim Cemetery	JRH
177.	Map No. 11 - Recife	Lonely Planet
178.	USS Albemarle	B. Goodell
179.	PBM 204-P-1 (Martin Mariner)	JRH
180.	Grumman Goose (J2F6)	JRH
	Chapter 14	
181.	Grumman Avenger (TBF)	JRH
182.	Model of Brewster Buffalo (1940)	JRH
183.	Grumman Wildcat (F4F)	K.G. Watland
184.	Lockheed Ventura (PV-1)	JRH
185.	OS2U (Kingfisher)	JRH
186.	PT Boat	K.G. Watland
	Chapter 15	
187.	The Commodores PV-1	JRH
188.	Secretary of Navy in Jeep	US Navy
189.	Ibura Field Photographers	US Navy

I - No.	Subject	Source
270.	Restaurante Bar Balalaika – Rio – 1944	JRH
271.	Unusual house – Copacabana – 1944	JRH
272.	A "Civilian Stroll" on Avenida Rio Branco	JRH
	Chapter 22	
273.	Aerial of Port of Natal, former RAMPA area and new bridge to Redinha	Eduardo Maia
274.	Ribeira shoreline from river showing old ships and Wonderbar location	F. Nicolau
275.	Close up of Ribeira shoreline showing former Italian Consulate building and treed area where Wonderbar once stood	F. Nicolau
276.	Aerial of Ribeira, Pan Am Archway building, and former US Navy ramp	Eduardo Maia
277.	Aerial of main dockside with ocean going container ship, part of Ribeira and high rise buildings at edge of Cidade Alta	Eduardo Maia
278.	Aerial of Praia do Meio looking northward toward Praia do Forte, Potengi River and New Bridge to Redinha	Eduardo Maia
279.	Aerial of New Bridge from above Redinha, eastward toward ocean and forte	Eduardo Maia
280.	Aerial looking south above Via Costeria toward Ponta Negra Beach	Eduardo Maia
281.	View from southwest showing Nordestao Grocery Supermarket, the Midway Mall and High Rise buildings	Eduardo Maia
282.	Aerial from above Government Office and Sports Complex south of 1940's Natal	Eduardo Maia
283.	Close up aerial of Parnamirim – Natal dual highway with state office campus entrance on the left	Eduardo Maia
284.	Marshall Jamison sitting on service road next to BR-101 (Parnamirim to Natal)	Marinho Neto
285.	Marshall Jamison at Parnamirim Field (now Augusto Severo Airport) alongside battle scarred World War II plane	Marinho Neto
286.	Marshall Jamison with Brazilian Air Force officers at Parnamirim	Marinho Neto
287.	Luxory high-rise residence building in Natal	Eduardo Maia
	Chapter 23	
288.	Boa Vista, Central Recife, and Recife Island	Hans von Manteuffel
289.	Rua Aurora - Recife	Hans von Manteuffel
290.	Aeroporto Internacional dos Guararapes – (Ibura Field)	Hans von Manteuffel
291.	Modern Boa Viagem Beach	Hans von Manteuffel
292.	Carnival Dancer – Recife	Hans von Manteuffel
293.	View of Olinda toward Recife	Hans von Manteuffel
	Chapter 24	
294.	View across Baia de Todos Santos from Cidade Alta	C. Fehr
295.	Dockside of Cidade Baixa, Lacerda Elevator and Cidade Alta from Forte do Mar	C. Fehr
296.	Aerial view of Salvador from above Forte do Mar	R.C. Pinto
297.	Aerial view of Southern tip of Salvador	R.C. Pinto
298.	The Pelourinho Historic District	C. Fehr